catalyst groupzine™
Volume 2. The Culture Issue

M000267108

Catalyst GroupZine™

Volume 2: **The Culture Issue**

Copyright © 2006 by Thomas Nelson, Inc. & INJOY

All rights reserved. No portion of this GroupZine™ may be reproduced, stored in a retrieval system, or transmitted in any form or by any means—electronic, mechanical, photocopy, recording, scanning or other—except for brief quotations in critical reviews or articles, without prior written permission of the publisher.

Published by Nelson Impact, a Division of Thomas Nelson, Inc., P.O. Box 141000, Nashville, Tennessee, 37214.

Scripture quotations marked NKJV are taken from the New King James Version®. Copyright © 1982 by Thomas Nelson, Inc. Used by permission. All rights reserved.

Scripture quotations marked NCV are taken from the New Century Version®. Copyright © 1987, 1988, 1991 by Thomas Nelson, Inc. Used by permission. All rights reserved.

Scripture quotations marked NIV are taken from the HOLY BIBLE, NEW INTERNATIONAL VERSION®. NIV®. Copyright©1973, 1978, 1984 by International Bible Society. Used by permission of Zondervan. All rights reserved.

Scripture quotations marked NLT are taken from the *Holy Bible*, New Living Translation, Copyright © 1996. Used by permission of Tyndale House Publishers, Inc., Wheaton, Illinois 60189. All rights reserved.

Scripture quotations marked as MSG are taken from *THE MESSAGE*. Copyright © by Eugene H. Peterson, 1993, 1994, 1995. Used by permission of NavPress Publishing Group.

Scripture quotations marked ESV are from *The Holy Bible*, English Standard Version, copyright © 2001 by Crossway Bibles, a division of Good News Publishers. Used by permission. All rights reserved.

Scripture quotations marked NASB are taken from the *New American Standard Bible®*, Copyright © 1960, 1962, 1963, 1968, 1971, 1972, 1973, 1975, 1977, 1995 by The Lockman Foundation. Used by permission. (**www.Lockman.org**)

All book excerpts and articles used by permission.

Creative Design:
FiveStone, Atlanta, Georgia
(**www.fivestone.com**)

Executive Editor Jeff Shinabarger
would like to thank:
Joanna DeWolf
It's been a blessing to learn from my sister for years.
Jason Locy
You and your team have a gift in creating beauty.
Andy Crouch
Your life is a taste of cultural understanding.
Kerry Priest
You are the glue that has put this entire project together.

Special thanks also to:
Wayne Kinde, Lori Jones, Neil Rogers, Brad Lomenick, Gabe Lyons, Richard Chancy, Chad Johnson, Melissa Kruse, Todd Cox, Beth Nelson, Amanda Hindson, Danielle Kirkland, Mark Cole, Reggie Goodin, Cindy Gould, Ben Ortlip and all our contributors.

For more information on the Catalyst Conference or to order additional copies of the **Catalyst GroupZine™**, call INJOY 1-800-333-6506 or visit **www.catalystspace.com**.

To find out how to exhibit or be a sponsor at the Catalyst Conference, contact Stacy Coleman (**stacy.coleman@injoy.com**).

ISBN-10: 1-4185-0322-3
ISBN-13: 978-1-4185-0326-0

Printed in the United States of America.

06 07 08 09 CJK 9 8 7 6 5 4 3 2 1

Welcome to *The Culture Issue*—the next volume in the *Catalyst GroupZine* series. Like consuming a subway map in a new metropolitan city, it's helpful to see the big picture to orient yourself … so here are some ideas on using this GroupZine with your community.

THE MAP

As you browse through this study you'll notice six sessions, representing each of the Elements of a Catalyst Leader: *Engaged in Culture, Authentic in Influence, Uncompromising in Integrity, Passionate about God, Intentional about Community,* and *Courageous in Calling.* Within each session you'll find …

Catalyst Study: The first article and primary curriculum for each session.

Group Discussion: Questions and journal space to reflect and prepare for group discussion.

Articles: Writings and stories from some of our favorite speakers and authors discussing the Elements through the lens of culture.

Catalyst Features: Check out the *True Story* profiles, read interviews from the *Christian Vision Project,* and hear other young leaders' *Perspectives.*

Engage Journal: Reflect and respond to the entire session and engage in the *Cultural Challenge.*

NAVIGATION

As a leader, you are often expected to have all the answers, but let's be honest, you don't. Understanding that from the start and sharing that is a great way to begin. However, you do tend to have the most questions, greatest commitment and the confidence to speak up and communicate your thoughts. So lead that way: Bring your questions to the group and explore the ideas together. Conversation is a starting point to form true community, and through your dialogue the group will grow.

HOW TO USE A GROUPZINE

1. Buy the GroupZine.　2. Get a group of people　3. Read a section and answer questions by yourself.　4. Convene at a cool spot.　5. Discuss your thoughts.

Catalyst GroupZine™
Volume 2: **The Culture Issue**

TABLE OF ELEMENTS

SESSION 01
ENGAGED IN CULTURE

Catalyst Study

10. The 7 Languages of Culture
by *Ben Ortlip*
How many do you speak?

18. William Wilberforce
by *James Emery White*
A name you need to know

Writings & Stories

20. Against All Foes? by *David Kinnaman*
Identifying enemies of the Christian faith

24. What's Your Posture? by *Andy Crouch*
Become creators—not copiers—of culture

Catalyst Features

28. Christian Vision Project
Mako Fujimura: The Poetry of Art

30. True Story: Erik Lokkesmoe
Founder of Brewing Culture

31. Perspective by *Tim Willard*
Brilliant Irrelevance

SESSION 02
AUTHENTIC IN INFLUENCE

Catalyst Study

36. I Smell Dead Fish
by *Ben Ortlip*
Cultivate the authentic fragrance of Christ

Writings & Stories

44. The Calcutta Paradox by *Tim Elmore*
Express humility and increase your influence

48. No Perfect People Allowed by *John Burke*
Stories from the search for authenticity

52. Strengths Revolution:
An Interview with Marcus Buckingham
Gain influence by living out your strengths

56. Green Light by *Jeff Shinabarger*
Influence is gained by doing something

Catalyst Features

60. Christian Vision Project
Reverend James Meeks: Redeeming a Needy Neighborhood

62. True Story: Josh Jackson
Co-founder of Paste magazine

63. Perspective by *Joanna DeWolf*
Life is Just So Daily

SESSION 03
UNCOMPROMISING IN INTEGRITY

Catalyst Study

68. Integrity at Risk
by *Andy Stanley*
Recognizing the four danger zones

Writings & Stories

76. Justicia para Yuri! by *Bethany Hoang*
Rise Up and Engage Injustice

80. How to Pay for a Free Cell Phone
by *Donald Miller*
Guard against wrong thoughts and actions

82. Love: The New Integrity by *Leonard Sweet*
Measure your life by love

Catalyst Features

86. Christian Vision Project
Frederica Mathewes-Green: Some Things are Ageless

88. True Story: Daniel Homrich
Founder of The Passport

89. Perspective by *Sara Raymond Cunningham*
Pedro's Question

SESSION 04
PASSIONATE ABOUT GOD

Catalyst Study

94. The End of the Spear …
The Beginning of the Lesson
by *Ben Ortlip (with Steve Saint)*
How one stone age church found its passion

Writings & Stories

102. Green-Thumbed Gardener
by *Jarrett Stevens*
Trusting the work of our Gardner-God

106. Sabbath *Shabbat* by *Lauren F. Winner*
Remembering and understanding the day of rest

110. The Rest of Time by *Mark Buchanan*
Stopping to number our days aright

114. Candid: An Interview with Eugene Peterson
Insights on *The Message*, church leadership,
and the Sabbath

Catalyst Features

118. Christian Vision Project
Brenda Salter McNeil: Radical Reconciliation

120. True Story: Naomi Zacharias
Director of Wellspring International

121. Perspective by *Ted Vaughn*
Art Surrendered

SESSION 05
INTENTIONAL ABOUT COMMUNITY

Catalyst Study

126. The Coming Loneliness Epidemic
by *Ben Ortlip*
What's at stake with our internal struggle
between privacy and community

Writings & Stories

134. The Simple Way by *Shane Claiborne*
An experiment in radical community

138. The Culture-Shaping Church
by *Gabe Lyons*
One Bahamian community is changing the face
of Christianity in culture

142. The Messy Blessing of Community
by *Rick McKinley*
Practicing the Presence of the Kingdom of God

146. Expand Your Circle—
Increase Your Influence by *John C. Maxwell*
Get out of your relational comfort zone

150. The People Factor by *Ben Ortlip*
How your network influences your Blue Print for Life

Catalyst Features

152. Christian Vision Project
*Chip Sweney & Bryan White: Separated at Birth,
Rejoined in Ministry*

154. True Story: David Hodges
Grammy Winning Musician

155. Perspective by *Eric Haskins*
Bryan's Freedom Day

SESSION 06
COURAGEOUS IN CALLING

Catalyst Study

160. Confessions of a Reluctant Leader
by *Bill Murray*
Finding the courage to lead even if
you're not wired that way

Writings & Stories

168. Flipping Coins by *Bill Hybels*
Choosing to trust God when at a
calling crossroads

172. No Gig is Too Small by *Margaret Feinberg*
Every small initiative in life is significant in the
Kingdom of God

176. Chazown by *Craig Groeschel*
Discover the vision for your life

180. God is Always Calling by *Andi Ashworth*
New aspects of our calling unfold with age

Catalyst Features

184. Christian Vision Project
Amy Laura Hall: For All Humanity

186. True Story: Brandon McCormick
Filmmaker

187. Perspective by *Tim Sanders*
The End of Suffering

ABOUT AFRICA …

190. What we are doing
A Special Report from the
Catalyst Rwanda Wells Project

198. What others are doing
A collection of stories from people of action

202. What are you doing?
Ways you can get involved

THE CATALYST STORY

CATALYST: THE LEADERSHIP FILTER FOR WHAT'S NEXT IN THE CHURCH
Catalyst exists to ignite passion for Christ and develop the leadership potential of the next generation, equipping them to engage and impact their world.

THE CATALYST STORY

In 2000, Catalyst was birthed out of a handful of young leaders at INJOY and Northpoint Community Church in Atlanta, Georgia who imagined a new experience—a leadership awakening that would revolutionize Next Generation Leaders for the Kingdom of God. What began as only a vision caught fire and over the past seven years, more than 40,000 young leaders have gathered for the annual Catalyst Conference.

Today, Catalyst is more than a conference—it's a creative community of young leaders who are passionate about their generation and eager to learn from wise communicators, mentors, and teachers to increase their influence. The community has grown to thousands of next generation leaders wanting to connect with the leadership filter for what's next in the church through events, podcasts, online magazines, resources, and blogs. To learn more about Catalyst resources visit **www.catalystspace.com**.

THE ELEMENTS
We believe that a Catalyst leader is:

Engaged in Culture

Authentic in Influence

Uncompromising in Integrity

Passionate about God

Intentional about Community

Courageous in Calling

catalyst
GROUPZINE ™

Dear Catalyst,

Thank you for choosing this journey. While Engaging the Culture has always been a key element for a Catalyst leader, with this issue we are putting it front and center. It is a deeply held value of our entire team. For several years, many of us have been wrestling through theories, studying culture, and trying to live by what contributor Andy Crouch calls one "posture" towards culture. We invite you to join us in our continuing exploration of engaging culture as a Christ-follower.

Let's start with a definition:
Culture: *the totality of socially transmitted behavior patterns, arts, beliefs, institutions, and all other products of human work and thought.*

The Culture Issue is a consideration of all these social artifacts, pieced together and shared to expand our scope, challenge our thinking, and spur us to action. After many conversations, we put together some of the best thoughts from a scope of differing minds for your consumption. These authors, artists, and practitioners love God and love others; but, as you'll discover, this is played out in many different ways. We hope some articles and ideas will keep you up at night as you wrestle with what all this means for your calling. We hope it stretches any previous notions on your role within culture. May the readings challenge you to seek God for how he wants you to relate to the greater culture in your everyday life.

Here's a thought for you to consider: the community you choose to explore this journey with will significantly influence your conclusions and solutions. It is easy to find yourself running in circles with people who think, act, dress, and live in neighborhoods just like you. Look back at the definition of culture and you will notice the word "totality." Unfortunately, we normally only see the whole of culture through the lens of our current worldview. Since you are about to embark on a study of the many pieces that make up culture, then we encourage you to surround yourself with a diverse people group that may help you understand the totality of the culture. Consider a working class person, a pastor, a teacher, a stay-at-home mom, a social worker, a businessman, a musician, maybe even a barista serving coffee at Starbucks (trust me, they understand social behaviors). By surrounding yourself with these differing opinions and views on life, you will experience a study rich in dialogue—not to mention it will expand your view of community. Let's face it, you probably won't agree with everything shared in this issue. You may, however, grow to understand another's perspective, see the genuine pursuit of God in another, expand the Kingdom of God, or make a new friend.

To introduce you to the importance of caring for our culture is a joy for us. The hope of our entire team is that you would take the time to consider what *The Culture Issue* means to you, that your community would be challenged, and that God would clearly communicate with you on how you personally can engage the culture.

May you cultivate the land with the gifts God has given you.

Jeff Shinabarger
Executive Editor and Experience Designer
jeff@fermiproject.com

Catalyst
PO Box 7700
Atlanta, GA 30357
www.catalystspace.com

Executive Editor
Jeff Shinabarger

Managing Editor
Kerry Priest

Editor
Joanna DeWolf

Design and Art Direction
FiveStone
Jason Locy
Patricio Juarez

Contributing Writers:

Andi Ashworth	Joanna DeWolf
Andy Crouch	John Burke
Andy Stanley	John C. Maxwell
Ben Ortlip	Lauren F. Winner
Bethany Hoang	Leonard Sweet
Bill Hybels	Marcus Buckingham
Bill Murray	Margaret Feinberg
Cory Lebovitz	Mark Buchanan
Craig Groeschel	Rick McKinley
David Kinnaman	Ryan Bricker
Donald Miller	Sarah Cunningham
Doug Klein	Shane Claiborne
Eric Haskins	Steve Saint
Eugene Peterson	Ted Vaughn
Gabe Lyons	Terry Wilhite
Gary Haugen	Tim Elmore
James Emery White	Tim Sanders
Jarrett Stevens	Tim Willard
Jeff Shinabarger	

If you have a story idea, question or feedback, email us at **info@catalystgroupzine.com**. For information on the Catalyst Conference visit us online at **www.catalystspace.com**. To purchase other INJOY or Catalyst resources call 1-800-333-6506.

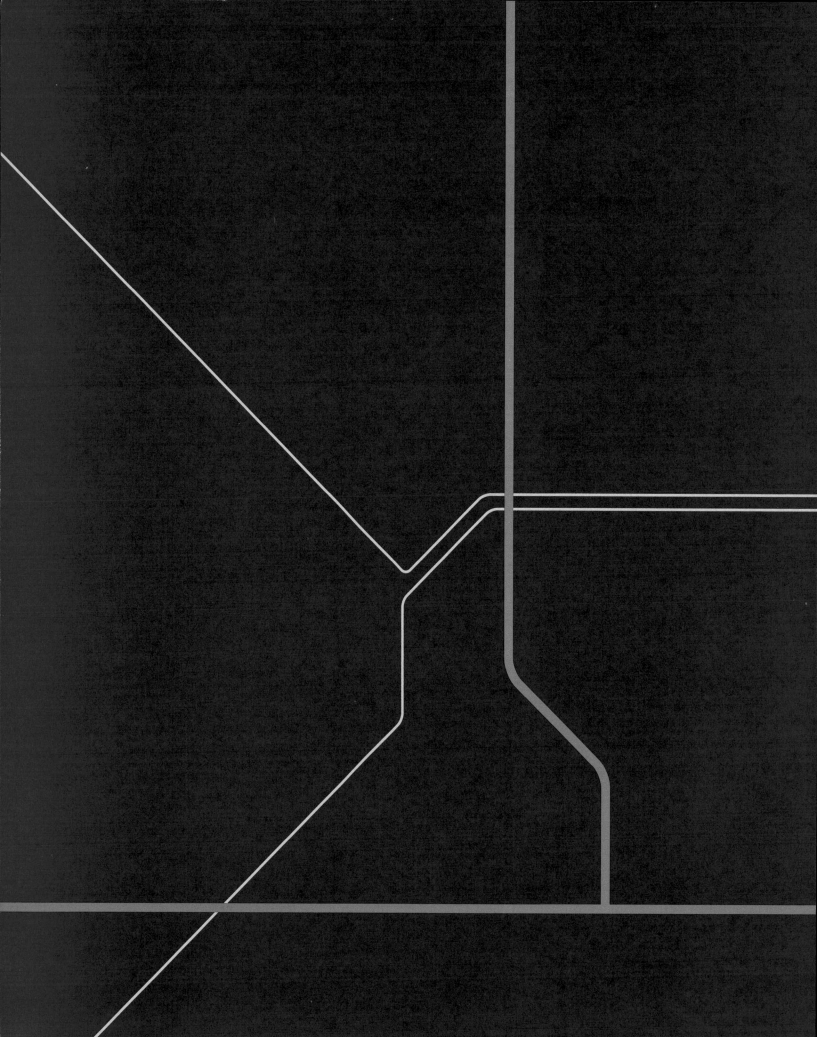

SESSION 01
Engaged in Culture

As a leader, I must understand the context God has placed me in. I must know the audience I am connecting with to have any opportunity of relevance. Because God desires that Christ-followers engage and influence their surroundings, I will be a source of hope, redemption, justice and peace in my community, demonstrating a piece of the Kingdom of God in a fallen world.

How do I respond to the cultural context I am living in?

THE 7 LANGUAGES OF CULTURE

By Ben Ortlip

HOW MANY DO YOU SPEAK?

To reach a culture, you have to speak their language.
To influence one, you have to speak all seven.

BEING A CHRISTIAN WASN'T EASY BACK IN THE 1300s. THE CHURCH WAS OUT OF TOUCH WITH EVERYDAY LIFE. THERE HADN'T BEEN AN UPDATED BIBLE TRANSLATION IN OVER 1000 YEARS. AND THE TERM "SMALL GROUP" WAS A REFERENCE TO THE ATTENDANCE ON SUNDAY MORNING. ENTER JOHN WYCLIFFE. HE UNDERSTOOD THE IMPORTANCE OF PUTTING SCRIPTURE IN THE LANGUAGE OF THE PEOPLE. SO HE TRANSLATED AN ENGLISH BIBLE. THEN HE SENT ITINERANT PREACHERS ALL OVER ENGLAND TO EXPLAIN WHAT IT MEANT TO HAVE A PERSONAL RELATIONSHIP WITH JESUS CHRIST IN THE 14TH CENTURY. IN ESSENCE, WYCLIFFE SPOKE THE LANGUAGE OF THE CULTURE. HE WAS SO FAR AHEAD OF HIS TIME THAT HISTORIANS NICKNAMED HIM THE "MORNING STAR OF THE REFORMATION." NEARLY TWO CENTURIES LATER, GUYS LIKE MARTIN LUTHER, JOHN CALVIN AND JOHN KNOX WOULD CHANGE THE WORLD USING SIMILAR IDEAS.

Speaking the language of the culture has always been the key to success for the church. But in recent years, the culture has become increasingly complicated. Creating a meaningful connection with the next generation requires more than painting the old fellowship hall in a hip new color. In some cases, it means re-thinking our whole calling to ministry. It's one thing to add a contemporary worship service. But it's another to truly comprehend the church's role in bringing the Gospel to life for an entire culture.

It reminds me of another complex relationship. There was a time when husbands and wives simply said, "I love you." Then Gary Chapman introduced us to the *Five Love Languages*[1]. And we discovered that saying, "I love you," is much more effective when you say it in a language your spouse can really relate to. As it turns out, many well-meaning husbands were saying, "I love you," the best they knew how. But none of it was getting through. The language made perfect sense to the husband. But the wife actually felt neglected. Unloved. Only when the husband learned to speak the wife's primary language did she begin to feel the love he intended all along.

In the same way, the language of culture is actually seven languages. And simply saying, "God loves you," is no guarantee that the person on the other end is getting the message. We churches are good at communicating God's love in our language. But not everybody gets the feeling that this God we're describing loves

them. And if we're honest, sometimes the church has actually made people feel more distanced from God. We need a better understanding of the culture's different languages in order to make people "feel" loved by God. And that's going to take a whole new way of looking at the church's role in culture.

THE SEVEN LANGUAGES OF CULTURE

In his forthcoming Fermi Project book, *The Brand of Christianity*, Barna Group vice-President David Kinnaman describes seven channels of culture that shape and influence life in modern society. These channels refer to the major influential industries and institutions that define vast portions of American life. They are: Government, Business, Education, Media, Arts and Entertainment, Church, and Family. Virtually every significant development in the life of a modern culture falls into one of these seven channels.

These channels that make up our culture are like seven languages constantly buzzing in the background of life. Every now and then, a key word or a phrase can be heard above the others, giving us a picture of the world in real time. As with love languages, people respond to culture-shaping events based on the channel of culture that produces it. To some, an event is more culturally significant if it comes from the business world. It speaks their language. After all, that's where the real action is. When something impacts the NASDAQ, it must be important.

For another group of people out there, developments are prioritized based on the amount of media coverage they draw. When an event makes it big in the news, it has a big influence on this group of people. For them, media is the channel by which they measure the pulse of culture. It's their language.

Obviously, we are impacted by more than one channel at a time. We are fluent in multiple languages of culture. Our minds use elaborate algorithms to process the information we collect from all seven channels. The result of these calculations is called a worldview. And the collective worldviews of all people form the culture.

THE VOICE OF THE CHURCH
The Church plays a prominent role in culture. It's even one of Kinnaman's seven channels. That means there are people out there with whom the language of church resonates. When the Church talks about an issue, they listen. Some people gather their entire worldview from the Church's interpretation of events and circumstances. While others are only moderately influenced by what goes on in the church. Still others are ambivalent toward the Church completely.

When it comes to engaging culture, it's important for church leaders to recognize that not everyone speaks the language of the church. But that doesn't mean they can't experience God through other channels. In fact, Jesus' model for discipleship involved penetrating the major channels of culture and speaking whatever language necessary to reach the people. He connected with the fishing business (Peter), government (Matthew), and even the local media ("Come, see a man who told me everything I ever did." John 4:29 NIV).

The more sophisticated our culture becomes, the more we need a strategy for using the other six channels to connect with the culture and communicate the love of God. Instead of viewing church as taking place on our campus, we need to start exploring ways to help others encounter the presence of God in everyday life. If we honestly evaluate the premise of the modern church, there's not much about it that's designed to engage the culture.

IT'S NOT ABOUT SUNDAY

For the most part, modern churches employ an invitational strategy for engaging the culture. The idea is to invite, entice, coerce, or otherwise lure the unchurched to become involved in church life. Basically, we try to lure them into learning our language. We set up shop and invite them to drop in. We create exciting worship services, produce broadcast-quality children's programs, and build fitness centers that rival Gold's Gym. But our success at impacting the culture hinges on our ability to get them to show up … for something. In this model, the engagement begins when the prospect moves into our world.

We tell ourselves that we're softening the barriers of entry to church by making it a natural extension of the broader culture. By blending in with the culture, we position the church as a useful and relevant part of life in the culture. And it is. Again, if we can just establish a connection with the culture, then the real transformation of the Gospel can begin. Nevertheless, we're still asking them to learn about God in our language.

THE CHURCH AS A CHANNEL

The invitational strategy is a great one. It has been the driving ideology behind

SIMPLY SAYING, "GOD LOVES YOU," IS NO GUARANTEE THAT THE PERSON ON THE OTHER END IS GETTING THE MESSAGE.

many vibrant movements of God. But we should acknowledge its limitations. The fact is that the church will never truly be an extension of the culture. By nature, it can't be. Therefore, even the most irresistible church is still a sub-culture within the broader culture. In this approach, the church will never be anything more than one of the seven channels within a culture. This is an enormous reality. And it bears huge implications. Basically, it means the unchurched still must take the first step and cross a cultural boundary in order to connect with God. That's the inherent contradiction in the invitational strategy. Granted, it works for many people. But Jesus always took the initiative to cross cultural divides in order to connect with people. He entered *their* world. He spoke their language. Not vice versa. And as the body of Christ, we must find a way to do the same for the culture around us.

When our concept of church is to make our sub-culture relevant to the culture at large, we make ourselves vulnerable to a very narrow approach to ministry. Our impact is limited to what we can accomplish on our campus on Sunday morning, or Wednesday evening. Meanwhile, the unchurched continue to exist in a world where Sunday morning is the time for playing golf or planting shrubs. In fact, there are some people who wouldn't go inside a church if it were the last bomb shelter in an all-out nuclear war. Should we just write those people off as not-in-mission? Or would Jesus have a strategy for speaking their language too?

THE CHURCH AS CONNECTOR OF CHANNELS

Beyond the invitational strategy, there is a more invasive strategy. Instead of putting the focus on getting people into church, this other strategy seeks to get the church into the culture. You see, while the church is a channel, it also has unique leverage with the other channels. Its members include representatives from each of the other channels. On any given Sunday, there are legislators, educators, journalists, businessmen, and artists in worship together. And it's not just prominent people who create this leverage either. There are also voters, consumers, readers, and viewers in attendance. Influence abounds. And the church forms the universal connecting point for all these channels.

As a connector of channels, the church has the potential to impact the other influential channels of culture. But before that can happen, we need a clear understanding of how to cultivate influence across those channels to engage the culture. Just to be clear, we're not talking about moving the church into those cultural channels. We're talking about moving the churched into the culture. That's how Jesus taught His disciples to do it. It's how the early church did it. And it's where our greatest potential lies today.

One of the best examples of this leverage took place at the beginning of the nineteenth century. The Clapham Sect, as they were called, was a collection of Anglican evangelicals representing different segments of culture. They were the influencers in their respective fields—authors, educators, politicians, clergymen, and business leaders. Together, they teamed up on a variety of projects that promoted social justice and cultivated a sense of dignity for the entire culture. They are credited with getting slavery abolished in England. They used their influence and strategic relationships to improve the quality of life for everyone. And the impact of their efforts was astounding. The sense of grace that pervaded their communities seemed to lift the spiritual ambitions of the nation. It is widely held that their efforts spurred a revival across England in the 1800s.

The church may be a prominent institution in society. But as this example shows, the church's greatest untapped potential lies in concerted strategies to minister through the other institutions (or channels) of society.

In order to gain that kind of influence, leaders will have to move beyond traditional paradigms of ministry. The church

is more than just an environment that impacts the people in it. It is a voice that impacts all other environments. The church needs more than a well-crafted message to voice its opinions to the culture. It needs a strategy to infiltrate the soul of the culture.

This is a whole new approach to engaging the culture. And it enables the members of culture to begin experiencing God without so much as mapquesting your church's address. Granted, it's probably not what you had in mind coming out of seminary. And it requires much more of a long-term approach to ministry. But combined with our existing invitational ministries, this may be just the ticket for engaging the culture.

THE WISDOM OF SERPENTS

The Clapham Sect is not the only group to launch a coordinated effort to exert influence across the primary channels of culture. In February of 1988, 175 leading gay rights activists met near Washington, D.C. to map out a plan to eliminate the social stigmas of homosexuality. The

group was led by a pair of Harvard-trained social scientists who drafted an official manifesto. It described a detailed plan for indoctrinating the American psyche and authenticating homosexuality as a viable lifestyle within our culture. They were out to earn social legitimacy. There were plans for four stages of re-branding our perceptions of gays, concluding with their acceptance in the mainstream. You already know the impact it has had on the way gays are portrayed in the media. And you're aware of the legislation that has been argued in recent months. In less than two decades, those gay rights activists are amazingly close to their goal. All because they orchestrated their influence and leveraged their connections within the influential channels of culture.

We're not suggesting that Christians should put together a cultural power play. But there's a lesson here. Imagine if we applied the same wisdom to re-brand people's perceptions of Christ. What impact could the Christians in your local culture accomplish if they leveraged their connections to serve the community around you?

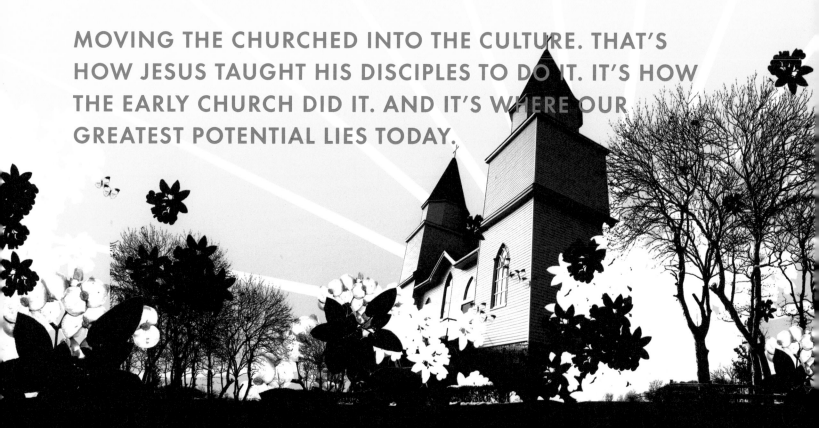

MOVING THE CHURCHED INTO THE CULTURE. THAT'S HOW JESUS TAUGHT HIS DISCIPLES TO DO IT. IT'S HOW THE EARLY CHURCH DID IT. AND IT'S WHERE OUR GREATEST POTENTIAL LIES TODAY.

STRATEGIES FOR THE OTHER SIX CHANNELS OF CULTURE

For some people, the only chance of meeting God will have to come through one of the other six channels. Their radar is up for anything that smacks of "church," and they're well-practiced in the technique of fleeing those situations. So, given those obstacles, how would Jesus move into that person's world? Each of these channels is a segment of culture in which members of the body of Christ should be active … not to fight for Christians' rights, but to reflect God's grace to a culture in desperate need of experiencing Him.

Engaging culture is more than speaking "church" to those in attendance on Sunday. It's about becoming an organic part of the culture itself. As we explore the following six channels in more detail, try to resist the impulse to think in terms of getting people from those environments to come to church. Instead, view them as legitimate venues for experiencing the grace and love of God in all its fullness.

BUSINESS

Business is one of the primary channels of cultural influence. For the average person, one third of his waking life is spent in the workplace. Compare that to the exposure of one hour in church on Sunday morning… if they even go at all. If the church could help to develop influence in a person's workplace, the impact can be enormous. Some of the greatest stories of personal change have come from the relationships between co-workers in which the love of Christ was lived out life-on-life. The church can learn to speak this language by equipping those in business to represent Christ in the workplace. This goes far beyond a sermon series on workplace evangelism. How would Jesus move into the world of the American laborer? What needs would He try to meet? And what logical opportunities exist for you to speak peoples' language in this channel?

POLITICS AND GOVERNMENT

When it comes to politics, the non-Christian's perception of Christianity is one of hatred and judgmentalism. The predominant image is of an angry person protesting either abortion or homosexuality. It's not the Biblical or political position that's in question here, but the spirit in which it is pursued. The language of politics is a language that influences people. And often what the culture hears is a message of hatred and rejection. Without abandoning our convictions about the unborn or God's design for sexuality, what are some ways the church could make the culture experience God's love through the channel of politics? Are there additional strategies that would transform politics into an arena that reflects attributes like grace? How would Jesus move into the world of the average citizen? How would He serve less fortunate citizens? How might the church cultivate vision for such strategies among believers? In addition to exercising our voice in politics, is there a way to leverage this channel to be a blessing to the unchurched in culture?

EDUCATION

Institutions of learning are among the most valued establishments in our culture. From the ground up, they are designed to speak into young lives and shape them. People have an inherent respect for the voice of education. Education speaks to culture. Unfortunately, our associations tend to revolve around highly-publicized issues like the battle over prayer in school. But aside from the battlefields, what strategies might exist to make education a voice that carries overtones of God's love? What are the areas of greatest concern in your local schools? Are there ways Christians could be serving important needs of the culture in this arena?

FAMILY

To influence the family is to influence one of the most important institutions in all of culture. As the fundamental environment of our social system, the family is the primary source of support and direction for personal development. A person's success or failure is often determined by conditions in the family in which he was raised. As the family goes, so goes the culture. Needless to say, winning the favor of families by serving them could result in a

WHAT IMPACT COULD THE CHRISTIANS IN YOUR LOCAL CULTURE ACCOMPLISH IF THEY LEVERAGED THEIR CONNECTIONS TO SERVE THE COMMUNITY AROUND YOU?

significant measure of influence. When it comes to considering strategies for engaging the culture, it's difficult to ignore the impact of reaching this important institution. What unique needs do families hold in common with each other? What overarching strategies might position believers to help the unchurched encounter God's love as a family?

ARTS AND ENTERTAINMENT

Does art imitate life, or does life imitate art? The answer is both. That's how much entertainment is integrated into our everyday lives. And that's why it's one of the most important channels of culture. It speaks our language. It influences our values, our lifestyles, and our behavior. Because it routinely touches our emotions, entertainment has the ability to motivate us at the deepest level. The presence of caring Christians in the entertainment community—combined with a strategy to impact the channel—could have an astounding impact on the culture at large. Your neighbor may never darken the doors of a church. But his appetite for entertainment will not go unquenched.

MEDIA

The joke goes, "Entertainment is fantasy with an agenda, but the media is an agenda with fantasy." In the wake of the information explosion, it has become clear that information is rarely shared without some overtones of bias. And given the volume of data we process each day, there's no shortage of opinions to influence our thinking. It is estimated that the average person is bombarded with as many as 5,000 messages every day. The sheer volume alone makes the media a powerful language of culture. And representatives of the media industry can be found in congregations across America every Sunday morning. Imagine the potential, not to cram a Christian message down the culture's throat, but to leverage this influential channel for the common good.

A NEW LANGUAGE

Essentially, there are two jobs that define the role of the church. The first is to speak the language of the church to the culture. And the second is to be the connector for the other six influencers. Doing church in a way that's culturally relevant is admirable. But the real impact lies in influencing all the other channels that reach into the life of the unchurched. Taking on this approach is like learning a new language. It's a whole new way of thinking. And it may feel awkward at first. But with a little practice, you'll be equipped to connect with people you'd never reach by speaking "church" alone. **C**

Ben Ortlip writes books and study curriculum for several prominent Christian authors and oversees creative projects for trend-setting ministries like Campus Crusade for Christ, Injoy, Family-Life, Walk Thru the Bible, and Northpoint Ministries. Ben is co-author of the breakout small group study *Blueprint for Life*. He and his wife, Lisa, live in Cumming, Georgia with their six children.

© 2006 by Fermi Project. Used by permission. **www.fermiproject.com**

WILLIAM WILBERFORCE
A Name You Need to Know

By James Emery White

WILLIAM WILBERFORCE (1759-1833) STRODE ONTO THE STAGE OF HUMAN HISTORY IN ORDER TO CALL THE WORLD BACK TO A TRUE VIEW OF HUMANITY IN RELATION TO GOD.

In 1970, after graduating from Cambridge with future prime minister William Pitt the Younger, Wilberforce entered the House of Commons. While many would look to later events in his life as more noteworthy, Wilberforce himself pointed to his "great change" during 1784-1785 when he embraced Christianity. "This transformation redirected the course of his life," writes biographer Kevin Belmonte, "and without it he would not have become the reformer he was."[1] Wilberforce himself writes, "The first years that I was in Parliament I did nothing—nothing I mean to any good purpose … My own distinction was my darling object."[2]

The "great change" changed that.

With his new faith Wilberforce scanned where history had brought the world, and he saw with new clarity the horrors of one aspect of its arrival—the slave trade. Arguing for a radical reversal of British policy, Wilberforce stood before Parliament on May 12, 1789, and for three hours poured out his heart and passion, conviction and resolve. Speaking to his colleagues of his own pilgrimage on the issue, Wilberforce said:

I confess to you …so enormous, so dreadful, so immediate did its wickedness appear, that my own mind was completely made up for its abolition. A trade founded in iniquity, and carried on as this was, must be abolished, let the policy be what it might—let the consequences be what they would, I from this time determined that I would not rest till I had [secured] its abolition."[3]

And he did not rest.

For twenty years Wilberforce devoted his life to abolishing Britain's slave trade, and another twenty-six years to abolishing slavery throughout British colonies and around the world. Undeterred by personal challenges to his health and family, death threats and persecution, world war and prejudice—though it arguably cost him the role of prime minister of Great Britain—Wilberforce's consistency, courage, disregard for reputation and position, and commitment to Christ allowed him to witness the abolition of Britain's slave trade throughout the colonies just days before his death.

A life given over to Christ saw the flow of history, and then gave its life to change it. And did. **C**

James Emery White is the president of Gordon-Conwell Theological Seminary. He holds M.Div. and Ph.D. degrees in theology, history and biblical studies. White is the author of twelve books, including *Embracing the Mysterious God, A Search for the Spiritual, Serious Times* and *The Prayer God Longs For.*

Photo from public domain.[4]

1. Which of the seven channels of culture speaks your language the most and why?

2. Which one speaks to your unchurched friends or neighbors? Give an example.

3. How well does your church engage the culture of the unchurched?

4. What would it look like for your church to infiltrate the soul of the culture?

5. What would need to change for that to happen?

AGAINST ALL FOES?

Identifying enemies of the Christian faith.
(It's not just the one with a pitchfork.)

By David Kinnaman

MOVIES OFTEN HINGE ON A GOOD-VERSUS-EVIL STORY LINE. THE JEDI WILL RISE AGAIN TO DEFEAT THE SITH. THE GLADIATOR FACES A DESPICABLE EMPEROR. JACK SPARROW CONFRONTS THE WRETCHED DAVY JONES.

When it comes to faith, many Christians embrace a similar kind of thinking—us versus them. But not necessarily the biblical notion of combating spiritual forces (described in Ephesians 6:12), which is the very real kind of spiritual entanglement that Christians should be engaged in.

Instead, many believers demonize the *people* with whom they disagree—atheists, homosexuals, environmentalists, political opponents, and even people from other faiths. For these Christians, their motivation is not bringing the Kingdom of God into sharper relief. Rather, they respond to the world and to others based upon impulses of fear and self-righteousness.

Unfortunately, we are in that boat more than we care to admit, aren't we? Mel Gibson's tirade against Jews was extreme, and public failures such as his certainly damage the image of Christianity. But the

reputation of the Christian community is not merely created at hands of high-profile leaders. Every one of us, as leaders, communicators and bearers of the image of God, are partly responsible. Do your thoughts and actions always reflect Christ's love toward others? When was the last time you made an off-handed, demeaning joke about homosexuality or some other area in which people struggle? Have you been kind and bighearted—without being condescending or compromising—toward people who believe differently than you?

I can vividly recall verbally hammering two young Mormon missionaries who came to my door. Another time, I remember making a joke about homosexuality, only to be reminded later that one of our houseguests had personally struggled with that lifestyle. I am ashamed at these memories—and others like it, when my behavior stole away a sliver of God's great fame.

A research study I have been working on examines this issue more deeply—how Christians are perceived today in our multi-faith, sophisticated culture. You probably would not be surprised at the findings: the "brand" of Christianity—the set of perceptions and imagery that people maintain about the Christian faith—is not flattering. Most non-Christians think of Christianity as hypocritical and judgmental (among other things) because we have misrepresented God's character by our lives and our words. **We have become famous for what we're against rather than Who we're for.** Just ponder that for a moment.

REAL RIVALS

I would ask you, based upon what we learned in the research, to re-orient your thinking about people outside the Church. They are not your opponents. It is not an us-versus-them thing; it's an *us-versus-us* crisis. People bearing the badge of Christ are often at the root of the problem. Yes, there are "mighty powers of darkness" that should motivate us to spiritual contention. But let's look at three ways that the Christian community bears responsibility for cheapening the image of God.

Spiritual Apathy – Lazy Christianity is devastating because it undermines the compelling difference Christ makes in people's lives. The vast majority of Americans are in this predicament: they call themselves Christians, but comparatively few have been transformed by that faith. Their lives are no different than the "average" American. Their Christian faith is a dusty trophy sitting on a shelf somewhere in a cluttered life.

The scope of this problem is huge. Our research suggests that seven out of every eight self-identified Christians and three out of every four born again Christians are dealing with significant levels of spiritual apathy. As an example: less than one in every 10 *churched* families spends any time in a typical month in spiritual pur-

suits in the home, aside from praying at mealtimes. So, when non-believers come in contact with a "Christian," the chances are good that they will come away with an apathetic, uninspiring, and theologically scrambled impression of what it means to be a Christ follower.

Spiritual Arrogance – The research points out that spiritually arrogant Christianity is also part of the problem that diminishes God's reputation in our culture. In the interviews, non-Christians explained that they are offended by the assumption that people who are not part of the Christian faith are immoral. They feel threatened by Christian posturing as morally superior. And they often take offense at the terms we use to define them, such as "lost" and "non-believers"—the implicit message of our terminology being that those outside of churches are not spiritually minded.

In a stunning but strategic maneuver of Satan, the people who are most susceptible to spiritual arrogance are the very ones who are least likely to be spiritually lazy. In other words, among the most biblically thinking and functioning believers in the country, much of their effort is undercut by a lack of love. This means that the ones who can best communicate the answers that Jesus provides are often neutralized by their own pride.

Self-absorption – Our research among non-Christians also shows that their perception is that Christians feel the world revolves around them. For instance, Christians sometimes complain about being a persecuted minority in America—that they are misrepresented in the media and other venues. While there may be some truth to this view, cries of abuse don't help non-Christians (who *really are* a minority) feel more endeared to a faith which draws allegiance from four out of five Americans and that continues to operate with significant opportunities in this country. Non-Christians believe our grumpiness is a reflection of an inflated

sense of self-importance. In their view, the nation's most dominant religion—the big faith on the block—shouldn't have (or need) special treatment. Besides, they feel as though Christians consistently misunderstand and mischaracterize *them*, so what's the big deal?

Another reason why non-Christians believe we are self-absorbed is that our efforts to share Christ often come across as insincere and one-sided. Here's a remarkable thought: How do you feel when Mormons come to your door? Do you believe that they are genuinely interested in you as a person—or do you believe they would very much like to see you convert? Do you feel that they really listen to what you have to say or do they pretty much have an agenda for their visit? Well, guess what? That's not far from the reputation we have among those outside the Christian faith. We have to take a long, honest look at our approach to spiritual conversations: are we operating out of a pure spirit to help people find the living Christ—or does our concern for others come with a not-so-hidden agenda, another notch in the convert belt?

SEEING THE FUTURE

There are no simple solutions or easy way out of the hot water we're in. But here are some guidelines for re-engaging people outside the church and reframing the Christian way of life. The first thing is to remember what our goal is <u>not</u>: popularity. Being well-liked doesn't make Christians more effective. Working harder, saying the right words, and trying the right combination of things doesn't help us break through to more souls. What does? Being more in tune with God's desires and His passion for people.

Instead, our main goal should be life transformation, molding people into the types of disciples Jesus shines through. This is easy to articulate, but very tough to do. Our research shows that transformation rarely happens through brief interactions, but through life-on-life modeling over a long period of time.

Next, you should realize that creativity is vitally important to the future of our faith. One of the undercurrents of non-Christians' perceptions of Christianity is indifference. It has no relevance. Good or bad, they simply don't care. But, for most of them, it's not for a lack of hearing the message of Christ. They have heard it, most of them, before. But the message never sank in; it had neither gravity nor buoyancy, neither humanity nor divinity. That's why creativity becomes so crucial in telling the story of the Christian faith—not just through hyped-up presentations or slick, well-run church services—but through honest people trying to tell the story of Christ's death and resurrection in remarkably relevant ways. If God has given you a passion for trying something new—maybe in your church, perhaps outside of it—keep pursuing that vision. It's not a mistake that you're feeling that way.

Finally, take stock of your own context. God wants to shape you into the best possible servant of His kingdom. If you want to reflect His glory brightly, He will show where to apply the polish. *Review the following questions as you think about this, or use them in a group to consider the work of your church.*

• Are there ways in which you are enabling spiritual laziness to exist in your life, your family's life or in your church?

• Has spiritual pride or self-absorption crept into your faith?

• Do you use language or phrases about people outside of Christianity that are demeaning and judgmental?

• What steps do you take to understand other people when you meet them—not just their spiritual journey and needs, but everything about their life?

• How much leverage do you give the Holy Spirit to show you blind spots in your life?

• Are you defined by what you oppose or Who you're for? It's easy to claim we are motivated by our love for Jesus—but how would other people describe you? In their view, do your words and actions help or hurt God's reputation?

• Is your life or your church a place where only perfect people are welcome?

• Since Scripture has the special ability to cut through us, what parts of the Bible are you rolling around in your brain regarding God's fame and how he wants us to treat others? How does Jesus react to people? Spiritually needy individuals? Prideful people?

We cannot ignore the poor reputation of our faith. You probably already had a sense of this problem. If not, I hope this article spurred your realization of the challenges that we face. And I hope it catalyzes your search for solutions in your life and ministry.

It is easy to live a spiritually lazy life, harder still to catalyze people to true spiritual maturation and transformation. It is a cheap excuse to complain that Christians are mistreated at the hands of the culture at large; it is much more difficult to make sacrifices for and serve that culture. Slowly succumbing to pride is a path of minimal resistance compared to humbly measuring our heartbeat every day by God's standards.

But, then, God is pleased when we accomplish big things that increase His fame in our time. Are you up to the challenge? **C**

David Kinnaman is Strategic Leader and Vice President of The Barna Group, Ltd in Ventura, California. (**www.barna.org**) His book on the "brand" of Christianity—how America's most dominant faith needs an injection of humility and love—will be released in 2007.

© *2006 by Fermi Project. Used by permission.* **www.fermiproject.com**

WHAT'S YOUR POSTURE?

By Andy Crouch

AS A GANGLY TEENAGER, I WAS OFTEN ADMONISHED BY MY MOTHER TO IMPROVE MY POSTURE. "SIT UP STRAIGHT!" SHE WOULD REMIND ME AT THE DINNER TABLE. I'D GRUDGINGLY STRAIGHTEN UP FOR A FEW MINUTES, THEN GRADUALLY SLIDE BACK DOWN, COMFORTABLE IN MY OLD FAMILIAR SLOUCH.

figure 1.

Our posture is our unconscious default position, the natural stance we take as we go through life. Our *posture* is different from our *gestures*. In the course of a day I may need any number of bodily gestures. I will stoop down to pick up the envelopes that came through the mail slot. I will curl up in our oversized chair with my 6-year-old to read a story. If I am fortunate, I will embrace my wife; if I am unfortunate, I will have to throw up my hands to ward off an attack. All these gestures and more are part of the repertoire of daily life.

Over time, certain gestures become habits, so ingrained that they become part of our posture. I've met former Navy SEALs who walk through life in a half-articulated crouch, ready to pounce or defend. I've met models and actors who carry themselves, even in their own home, as if they are on a stage. I've met soccer players who bounce on the balls of their feet wherever they go. And I've met teenage video-game players whose thumbs are always restless and whose shoulders betray a perpetual hunch toward an invisible screen.

What *posture* do we Christians find ourselves taking toward the culture around us? What *gestures* are we making? And are some of those gestures becoming such a habit that they are turning into postures—default attitudes that don't do justice to the world around us? Here are a few examples.

GESTURE 1: CONDEMNATION
Some cultural artifacts can only be condemned. The international web of power and lawlessness that sustains the global sex trade is culture, but there is nothing to do with it but eradicate it as quickly and effectively as we can. As Karl Barth,

Dietrich Bonhoeffer, and other courageous Christians saw in the 1930s, Nazism demanded Christian condemnation. It would not have been enough to form a "Nazi Christian Fellowship" designed to serve the spiritual needs of up-and-comers within the Nazi party. Instead, Barth and Bonhoeffer crafted the Barmen Declaration, an unequivocal rejection of the entire cultural apparatus that was Nazi Germany.

Among cultural artifacts that are prevalent among us right now, there are no doubt some that merit condemnation. Pornography creates nothing good and destroys many lives. Our economy has become dangerously dependent on factories in far-off countries where workers are exploited and all but enslaved. Our nation permits the murder of vulnerable unborn children and often turns a blind eye as industrial plants near our poorest citizens pollute the environment of born children. The proper gesture toward such egregious destruction is an emphatic *Stop!* backed with all the legitimate force we can muster.

GESTURE 2: CRITIQUE
Some cultural artifacts deserve to be critiqued. Perhaps the most clear example is the fine arts, which exist almost entirely to spark conversation about ideas and ideals, to raise questions about our cultural moment, and to prompt new ways of seeing the natural and cultural world. At least since the Renaissance, artists in the Western tradition *want* the rest of us to critique their work. Indeed, the better the art, the more it drives us to critique. We may watch a formulaic blockbuster for pure escapism, laugh ourselves silly, and never say a word about it after we leave the theater. But the more careful and honest the filmmaking, the more we will want to ask one another, "What did you make of that?" Critique is the gesture that corresponds to the particular calling of art and artists.

GESTURE 3: CONSUMPTION
When I make a pot of tea or bake a loaf of bread, I do not condemn it as a "worldly" distraction from spiritual things, nor do I examine it for its "worldview" and assumptions about reality. I drink the tea and eat the bread, enjoying them in their ephemeral goodness, knowing that tomorrow the tea would be bitter and the bread would be stale. With many wonderful things in this world, the only appropriate gesture is to consume them with a grateful heart.

When *all* we do is copy culture for our own Christian ends, we aren't loving or serving our neighbors.

GESTURE 4: COPYING

When we set out to communicate or live the gospel, we never start from scratch. Even before church buildings became completely indistinguishable from warehouse stores, church architects were borrowing from "secular" architects. Long before the Contemporary Christian Music industry developed its uncanny ability to echo any mainstream music trend, Martin Luther and the Wesleys were borrowing tunes from bars and dance halls and providing them with Christian lyrics. Why shouldn't the church borrow from any and every cultural form for the purposes of worship and discipleship? Copying culture can even be, at its best, a way of honoring culture, demonstrating the lesson of Pentecost that every human language, every human cultural form, is capable of bearing the good news.

So all of these gestures—condemning, critiquing, consuming, copying—can be appropriate responses to particular cultural goods. Indeed, each of them may be the *only* appropriate response to a particular cultural good. But the problem comes when these gestures become too familiar, become the only way we know how to respond to culture, become etched into our unconscious stance toward the world and become postures.

POSTURE 1: CONDEMNATION

While there is much to be condemned in human culture, the *posture* of condemnation leaves us closed off from the beauty and possibility, as well as the grace and mercy, in many forms of culture. It also makes us into hypocrites, since the culture of our churches and Christian communities is often just as lamentable as the "secular" culture we complain about. The posture of condemnation leaves us with nothing to offer even when we manage to persuade our neighbors that a particular cultural good should be discarded. And having condemnation as our posture makes it impossible for us to reflect the image of God who called the creation "very good" and, even in the wake of the profound cultural breakdown that led up to the Flood, promised never to utterly destroy humankind and human

culture again. If we are known mostly for our ability to poke holes in every human project, we will probably not be known as people who bear the hope and mercy of God.

POSTURE 2: CRITIQUE

Similarly, there is much to be said for critiquing particular cultural goods. But when critique becomes a *posture*, we end up strangely passive, waiting for culture to give us some new item to talk about. We also become strangely unable to simply *enjoy* cultural goods when we are preoccupied with interrogating their "worldview" and "presuppositions." The posture of critique also tempts us toward the academic fallacy: believing that once we have analyzed something, we have understood it. Often true understanding, of a person or a cultural good, requires *participation*—throwing ourselves fully into enjoyment and experience without reserving an intellectual, analytical part of ourselves outside like a suspicious and watchful librarian.

POSTURE 3: COPYING

It is good to honor the excellences of our cultures by bringing them into the life of the Christian community, whether that is a group of Korean-American chefs serving up a sumptuous church supper of *bulgolgi* and *ssamjang* or a dreadlocked electric guitarist articulating lament and hope through a vintage tube amp. But when our dominant mode of relationship to culture becomes imitation, when copying becomes our posture, a whole host of unwanted consequences follows. Like the critics, we become passive, waiting to see what interesting cultural good will be served up next for our imitation and appropriation. In fast-changing cultural domains, those whose posture is imitation will find themselves constantly slightly behind the times, so that church worship music is dominated by styles that disappeared from the scene several years before. Our copy-culture by definition will never be seen by the vast majority of the mainstream culture. When *all* we do is copy culture for our own Christian ends, we aren't loving or serving our neighbors.

> If we are known mostly for our ability to poke holes in every human project, we will probably not be known as people who bear the hope and mercy of God.

The greatest danger of copying culture, as a posture, is that it may become all too successful. We create an entire subcultural world within which Christians comfortably move and have their being. We breed a generation that prefers facsimile to reality, simplicity to complexity (for cultural copying almost always sands off the rough and surprising edges of any cultural good it appropriates), and familiarity to novelty. Not only is this a generation incapable of genuine creative participation in the ongoing drama of human culture-making, it is dangerously detached from a God who is anything but predictable and safe.

POSTURE 4: CONSUMPTION

If the fundamentalists were known for a posture of condemnation, the evangelicals were known for their critiques, and the musicians and merchants of the 1970s were known for their copying, in recent years American Christians have adopted the posture of consumption. We no longer forbid going to the movies, nor do we engage in earnest cri-

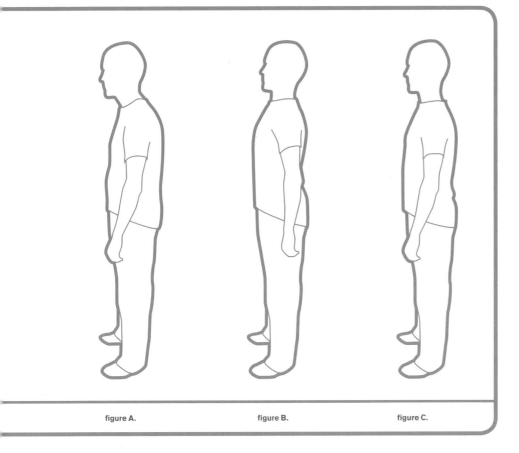

figure A.   figure B.   figure C.

tiques of the films we see—we simply go to the movies and, in the immortal word of Keanu Reeves, say, "Whoa." We walk out of the movie theater amused, distracted, or thrilled, just like our fellow consumers who do not share our faith.

Consumption is the posture of cultural denizens who simply take advantage of all that is offered up by the ever-busy purveyors of novelty, risk-free excitement, and pain-avoidance. Not that consumers are entirely undiscerning in their attitude toward culture: someone whose posture is consumption can spend hours researching the most fashionable and feature-laden cell phone; can know exactly what combination of espresso shots, regular and decaf, whole and skim, amaretto and chocolate, makes for their perfect latte; can take on extraordinary commitments of debt and commuting time in order to live in the right community. But while all of this involves care and work—we might even say "cultural engagement"—it never deviates from the core premise of

consumer culture that we are most human when we are purchasing something someone else has made.

Condemnation, critique, copying, consumption: all are essential gestures, and terrible postures. What posture were we made to take toward culture? The answer is at the very beginning of the human story, according to Genesis: like our first parents, we are to be **creators** and **cultivators**. Or to put it more poetically, we are artists and gardeners.

PROPER POSTURE: ARTISTS & GARDENERS

The postures of the artist and the gardener have a lot in common. Both begin with contemplation, paying close attention to what is already there. The gardener looks carefully at the landscape; the existing

plants, both flowers and weeds; the way the sun falls on the land. The artist regards her subject, her canvas, her paints with care to discern what she can make with them.

And then, after contemplation, the artist and the gardener both adopt a posture of purposeful work. They bring their creativity and effort to their calling. The gardener tends what has gone before, making the most of what is beautiful and weeding out what is distracting or useless. The artist can be more daring: she starts with a blank canvas or a solid piece of stone and gradually brings something out of it that was never there before. They are acting in the image of One who spoke a world into being and stooped down to form creatures from the dust. They are creaturely creators, tending and shaping the world that original Creator made.

I wonder what we Christians are known for in the world outside our churches. Are we known as critics, consumers, copiers, condemners of culture? I'm afraid so. Why aren't we known as cultivators—people who tend and nourish what is best in human culture, who do the hard and painstaking work to preserve the best of what people before us have done? Why aren't we known as creators—people who dare to think and do something that has never been thought or done before, something that makes the world more welcoming and thrilling and beautiful?

Changing our posture takes time, lots of time. Once you've gotten used to being a critic or a consumer, once you've been bent into that shape, you can only unbend slowly. But unless you unbend and begin to learn the posture you were made for, you'll never experience what it is to be fully human. It's long past time that we began to unbend, and began to be cultivators and creators in the image of God. **C**

Andy Crouch is editorial director of the Christian Vision Project (**www.christianvisionproject.com**). Read more of his writing at **www.culture-makers.com**.

This article is excerpted from the upcoming book, Culture Makers, *© 2006 by Andy Crouch. All rights reserved. Used by permission.*

NATURAL: THE POETRY OF ART BEFORE THE FALL

AN INTERVIEW WITH MAKO FUJIMURA

MAKO FUJIMURA'S ART, WHICH FUSES THE JAPANESE TECHNIQUE OF NIHONGA WITH WESTERN ABSTRACT EXPRESSIONISM, IS COLLECTED AROUND THE WORLD. BUT MAKO IS MORE THAN JUST A WIDELY RE-SPECTED ARTIST. A NATURAL BRIDGE-BUILDER, HE FOUNDED THE **INTERNATIONAL ARTS MOVEMENT (WWW.IAMNY.ORG)** TO HELP ARTISTS WORK FOR THE RENEWAL OF THEIR CULTURE. A SEASONED LEADER, HE HELPED TO PLANT THE VILLAGE CHURCH, IN GREENWICH VILLAGE. MAKO HAS BECOME A MENTOR FOR A GENERATION OF ARTISTS EVEN AS HE HAS BECOME INCREASINGLY IN DEMAND AROUND THE COUNTRY— HE SERVES ON THE COUNCIL OF THE NATIONAL ENDOWMENT FOR THE ARTS—AND IN EUROPE AND ASIA. IN THIS INTERVIEW FOR THE CHRIS-TIAN VISION PROJECT HE TALKS ABOUT THE REALITIES OF THE ART WORLD AS WELL AS THE BIBLICAL BASIS FOR TAKING THE ARTS MORE SERIOUSLY IN OUR CHURCHES, AND IN OUR EVANGELISM.

CVP: *What advice would you give to a young artist who is wary of "selling out"?*

FUJIMURA: Well, my artist side will say, art is sacred, it's precious. But if you want to make a living as an artist, if you feel that is the best way you can sustain your creativity, then it *is* a business. Yet the business side can be just as creative and artistic and beautiful as the art side. It's just a different challenge. You can have a business practice that speaks of your humanity, speaks of your creativity. It's not like you throw your creativity out the window.

The idea of stewardship is a very impor-tant concept for Christians. Steward-ship assumes that there are transactions somewhere. Somebody's going to benefit from your work and your work will be re-warded. So if you believe that you have a gift that God will sustain—which means, among other things, he is going to pay your bills through that gift—then you have to trust that God is going to be in the process of selling your work. Steward-ship demands that we see what we do as not our own, but belonging to Christ. We are simply there to take care of it, nurture it, cultivate it, work it—and our respon-sibility then is to let it go. If you are the caretaker of the garden, but you don't let your fruit be enjoyed by a community, you're not a good caretaker. So our art always needs to be engaged with the outer world, and that often means, in our capi-talist system, that it will be seen and sold as a commodity.

I also believe very strongly in doing things that don't sell. I am very passionate about collaborating in cases where you really don't have any business sense of whether it will be received well. I ask, "Is this going to be work that I can be proud of, that I can put my name on, that speaks of truth, goodness, and beauty in a way that I want to convey to the world?"

CVP: *What are the key elements of a Christian theology of the arts?*

FUJIMURA: I am convinced that fulfilling Matthew 28—the Great Commission—requires understanding Genesis 2.

Before the Fall, God begins to tap into Adam's creativity by giving him this garden to steward. Indeed, the text lists these precious minerals he will find under the earth, which assumes that he will have to work to get there. Then God brings a relational element into the picture, by bringing the animals to be named, which is really what poets do: to name experiences. And in the midst of that creative activity God reveals lack, of a mate, and Adam realizes the lack, and God immediately answers by creating Eve, and you have your first ecstatic poetry! So unceasing creativity flows out of the Garden—tied in with the marriage relationship and with community all before the Fall..

So what I do as an artist is not reparative work, like dentistry or road construction. Art is always generative. It creates. So it was, and is, and will always be. We will always be creators. That's just our natural state.

Now imagine a *lack* of those things: of creativity, of love, of the marriage covenant. Imagine an evangelist who is uncreative, dull, a black-and-white thinker, judgmental, intolerant, and his marriage is falling apart! And he comes to you to share the gospel. How persuasive is that?

I think that's the picture of the church right now, as seen from the outside. That's exactly what people feel: these are not creative people, they are the first to have an affair and fall apart, except a few very dedicated instances. And I think that shows that we have not done a good job as a church of living out the Genesis covenant—that's why we can't fulfill the Great Commission.

The church should be a place where people come for inspiration. Media companies, writers, filmmakers—they should come to church to be trained in how to think about creativity, how to find beauty. We have what the world wants. And we should be the first people group seeking answers about marriage relationships, about community, and that's not often the case.

I find it perplexing. If Genesis 2 is where we really find our foundational principle, why are we so distant from it? What are we doing wrong? It's the church's job to frame that question, and to come up with local answers. They may be different for each church, but every church should be concerned with this. Every mission organization should be concerned with this.

Let's say we all were to take a week of fasting from evangelism, and instead take Genesis 2 seriously. So you take your family to the zoo and name the animals. You go to a museum. You take your wife out on a date. You take your roommates out to dinner. You create, you make something, you write poems. If you don't know how

to write poems, you take a workshop in how to write poems. Whatever! Just take a week doing that.

And then on the eighth day, go out with the intent to evangelize. My guess is that you are going to be far more effective on the eighth day than we would have been before. Because you will have a narrative. You will be able to tell the person that you're sitting next to: "You know what I did last week? I took my kids to the zoo?" They'll say, "What?" Or they'll say, "I haven't been to the zoo in such a long time!"

Now that person is more likely to want to be part of our lives. "Hey," he'll think, "This guy is taking his kids out—maybe I could use his guidance." "She's talking about loving her husband, while I'm about to break up with my boyfriend—maybe I need her advice." These narrative contexts allow the gospel to become real to people. If we're not really enjoying life, why should people want to listen to us? Why should people want what we have if we don't have anything to give, if we don't have any stories about life, about what makes us truly human?

The idea of play is very important in Genesis 2. There's this eternal sense of freedom that gives Adam enormous ability to take risks—total freedom. God is giving us that, and I don't think we enjoy it enough. When we begin to enjoy his world, to fulfill the Genesis 2 covenant, the Great Commission will come much more naturally. ▣

For more from the Christian Vision Project and Mako Fujimura, visit **www.christianvisionproject.com**.

© *2006 Christianity Today International. All rights reserved. Used by permission.*

ERIK LOKKESMOE

FOUNDER OF BREWING CULTURE
Age 33, Washington D.C., www.brewingculture.com

AFTER SERVING IN POLITICS FOR SEVERAL YEARS, ERIK DISCOVERED THAT CULTURAL CONTENT, NOT POLITICAL ACTION, SHAPES THE HEARTS AND MINDS OF OUR NEIGHBORS. IF WE LOVE THEM AS WE ARE CALLED TO DO, THEN WE MUST FIND WAYS TO REDEEM THE CREATIVE SPHERES. BREWING CULTURE INVITES CREATIVES OF ALL BACKGROUNDS AND BELIEFS INTO A SAFE PLACE FOR AUTHENTIC COMMUNITY, CONVERSATION, AND CREATIVITY. IT IS WHERE PEOPLE GATHER TO WONDER ALOUD, "WHAT DOES IT MEAN TO BE HUMAN AND MORE THAN HUMAN?"

REDEEM THE CREATIVE SPHERES

I dream of a day when the Church—the people, not the building—is the most creative force in the world. Art and media should lift the eyes, give us a sense of our place, a sense of direction, and fill space with meaning, beauty. I am passionate about the whole idea of redeeming space. How do we take a building and use it for some great purposes? How do we take this barren landscape that we call television, and redeem it with content that, as Cicero said, "teaches, delights, and moves audiences"? How do we use our homes for hospitality, as a means of grace? These questions haunt me.

BUS STOP GRACE

Like Christ, we engage culture by entering time and space with excellence, substance, grace, and prayer. We are called to love our neighbor through our creations. An urban designer reminded me that a well-placed tree at a bus stop is a grace to the weary traveler. The same is true with a short story or a truthful advertisement or a song on the radio. It reminds us of something more, or as Os Guiness says, "that the world should have been otherwise." It means accepting art that is simply descriptive—it shows the world as it is, not how it should be. We must diagnose the world before we can give it the medicine. Most of all, however, we engage culture with holiness. Not cleverness, not better marketing or cooler haircuts, not the right words. We need holiness.

LEARNING THE CURRENTS

Almost daily I will encounter someone who will talk about a movie or a music group or a book—often a very popular cultural happening—with the expectation that I have seen or heard or read the work. I smile and nod with this nagging thought that, "I am so uncool. I don't even know what this person is talking about." It is a daily reminder that it is impossible to stay up on every cultural event, the latest group or bestselling book. Any attempt would be exhausting. I was a river guide for one summer. Good guides study the river. They know the currents, the rate of the flow. The way the water pushes against the rocks. The trick is to know the currents, not watch the rafts floating down the river ahead or behind you. Watch how the water flows over the rocks, how the river changes, how it is constantly creating.

FOUR THINGS

First, the world says it is all about you. It's not. It is about God and others. Something I learn every day. Second, you will not do anything great without friends by your side. Third, we need people with long-term vision for their work. A patient, persistent vision for change. And fourth, safe is not a word in the Christian vocabulary. This missionary named C.T. Studd said, and I paraphrase, "some want to serve within the sound of church and chapel bell, I want to run a rescue shop a yard from hell." That is where the leader should be—a yard from hell. **C**

Brilliant Irrelevance

By Tim Willard

Like screaming children on a teeter-totter, Christianity teeters on the fulcrum of relevance, deciding the best ways to reach the world for Christ. Imagine this scene on a busy playground … oblivious to those on the teeter-totter there is a little boy holding his bleeding knee. Beside him is his neighbor, helping him to the fountain to wash the cut, giving him the lollipop from his lunch and picking him for his kickball team. Meanwhile, the kids on the teeter-totter are still screaming at each other as the bell rings and the two new friends walk in from the kickball field. A new relationship grows now, one that is founded on the transference of love—one to another. It is messy, and not too many people even know about it. Thus is the brilliance of evangelism's new irrelevance.

Evangelicalism has oft struggled with how to make the Good News relevant to the swirling eddy of culture. Perhaps in today's turbulent society the answers to our questions on evangelism do not come from looking within evangelicalism but from without.

The church that survives and thrives goes beyond the classroom and headlong into culture. The more people I talk to, the more I pick up a general understanding that relevance doesn't equal what the church service does for unbelievers as much as how well the service equips believers to "be" in the world.

A friend of mine told me his church was contemplating ending weekly communion because it might offend a visiting unbeliever. He told his church that communion wasn't for the unbeliever; it was for Christians. There is this shift—from luring people into the church to hear preaching, to preaching the Good News with our lives and letting the world see that.

The new evangelism does not look like it used to; rather, it comes neatly packaged in the mess of redemption. But not only redemption … go one-step further: restoration. Think Narnia. It comes with what Kenneth Boa describes as the Cosmic Architecture—God's tapestry of creativity interwoven with man's life purpose. We are beginning to understand what it means to just "be"—"be" with God, "be" with our fellow man.

The Apostle James describes this as faith defined by works. This new shift goes beyond trends of 'cool' and the questions of what makes a church approachable. Instead it teaches believers that being relevant in America equals irrelevance to the world. Christ does not care if His bride is trendy; He cares for those in the child brothels of Cambodia, the killing fields of Rwanda, and those dealing with the devastation of Katrina.

People like Bono are harnessing celebrity currency and pressing entire governments to recognize this paradigm shift. Leaders such as Rick Warren, Gary Haugen and Sara Groves are bringing awareness to the needs of the world so that the church can lead the way in the effort to reach those in need.

Theologians and musicians alike recognize that Christianity may be on the verge of another Great Awakening—the threshold of revolution. God is moving, like ocean swells before a great storm. There is something on the horizon, past the waiting room of postmodernism, and it is closer to the heart of Christ than we have ever come. Many of us will die, but those who make it will see a raging love … come, Lord Jesus, come. **C**

Tim Willard is a staff writer and editor at Walk Thru The Bible Ministries. He also does freelance work for **www.relevantmagazine.com** and **www.lowercasepeople.com**. Tim only drinks french pressed dark roast and exclusively rides Kona mountain bikes. He lives with his wife, Chris, in Atlanta Georgia. Read more from Tim at **www.flickernail.com**.

ENGAGED IN CULTURE:

Celebrate the beauty of art. Take an afternoon or evening and find an art exhibit in your city or at a local university. As you study the art, try to discover the story behind it—who was the creator? Imagine the process they went through to create the piece. Journal your thoughts about Creation and how through redeeming the arts we can redeem the culture.

Authentic in Influence

Leadership is influence. I am not a leader if others are not following. Influence can't be forced or contrived. It can only be won over time. If I am living out the elements of a Catalyst Leader, influence will be natural, compelling, and attractive. If not, it will be challenged by others and ineffective. My prayer is that God would continue to expand and entrust me with greater influence.

What area of culture am I currently influencing? How do I lead others to influence culture?

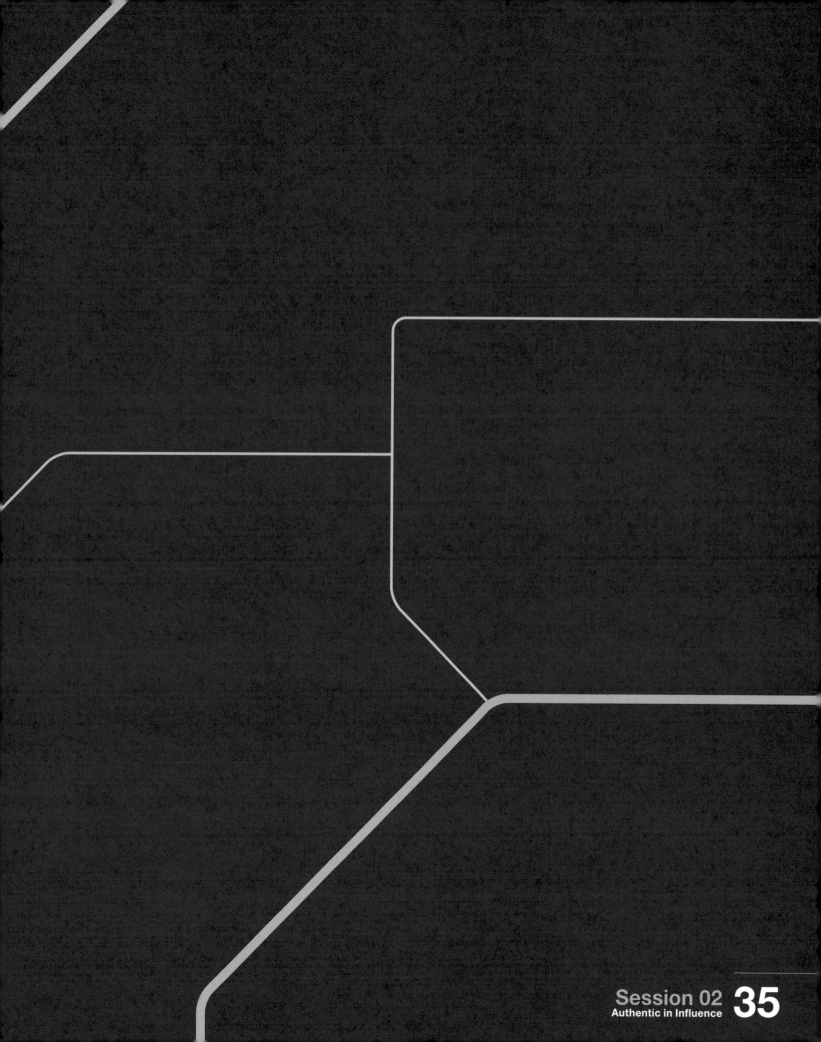

Authentic in Influence

I SMELL DEAD FISH

Cultivating the Authentic Fragrance of Christ

By Ben Ortlip

IN THE BEGINNING, THERE WAS THE ICTHUS. WHEN ADHERED TO YOUR BUMPER, THIS UNDERSTATED EMBLEM ALLOWED YOU TO SPREAD GOD'S LOVE WHEREVER THERE WAS ASPHALT. IN A GLARING OVERSIGHT, HOWEVER, IT ALSO TURNED OUT TO BE A SUBTLE WAY TO LET OTHER MOTORISTS KNOW THAT THEY'D JUST BEEN CUT OFF BY A CHRISTIAN. NO DOUBT, THAT'S WHEN THE COGWHEELS STARTED TURNING IN THE MINDS OF THE EVOLUTIONISTS; AS NOT LONG AFTERWARD, ICTHUS HAD GROWN FEET AND WAS WORKING FOR DARWIN. BUT THE EVOLUTION WAS JUST BEGINNING. NOT TO BE OUT-WITTED, CHRISTIANS QUICKLY ASSUMED THE ROLE OF BIG FISH IN THIS LITTLE POND OF DEBATE, AND DARWIN BECAME A MERE APPETIZER FOR A MUCH BIGGER "TRUTH" FISH. TALK ABOUT SURVIVAL OF THE FITTEST.

You already know the rest of the story: with their hearts broken from conviction, heathen motorists everywhere fell to their knees and begged to be told how they might repent of their sins. Unable to see over their steering wheels from their penitent position, massive pile-ups were occurring on highways all across the country. In the ensuing gridlock, Christian motorists had ample time to exit their vehicles and explain the four spiritual laws to the heathen evolutionists, who were still pinned inside their cars (though miraculously unharmed). They prayed the prayer and signed up for discipleship class right on the spot. It became the greatest evangelism outreach in the history of Christianity. They even made a television show about it, called "Highway to Heaven."

Okay, so maybe the whole Icthus bumper sticker ministry wasn't exactly the fulfillment of the Great Commission. But it did stimulate the creativity of the sticker industry. Stickergiant.com now carries more varieties of fish than the Georgia Aquarium. On a clever side note, they offer one fish that says "Sushi," one that says "Gifelte," and another that says "Lawyer" (in the shape of a shark). My favorite is the one that says "N Chips."

I had a fish on my car years ago. I took it off because I thought God would prefer not to have the publicity if it meant being glued to the back of an old rust bucket like mine. After all, just riding in the passenger compartment was enough of an attack on one's dignity. Plus, I didn't want people thinking that becoming a Christian would make them turn out like me. As a result, I missed out on the battle of the emblems. I'm glad, too. Frankly, I think that whole fish debate leaves a bad smell in the nostrils of the culture. In fact, I'm starting to think there's an entire element of American Christianity that reeks of rotten fish.

Let's face it. There's a big difference between Christ and Christianity. Christ is a person. And when someone encounters the person of Christ, there's no mistaking the fragrance of His Spirit. Christianity, on the other hand, is a name we call the sub-culture that claims to be affiliated with the Savior of the world. At least that's how non-Christians see it. Sometimes we manage to resemble the aroma of Christ Himself. But as a sub-culture, most of the time we smell no different from the unwashed. Our statistics for divorce are the same. Our practices in the workplace are no holier. And our reputation in traffic doesn't help us either. In fact, when it comes to things like taking care of the earth and recycling our milk jugs, we probably score lower than the national average.

This points us to a common misunderstanding for many well-meaning Christians. Believers often think that progress of the Christian sub-culture means progress for the name of Christ. When our sub-culture gains ground and is embraced by the culture at large, we consider it a success. If a Christian gets elected, we feel good about the state of the Kingdom. When an athlete acknowledges God after a big win, we well up inside. And when the Gospel finds its way into mainstream media, we feel like our work on this planet is almost done. Such events may be cause for celebration. But Christ-followers were not called to build a country, a compound, or any other sub-culture. We are called to make disciples. And often, those two objectives are in opposition to each other.

CHRIST IN THE CLUTTER
In fact, there's a big down-side to cultivating the culture of Christianity. The more prominent the culture of Christianity becomes, the more difficult it becomes for outsiders to see Christ in all of it. The more our faith is defined by the things Christians *do*, the less it will be distinguished by what Christians *are* on the inside. Suddenly, Christianity means nothing more to outsiders than another lifestyle to choose from. To them, Christians dress a certain way, they act a certain way, they listen to a certain kind of music, and they put fish stickers on their cars.

Of course, we don't foster this perception intentionally. But when we gather together at the cross, it's just a matter of time before our social instincts kick in and we form a people group … complete with unwritten social protocols for how to think, talk, act, dress, etc. The greatest challenge for Christians is not to help unbelievers get religion, but to help them get the difference between religious people and the person of Christ. Likewise, the greatest challenge for church leaders is to make disciples who understand the importance of this distinction. Frankly, playing the role of a Christian comes more naturally than pursuing a deep, personal connection with Christ … the kind that causes you to mimic His fragrance to the world around you.

AUTHENTIC IN INFLUENCE

One of the tenets of a Catalyst Leader is to be authentic in influence. But unless the next generation of leaders figures out how to rally believers around the flagpole of authenticity, we could be headed for a dark and disturbing era for the church's legacy.

If we allow our faith to be perceived as just another sub-cultural lifestyle, we risk burying the nucleus of our faith beneath the garments of our faith. Ironically, we hide our lamps under bushels that are smattered with Jesus stickers.

If you think about it, it's ironic when Christians talk about "engaging the culture." The minute we start using such terms, it suggests a comparison between our way of life and everyone else's. In essence, we reduce Christianity to a mere issue of sub-culturalism. And evangelism is basically an effort to recruit unbelievers away from their sub-culture and into ours. The first step is to get them to join our sub-culture on Sunday … to go to church and sing the songs and carry a Bible. With any luck, the other days of the week will start to resemble our lifestyle as well. The problem with that mentality is that it has nothing to do with sharing the Gospel. In fact, it's one of the biggest distractions from it.

These days, culture has more labels than ever. The biggest obstacle is getting past the culture's foregone conclusions about Christianity. Somehow, we have to rely less on sharing the gospel and focus more on living it.

When it comes to the church, that's pretty hard to do. The sign out front says Church. The steeple says Church. In fact, the bigger and more "successful" your ministry becomes, the tougher it becomes to see Christ in the middle of it. As sincere believers flock around it, your

mission statement becomes obscured by the social protocols of the people groups that develop in their midst. And instead of being drawn to the fragrance of Christ, outsiders can feel alienated by the cultural boundaries it creates.

THE LABEL-PROOF CHURCH

In essence, unbelievers are constantly looking for labels to place on things they don't understand. All humans do this. It's how we construct a personal worldview that enables us to function in society. As a result, every time Christians re-invent church, non-Christians are taken aback at first. Then, gradually, they learn to recognize it as the "God thing" knocking on the door of their heart again. Over time they assure themselves, "Oh, it's just those Christians trying to act cool again." Labeled. As long as there are tidy labels on everything, there's nothing to rock their worldview … nothing to challenge their personal theology … nothing to allow the need for Christ to come to the surface. That's why the job of church leaders doesn't permit us to rest on tradition—even new traditions. Our job is to stay one step ahead of the label-maker … to keep presenting the indescribable glory of God in fresh, relevant ways … until they conclude that the only label to give it is "Lord Jesus Christ."

For we are to God the aroma of Christ among those who are being saved and those who are perishing. To the one we are the smell of death; to the other, the fragrance of life.
-2 Corinthians 2:15-16a (NIV)

Labels can be powerful things. Corporations will spare no expense to make sure their labels portray just the right message to the public. In the 1990s, First Union National Bank had developed a terrible reputation, primarily for lousy customer service. They were losing customers left and right. With a crisis on their hands, they scrambled to save the company. They hired key people to revamp their whole approach to customer service. Essentially, they reinvented themselves, and within just a few months they had built a new bank that could once again be competitive in the marketplace. But one problem remained. The label still read "First Union." And despite all the positive things going on inside the bank, customers still saw the same old signage on the outside. They had already made up their minds about the brand. Eventually, First Union bought Wachovia Bank for a few billion dollars and converted all their locations into Wachovia branches. The First Union brand was retired, and Wachovia signs were put up everywhere. With the old label gone, their business finally rebounded.

That's the problem with labels. They tell stories before we have a chance to experience reality. And they can lead people to make decisions based on information that is no longer accurate ... or never even was.

In a way, Jesus' entire ministry was about changing all the labels. Back around 30 A.D., the culture had deeply-held perceptions about God and the church. Jesus not only changed everything about the church's infrastructure, but He also had

the task of announcing that things were different. The old labels no longer applied. For Jesus, engaging the culture meant recognizing the current perception and executing a strategy to re-inform it. For example, the old perception of God was that He never crossed cultural lines. So Jesus pursued relationships with those outside his prescribed circle.

That sounds a lot like the challenge of the Great Commission today ... to cross the line of "Christianity" to reach a world that's never met the real Christ.

THE PASSION OF THE CHRISTIANS
But like we said, it's easier to get excited about being a Christian than bridging cultural divides the way Christ would. The release of Mel Gibson's movie, *The Passion of the Christ*, was a great example of this. The first time I saw a trailer for the film, I was in a darkened theater equipped with Dolby surround sound. It was so powerful, the hair on my neck stood up and sang *Amazing Grace* in four-part harmony. I couldn't get a comb through it for a week. But I have to admit, a big part of my enthusiasm was about being part of a sub-culture that was finally getting some proper airtime on the silver screen.

I wasn't alone. Christians everywhere were starting to buzz about the film's release. What happened next was a classic case of wrapping Christ up with the labels of sub-culture. Christians across the country began huddling to make their game plans. Pastors were meeting with film company executives and Gibson himself. Churches were buying out

entire theaters. And all of these facts were widely publicized. By the time the movie came out, it had been clearly branded as a movement of the evangelical sub-culture. Fully aware of who was behind it, non-Christians made up their minds about the film without ever having to see it. And despite its huge success at the box office (almost all Christians), can we claim that it truly engaged the culture—penetrating their defenses, disarming their objections, and winning their trust ... the way Christ would?

I'm not discounting the film's sincere impact. But we should also be honest about how the situation devolved into a cultural stand-off. Jews claimed anti-Semitism. Catholics talked about blasphemy. Christians pledged allegiance to Mel. And non-Christians wrote it all off as a religious culture war based on selfish capitalism. As one cynic expressed, "Christian popular culture has always been rooted in an evangelistic impulse: from Warner Sallman's 'Head of Christ' portrait to the Contemporary Christian Music complex to WWJD paraphernalia, Christian popular culture is a cornucopia of evangelistic outreaches that have grown up to become consumer goods ... Evangelicalism will no doubt someday have its own filmmaking industry."[1]

Perhaps we thought *The Passion* would drive people into church the way the movie *Jaws* drove people out of the ocean. But apparently, that's not the way it works. In fact, it seems the Gospel will never gain ground through cultural channels. Instead, it plods steadily forward through individuals within those channels.

Our job is to stay one step ahead of the label-maker ... to keep presenting the indescribable glory of God in fresh, relevant ways ...

The lifestyle of Christianity makes a great path for believers to follow; but as a sub-culture, there's not much about it that begs the broader culture to approach the person of Christ. To them, it's just another way of life. So when it comes to engaging the culture, we have to recognize that there's not much power in Christianity as a sub-culture. The real power is in the authentic impact of Christ Himself in the meta-cultural realm—one person, face-to-face with God. Sure, some people will visit a church just because their neighbor attends. But for the most part, the culture is not influenced toward faith in Christ because of our fish stickers, even if they're stuck to the back of a brand new Lexus.

PR FOR JESUS

What is it that drives us to adopt a Public Relations approach to sharing our faith? I guess we somehow think it's a way of answering the directive: "let your light so shine among men." Perhaps it's a Western thing. We live in a world where rooting confidently for your team is somehow associated with helping them become "#1" in the world's eyes. We wear our school's sweatshirts and drink from their coffee mugs. In some towns, they'll even paint their bodies and rip off their shirts in sub-zero weather to prove their point. And what is the point, exactly? Is it that I think my team is the best, and therefore you should too? Or since I yell louder? Or act more insane? What if you don't want to be an idiot like me? Does that mean you should pull for the other guys instead?

At any rate, that's our mentality when it comes to promoting things in the West. We use buttons and stickers and yard signs to persuade voters to support our candidate. We speak out on behalf of a favorite hobby, a breed of dog, or an obscure club that we belong to. And perhaps strangest of all, we help corporations gain market share by brandishing their logos on our personal property. At our own expense, too. I guess aligning ourselves with a successful organization somehow feeds our need for significance and acceptance.

Maybe that's why it smells funny when we use the same approach to promote Jesus. To non-Christians, it's like we're witnessing out of a need for approval ... or worse yet, a hunger for significance. What kind of message does that really send? That's not where Jesus was coming from when He reached out to the culture. He didn't seek popularity to accomplish His mission. He proved His authenticity through His unpopularity.

THE IDOLS OF SUB-CULTURE

But the instinct to organize ourselves into like-minded sub-cultures is as strong as ever. And because of this tendency to form social groups, Christian leaders must constantly be on the lookout for the "idols of sub-culture"—those practices, mannerisms, or paraphernalia that invite labels ... the ones that define the lifestyle of

Christianity but obscure the invitation to life in Christ. And leaders must be willing to remove and replace them ... to redefine what it means to follow Christ. It's not likely that authentic, lasting impact will come through a massive movement of the sub-culture. "Making disciples" means more than introducing people to the Gospel. It means growing them toward mature citizenship in a kingdom that supersedes all cultures and classes.

To this day, I'm not comfortable putting stickers on my car. Maybe I'm too socially sensitive; but the idea of labeling myself with one sub-cultural group makes me think I'll only be alienating myself from all the rest. I don't want people making up their minds about me based on a few labels. So there's no sticker from my alma mater, because I want a clean slate when I encounter someone who attended our arch-rival school ... or never went to college at all. I even paid an extra $25 for one of those license plates that doesn't say which county you're from (my county made national news for its racism back in the 1980s). And there's no fish. When I meet a non-Christian, I don't want their preconceived notions about Christianity to keep them from seeing the real me (such as it is). Besides, it may be the only way I get close enough to tell them about the real person of Christ. **C**

Ben Ortlip writes books and study curriculum for several prominent Christian authors and oversees creative projects for trend-setting ministries like Campus Crusade for Christ, Injoy, FamilyLife, Walk Thru the Bible, and Northpoint Ministries. Ben is co-author of the breakout small group study *Blueprint for Life*. He and his wife, Lisa, live in Cumming, Georgia with their six children.

1. **What aspects of your sub-culture (your Christian sphere of influence) are most likely to be labeled by non-Christians?**

2. **Describe a time when non-Christians have been pleasantly surprised by an encounter with Christians.**

3. **What things would need to change to alter the way non-Christians view Christianity?**

4. **What does it take to engage someone with an authentic representation of Christ?**

5. **If you could do anything you want in ministry to engage culture, what would it be?**

6. **Did the movie *The Passion of the Christ* engage culture the way Christ would? Why or why not?**

THE CALCUTTA PARADOX

By Tim Elmore

IN 1997, I WAS PART OF A TEAM WHO WAS INVITED TO COME AND TEACH LEADERSHIP IN INDIA. ONE OF THE HIGHLIGHTS WOULD BE A SPECIAL MEETING WITH MOTHER TERESA IN CALCUTTA. UNFORTUNATELY, SHE DIED IN AUGUST, JUST THREE MONTHS BEFORE WE ARRIVED. ALTHOUGH IT WAS ONE OF MY DREAMS, I NEVER DID GET TO MEET THAT GREAT, LITTLE WOMAN.

We did, however, visit her headquarters, the Missionaries of Charity. It was tucked back into an alley, away from the main street. I was struck by how simple it was. There were Sisters, all on the floor, serving lepers, or wiping the sores from children's arms and legs or feeding homeless men. That's it. No neon lights. No flashy websites advertised. No plush toys to buy as souvenirs. We could tell the leadership Mother Teresa modeled for fifty years was simple and humble.

Maybe that's what made her so attractive to the world. She led, but she never called attention to herself. I discovered on the trip that Mother Teresa entered the world of the poor on August 17, 1948. She started alone, with no funding from St. Mary's High School where she'd been the principal. She left the famous, comfortable, elite school which served rich families to go to a slum where people lived in misery among rats and cockroaches, teaching the children of the nobodies... and serving anyone who needed help. She remembers, "One day, in a heap of rubbish I found a woman who was half dead. Her body had been bitten by rats and ants. I took her to a hospital, but they told me that they didn't want her because they couldn't do anything for her. I protested and said I wouldn't leave unless they hospitalized her. They had a long meeting and finally granted my request. That woman was saved. Afterwards, when thanking me for what I had done for her, she said, 'and to think it was my son who threw me into the garbage.'"[1]

Teresa felt she'd passed from heaven to hell. But she did it on purpose. When asked why she moved to the slums, she replied: "How can I serve the poor effectively unless I understand what they experience each day?" One by one, her former students at the high school began to join her. It grew over the years to become the largest order of its kind, with locations worldwide. She launched or inspired seven other organizations for both men and women, clergy and laypeople, to be involved. She won a Nobel Peace Prize in 1979. She spoke at Harvard's graduation. She spoke to presidents, and for several years she was voted the most influential woman in the world.

It's an amazing story. But what enabled Mother Teresa to attract so many people? I call it the Calcutta Paradox. It was the

fact that she was humble and didn't like attention—that magnetically drew others to her. It was the fact that she didn't pursue fame that made her famous. It was the fact that she downplayed her importance—that made her so irreplaceable as a leader. Several times she was asked about the secret to her work. She would only smile and sheepishly say, "I am just a little pencil in the hand of a writing God who is sending a love letter to the world."

Think about this principle. Have you ever heard someone ask an outstanding leader about her work or about the book she recently wrote—and that leader humbly brushed it off as nothing spectacular? How do listeners who know the truth respond? It makes them want to talk about how great that leader is or how great that book is. Why? Because the leader didn't do it. People tend to fill what is lacking in a leader's description of himself, and empty what is too full. It's the Calcutta Paradox. When we brush fame aside,

when we downplay our accomplishments, it is actually winsome and magnetic to people. They will start talking. People tend to over-speak about the leader who will only under-speak.

This principle shows up in all sorts of contexts. A few months ago, our organization, Growing Leaders, hosted a Leadership Forum for college deans. During the Forum, one dean, Mike, commented that his top student attended our leadership camp (Converge Atlanta) the previous May. He raved about how that student's life had been transformed. He went on and on about it. Hearing him talk deliriously about it, one of our team members asked him to share a testimony after the next session. That, however, is when we saw the Calcutta Paradox work in reverse. While introducing Mike, our team member began to talk about how this student's life had been incredibly transformed by our leadership camp. He didn't say anything that Mike hadn't already said,

but he stole Mike's thunder. Our team member unwittingly took the "rave" out of this dean. After the long introduction, Mike stood up and under-spoke about his student. Ouch. It totally ruined the moment. Why? Because we had over-spoken (Proverbs 27:2). This caused him to want to balance the comments so as not to distort them. Our team member should have humbly introduced him by saying, "We'd like to introduce a dean to you whose student attended our leadership camp. He mentioned it had a somewhat positive effect on him. Would you share about your student, Mike?" Can you guess what kind of testimonial that dean might have given? He would have raved again, because we under-spoke. Remember: people fill what is lacking and they empty what is too full.

Many of the greatest leaders in history—the ones we yearn to be like—are humble leaders. Why? The Calcutta Paradox. We're drawn to humility. Billy Graham won over the skeptical press when he first visited England in 1954. Those reporters mocked him at the beginning of his crusades there in Britain, yet by the end—they were praising him. And it wasn't his flashy preaching that changed them. In fact, Jesus himself was described as lowly and humble. Today, more people follow him than anyone else in history. In Jim Collins' book, *Good to Great*, he talks about Level Five Leaders: those who reached the top; leaders who took their company from being "good" to being "great." His research team was shocked by what they found in these leaders. He said he expected those companies to be led by charismatic leaders, with huge personalities and even bigger egos. Instead, he found the opposite. They were leaders with "windows and mirrors." When something went right, they looked out the window and said: Look at this team. Look at what they achieved. When something went wrong, they looked in the mirror and said: How can I improve to lead this team better?[2]

Humility doesn't mean weakness. These kinds of leaders are strong—but they're secure enough to see beyond themselves. They're not worried about their images. They know their value, but it isn't about them. It's about a cause much bigger than them. Humility doesn't mean leaders think less of themselves. It means they think of themselves less. And this … makes others think more of them.

A Look at the Book

Check out the scripture below and respond to the biblical references to this truth.

1. In this paraphrase of Luke 14:7-11, Jesus introduces the Calcutta Paradox in His own way. He tells people:

When you are invited by someone to a wedding feast, do not take the place of honor … but when you are invited, go and recline at the lowest place, so that when the one who has invited you comes, he may say to you, "Friend, move up higher." Then you will have honor in the sight of all who are at the table with you. For everyone who exalts himself will be humbled, and he who humbles himself will be exalted.

Why do people tend to insist on taking places of honor or seeking words of honor for themselves?

_____

Why does following Jesus' instruction require trust on our part, as leaders?

_____

2. Why is it that leaders who humbly "under-speak" about themselves are so attractive?

_____

Humility doesn't mean leaders think less of themselves. It means they think of themselves less. And this … makes others think more of them.

Getting Personal

Now assess how well you practice this principle with others. From whom do you seek recognition? From where do you receive your sense of identity? God saw fit to humble Jacob and break him of his self-promotion, self-righteousness, and self-sufficiency over time. In Genesis 32:24-32, Jacob wrestled with God—seeking His blessing. He finally got what he sought, but only when…

1. Jacob was alone with God. He couldn't depend on anyone else as his source.
What do you depend on as your source of identity and affirmation?

_____

2. Jacob was honest with God. He couldn't pretend he had no needs or struggles.

_____

How often do you attempt to project an image that appears to have it all together?

_____

3. Jacob was broken by God. He couldn't depend on his own strength or resources.
Do you often depend on your own strength and wisdom instead of God's?

_____

4. Jacob was hungry for God. He finally admitted he was desperate for God to meet his need.
Are you able to publicly acknowledge your weakness and your need for others and for God?

_____

Practicing the Truth

This week, attempt three acts of kindness—anonymously. Don't let anyone know what you're up to, including the ones you're blessing, if possible. It may be as simple as sending them an encouraging Bible verse in the mail, or as creative as restocking the fridge with their favorite cola. Jesus spoke of giving and not letting your "left hand know what your right hand is doing" (Matthew 6:3). It's a motive check. Next, examine your heart. How did this make you feel? Are you okay with serving without getting any credit? Journal your thoughts and feelings.

During this same week, practice The Calcutta Paradox. Under-speak any good deeds you may do, and express humility whenever one of your accomplishments comes up in a conversation. Don't deny the praise of others; thank them for it, but don't play into it. See what it does to your heart. See what it does to others. Do they find it attractive? Write down what happens. **C**

Tim Elmore is founder and president of Growing Leaders, Inc. He has worked with students for over 25 years and is committed to developing next generation leaders who love God and know how to influence their world. Tim is the author of several other books, including *Habitudes: Images that Form Habits and Attitudes* (2004). For more information on these resources check out **www.GrowingLeaders.com.**

Reprinted from Habitudes #2: The Art of Connecting With Others, *©2006 by Tim Elmore. Used by permission of Growing Leaders.*

no perfect people allowed

By: John Burke

When my wife, Kathy, was in preschool she fell in love with a comic strip character, Zelda. Kathy wanted to be like Zelda. She wanted to do everything Zelda did. Then Kathy decided she *was* Zelda. Her teachers came to her mom concerned because Kathy would no longer answer to the name Kathy, she wanted to be called Zelda. We've all pretended to be someone we're not. It's fairly common for kids to pretend they are someone else. And it's acceptable if kids pretend because they are still forming their identities. But the goal is to learn to be yourself by the time you are an adult. Unfortunately, few adults seem to be comfortable enough with themselves *not* to pretend.

Our generation longs for something authentic. They are searching for "the real thing," though they don't really know what "the real thing" is. Because

this generation has endured so much "me-ism" and letdown from those they were supposed to follow and trust, they want to see a genuine faith that works for less-than-perfect people before they are willing to trust. They want to know this God-thing is more than talk, talk, talk. They desperately want permission to be who they are with the hope of becoming more. They aren't willing to pretend, because hypocrisy repulses them. Most have yet to realize that every person is a hypocrite to some degree—the only question is whether we realize it and are honest about it.

IT STARTS WITH AUTHENTICITY

When we launched Gateway Community Church in 1998, the first service was entitled "Losing My Need to Pretend." Everything we did that morning contrasted the inauthentic ways of the religious leaders whom Jesus deemed hypocrites with an authentic spirituality of the heart. The religious leaders of Jesus' day were focused on religious rule-keeping. Jesus reserved his harshest words for these pretenders: "Woe to you Pharisees, because you give God a tenth of your mint, rue and all other kinds of garden herbs, but you neglect justice and the love of God. You should have practiced the latter without leaving the former undone."(Luke 11:42 NIV)The religious leaders of Jesus' day

were so focused on the traditions they had formed around the heart of God's message that they were neglecting the things most on God's heart.

That September morning in the delivery room of our new church, I told our new-born congregation that these stories are a warning against inauthentic, incongruent living. Jesus is basically saying, *Lose the religious pretense; it's destructive to authentic faith. Shed the mask of hypocrisy you hide behind. I want honest, authentic people—not hypocrites who pretend to be something they're not.*

I asked the congregation a question at the end of the message: "Can we be this kind of a church? The kind where people don't have to pretend? Where we can be ourselves and stop pretending we're more or less than what we are right now? That's the only way we can help each other grow to be all God intended us to be. If we can't do this, we're just playing church!"

SO YOU WANT TO BE AUTHENTIC?

I got an email that first Sunday afternoon from a woman who attended our first service:

Today for the first time ever I felt like I had found a place to explore spirituality where I would be accepted. Thank you! I hope to be able to talk my husband into trying our church. We both have tattoos and piercings and have always felt uncomfortable in traditional churches. You are just what I've been asking for. P.S. I almost used my work email to send this, but then I thought, why use a mask? This is me.

I hadn't noticed her email address, so I glanced at it: *browneyedbi*. Tia was bisexual! And she had taken me seriously—she wasn't going to hide it from her new church that valued authenticity! Later that month, she invited my wife, Kathy, and me over for dinner. I thought, *Okay Lord, lead us to represent you.* They were a young family, in their late twenties with three children, living in a nice neighborhood. Tia had been a single mom before marrying Jim, the father of the youngest boy.

Over dinner I found out that Jim had grown up in the wealthy part of town but had pretty much been disowned by his family when he kept getting busted for drugs. He now worked as a valet in a strip club because it paid better than any other job he could get. Jim and Tia had both been into spirituality but not into God. They dabbled in the occult and even got married in a "haunted house."

After dinner, we all went into the living room and after small talk, Kathy and Jim began conversing about Jim's occultic past and the hypocrisy of Christians.

Tia began to tell me how much she was growing since coming to Gateway.

"I loved the series, 'If You Really Knew Me,'" Tia said. "I know that's exactly why we've been scared of churches—fear that we'd be judged if they really knew us. That's why I love Gateway. I feel so welcome. And the message you did two weeks ago has really helped me already. I've patched things up with my best friend as a result of it. I hadn't talked to Shelly in over a year, and that Sunday I went home and called her, and we were able to patch things up. And I never thought that would happen," Tia replied shaking her head.

"Why? What happened between the two of you?" I asked.

"Jim got Shelly pregnant," Tia said as if telling me the weather forecast. I thought she was going to laugh and say, "Just messing with you," but as she continued to expound, I realized she was completely serious. "When Shelly found out, she was furious. Still, ever since that nasty fight we had afterwards, we hadn't talked at all in over a year. And now I've apologized, she forgave me, and we're friends again! I really feel like I'm growing spiritually!"

Whoa, hang on there a minute—my mind was spinning.

What was it they taught me in seminary about how to handle a situation like this? Nothing came to mind. So I prayed. "Lord, how do I respond? She's being authentic, and I don't know what to say. You knew all this already, so show me how to re-present you."

As we continued talking, my heart started to break for this woman. At an earlier time she had told me that she knew bisexuality was wrong for her, and she wanted to stop for her kids' sake. There had to be something very painful that led her into such a destructive lifestyle. I sensed I needed not to react but to listen. So I asked questions. "Tia, you said you felt

like bisexuality was unhealthy, and you knew you needed to make a change. What made you start down that road in the first place?" I hesitantly inquired.

"My parents divorced when I was a baby, and my mother remarried a wonderful man who was like a dad to me since I was three. But I would spend every summer with my biological father, who started sexually molesting me when I was nine. Once I turned thirteen, I refused to see my biological father anymore, but I didn't tell Mom why until I was in my twenties. That wasn't the end of it, though," Tia recalled, as I noticed a sadness bleeding through an otherwise hardened exterior. "I was later gang raped by some of the football team in high school. That probably had some effect."

God's heart broke for Tia, who learned from an evil world her value is purely sexual. All of her self-worth centered on her ability to attract others sexually, male or female . . . it was the closest substitute for real love she could find.

"Tia, where are you at spiritually?" I asked later in the evening.

"I'm good with God, but I don't know about the whole Jesus thing. It kind of makes me feel creepy for some reason," Tia confided. "I don't see why it's so important to believe in Jesus."

"The whole reason God sent Jesus was so we could know God in a personal way. So we can know why he will forgive us and make us clean no matter what's happened in the past. He wants a relationship with you, Tia, because he loves you. Do you know that?" I asked.

"That hasn't really been my impression, especially from Christians," Tia quipped.

"Well, Tia, you're on the right path," I took a leap of faith to encouragingly say. "I think God is trying to draw you close so that he can begin a healing process in your life. He's already working in your life, Tia. And I really believe, if you'll stay open and start seeking to understand who he is, you'll find the love you've been seeking."

Tia managed an uncomfortably soft smile as her eyes wandered off to some distant place. "You think so?" she semi-sarcastically ventured after a moment of silence.

"I'm sure of it."

AUTHENTICITY STARTS WITH ME

The longer I walk with Christ, the more I see the Pharisee in me. I'm convinced the most important work of spiritual leadership is leading a spiritually authentic life. But to do this, I must break through the deception that I am somehow better than others. That I am somehow a little less in need of God's mercy and grace than the Tias and Jims of the world.

A culture of authenticity starts with me. I must first recognize that I'm no less capable of being deceived than were the religious leaders of Jesus' day. I must constantly remind myself that the apostle Peter was deceived in his zealousness and called down the rebuke of Jesus. I must realize that Paul was deceived in his zeal for God's righteousness to the point of condoning the murder of Christ-followers. I must recount the corrupt yearning for power and self-aggrandizement that stalked the sons of Zebedee, James, and John, as they fantasized and plotted a path to greatness as Jesus' disciples. (Mark 10:35-40)

Who am I to think I am somehow incapable of being deceived by my own brand of cultural religious piety? I try to read daily from a one-year Bible for this reason. It usually takes me two years. My goal is not to read through it but let it read through me, knowing I can be deceived if I'm not ruthlessly taking inventory before God. And I must always remember that if I am deceived, I'll be the last to know about it.

Authenticity is hard work. It always works from the inside out. It begins with the inner life of the leader, being authentic with God. It manifests itself in personal vulnerability before others as an intimate connection with God displaces the fear of transparency. This opens for others a view into an authentic spiritual life of a real human—not a religious salesperson. Finally, it becomes embedded in a culture so that authentic, growing communities of people can be formed and transformed. **C**

John Burke is pastor of Gateway Community Church in Austin, Texas (**www.gatewaychurch.com**) and president of Emerging Leadership Initiative (**www.elichurchplanting.com**). He and his wife, Kathy, have been married for 17 years and reside in Austin with their two children.

Taken from No Perfect People Allowed: Creating a Come As You Are Culture in the Church, *copyright ©* *2005 by John Burke. Used by permission of Zondervan.* (**www.zondervan.com**)

I'm convinced the most important work of spiritual leadership is leading a spiritually authentic life.

STRENGTHS REVOLUTION
An Interview with Marcus Buckingham

DO YOU SPEND THE MAJORITY OF YOUR TIME AT WORK PLAYING TO YOUR STRENGTHS? DO YOU EVEN KNOW WHAT YOUR STRENGTHS ARE OR HAVE THEY BEEN LOST IN THE "TO DO YESTERDAY" PILE? RECENT POLLS REVEAL THAT LESS THAN TWO OUT OF TEN PEOPLE SAY THEY SPEND THE MAJORITY OF THEIR DAY "PLAYING TO THEIR STRENGTHS". CONSIDER THIS: IF YOU DEVOTE 25% OF YOUR DAY TO THE THINGS YOU DON'T LIKE TO DO, OR THAT BORE YOU, OR FRUSTRATE YOU—THIS STILL LEAVES 75% OF YOUR WORK HOURS TO FILL WITH ACTIVITIES THAT CALL UPON YOUR STRENGTHS. AND YET SO FEW OF US DO.

MARCUS BUCKINGHAM WANTS TO CHANGE THAT.

AFTER YEARS INTERVIEWING THOUSANDS OF EMPLOYEES AT EVERY CAREER STAGE, HE MADE A DISCOVERY: *COMPANIES AND ORGANIZATIONS THAT FOCUS ON CULTIVATING EMPLOYEES' STRENGTHS RATHER THAN SIMPLY IMPROVING THEIR WEAKNESSES STAND TO DRAMATICALLY INCREASE EFFICIENCY WHILE ALLOWING FOR MAXIMUM PERSONAL GROWTH AND SUCCESS.*

IF SUCH A THEORY SOUNDS REVOLUTIONARY, THAT'S BECAUSE IT IS. HE CALLS IT THE "STRENGTHS REVOLUTION."

CATALYST: *Your research shows that more than 80 percent of people are unfulfilled in their jobs or careers. Do you think people settle when it comes to picking a job or a career?*

BUCKINGHAM: Oh, no. I don't think people settle at all. I just think most of us don't have a clue as to how to bring the best of ourselves to work. We might have known when we were children—when our strengths were really clear and strong. You might not have called them strengths then, but when you were a kid you knew what got you out of bed every day, what process you wanted to take, and what situations kind of thrilled you and which ones you hated—and you trusted that.

But between then and now, you listen to parents to tell you what job you should have. You go to pay the bills or pay off a loan. You've got to have a boss, and the boss tells you to do this, that and the other. And what tends to happen is you listen to the outside world more closely than you listen to yourself … and the majority of us end up in a job where we don't have a chance to express the best of ourselves.

So, I don't think we settle. I just think we aren't taught how to identify our strengths and weaknesses, and then ensure that, week by week, we're spending more time playing to our strengths and less time on activities that weaken us.

CATALYST: *Why do you think people tend to give more attention to growing in their areas of weakness, rather than focusing their strengths?*

BUCKINGHAM: Well, my theory is that there are three myths that we believe to be true regarding weaknesses. The first myth is this: *As we grow, our personality changes.* The truth is, as you grow, you become more of who you already are. You might be able to change your values, your manners, or your aspirations; but in terms of the core of the positive personality, those things don't change as you grow.

Second, we believe *we will grow the most in our weaknesses.* The truth is the opposite of that— that for each of us, our greatest opportunity

for growth happens in our areas of strength. And by growth, I mean we'll be most creative, most inquisitive, come up with the most new ideas, and learn the most in the areas where we're already strong. Our weaknesses are— contrary to what's written on most employee appraisals—not areas of opportunity. They are areas of *least* opportunity.

The last myth is that *to be a great team member, you should chip in and do whatever it takes to help the team.* Ninety-one percent of people believe this myth. The truth is that productive team members find out what their strengths are and contribute those most of the time. That's really the most responsible thing you can do to help your team. Occasionally, you may have to step out of your strength zone, of course; but, as any great coach will tell you, that isn't the essence of teamwork. That's the exception to teamwork.

CATALYST: *If you had a minute to tell us one life principle, what would it be?*

BUCKINGHAM: Discover what you don't like doing and stop doing it. Deep down, the world is basically ambivalent about you and your strengths. If it helps get something done, then people like the strengths. But as soon as your strengths move you off in a slightly different direction, then they're annoyed by your strengths. So really, the only person who's going to keep you on your strengths track is you.

But the problem with strengths is they help you get things done, and soon people start offering you new opportunities. New doors will open and you get a bigger title and more money and a bigger desk. Some of those opportunities will continue to play to your strengths, but many won't. So, really, it's your job to keep yourself sufficiently clear-headed to know which doors you shouldn't go through.

So much of this is the function of what you choose not to do; those things you manage to edit out of your life. We need to be much more disciplined to stop doing those things that weaken us. That's what a weakness is:

an activity that weakens you, that bores you, drains you, or depletes you. The annoying thing is that you might be actually quite proficient at it. So if you want to make a long and lasting contribution, learn how to edit out your weaknesses, because no one else will. If you don't want to make a long and lasting contribution, then all this is irrelevant.

CATALYST: *So how does this living out our strengths play out in the emerging generation?*

BUCKINGHAM: The way to succeed for a species, whether it's plant, insect, animal, or human, is you find an unoccupied niche and you exploit it. Each cell in our body has a specialized function, and it works symbiotically with the one next door to it. It's nature's strategy for winning.

What is true for our bodies is true with your workplace. You look to whether there is an unoccupied niche, you figure out where your natural advantage is, and you find ways to make those two things converge. It's particularly true for Generation Y. Generation Y's are always looking for an award if they manage to show up to work six weeks on time, and expect to be the next vice president at age 23. They're always looking to sort of own it and claim it right now.

And that's okay. We shouldn't fight against that. What that means, though, is you need to figure out how to take control of your time at work and tilt it deliberately towards your strengths and away from your weaknesses. Without telling someone, "Hey, do whatever you want to do", the best companies will be ones to figure out a way to say to the Generation Y person, "Hey, we want you to rewrite your job description under your boss's nose, and we want you to do that each week, but not until you do it through the filter of a deep understanding of your strengths."

Why? Not because it'll make them feel better, but because they'll contribute more that way.

And, by the way, it *will* make you feel better; and companies will do it because it's just more productive.

CATALYST: *Let's talk about leadership for a moment. Many people use "manager" and "leader" interchangeably. You make a very clear distinction, however, between managing and leading. What are the key distinctions?*

BUCKINGHAM: The qualities of each are not mutually exclusive; however, having the qualities of one role does not suggest that you have the qualities of the other. The distinctions are found in the job roles. The key skill of a man-

1. *Who are you trying to serve?* That's what every great leader needs to answer. Vividly describe stories that describe who we are serving. When Howard Schultz talks about who Starbucks is trying to serve, he doesn't talk about coffee. He says, "We're trying to serve people who want a third space. Home is the first space; work is the second space; they need a third space. Starbucks is a third space." Well, that's beautifully vivid.

2. *What's your one advantage?* Don't give me

CATALYST: *Tell us about your new film series, Trombone Player Wanted. What was your motivation in creating this series and what do you hope will be the result?*

BUCKINGHAM: We wanted to find a way to reach more people. If you look at Google Video, Yahoo Video, YouTube, and the success of iTunes' video component, this is going to be the way that we reach Generation Y. While this is designed for busi-

---

"Discover what you don't like doing and stop doing it."

---

ager is individualization. It is the manager's job to find out what is unique about each person and capitalize upon each individual's strengths. Simply stated, great managers know how to turn one person's unique talents into performance.

Great leaders do the exact opposite of what managers do. The leader's job is to uncover what is universal, what we share as human beings—love of family, freedom, fear of the unknown—and capitalize upon that. Great leaders tap into higher order truths, create a vision of the future, and rally people around that better future.

CATALYST: *What advice would you have for a young, emerging leader, somebody that doesn't have the authority to cast that full organizational vision, but has influence within an area or people group?*

BUCKINGHAM: Remember, first of all, people are frightened of the future—and they should be. Don't label it a weakness. It isn't. It's an adaptive human trait. A young leader should know the challenge of leadership isn't to deny the change that's frightening. It's to engage with that fear and somehow bring confidence through clarity.

What are you clear about? There are three questions that a leader must answer to their followers, even if you don't have a job title as a leader; if you are simply trying to create influence:

five strengths. Give me one strength. The more strengths you give me, the less persuaded I am. The strength of Apple Computer is its design. Stephen Jobs says, "We design simple things to use. We are not very good at partnering with other software companies. We're not that good at partnering with large corporate IT departments. We are great at designing things that are incredibly simple to use."

3. *Why will we win today?* A good leader today needs to understand that what their followers need most of all is tell me why we will win, and there aren't three answers to that question—there's one vivid one. Think of Rudy Giuliani after 9/11. He was able to rally the city of New York by turning fear into confidence. The strength of New York City was all about exploiting their strength.

The best leaders are brilliant in painting vivid pictures of where we're going, and that transforms our fear into confidence. Great leaders pick one value, one organizational strength, one great cause, and talk about it vividly.

nesses, it's going to be the way to reach school kids. I was always conscious that this message about strength is something that we need to teach people earlier than when they get into the workforce. We need to indoctrinate them really quickly because, otherwise, they can get way off track and just not contribute what they should contribute.

And books are fine, talks are fine, but what this generation is used to are compelling, visually arresting images. So we joined up with the creative forces behind Rob Bell's successful *Nooma* series, which are just so compelling, so beautifully done, and so intimate without being fake.

My hope is that they will spread this strength message farther and faster than purely books can do. We've got to figure out a way to get these films in as many peoples' hands as possible. I'm very excited about them. **C**

Marcus Buckingham graduated from Cambridge University in 1987, with a master's degree in social and political science. During his seventeen years at The Gallup Organization, he helped lead research into the world's best leaders, managers, and workplaces. He is the author of three books, including *The One Thing You Need to Know* and *Now Discover Your Strengths*. He lives with his wife and two children in Los Angeles. For more information, visit **www.marcusbuckingham.com**.

For more information on Trombone Player Wanted, visit **www.simplystrengths.com.**

By Jeff Shinabarger

GREEN LIGHT
Influence is gained by DOING something

THE CATALYST COMMUNITY IS FILLED WITH AMAZING STORIES OF DREAMS COME TRUE. IN A SHORT TIME, WE'VE SEEN COUNTLESS EMERGING LEADERS GAIN INFLUENCE ALL OVER THE NATION AND WORLD. PASTORS HAVE PLANTED CHURCHES THAT GREW TO SERVE THOUSANDS, COLLEGE STUDENTS WITH LINT IN THEIR POCKETS HAVE RAISED MILLIONS OF DOLLARS FOR ORPHANS IN AFRICA, AND WRITERS WHO ONCE WERE JOURNALING RECKLESS THOUGHTS IN COFFEE SHOPS ARE NOW HEARING THEIR WORDS QUOTED ON SUNDAY MORNINGS. ALL OF US HAVE DREAMS ... BUT WHAT MAKES THESE INFLUENCERS DIFFERENT THAN THOSE OF US WHO ARE STILL WAITING FOR THE BIG BREAK? IS IT TALENT, PASSION, OR POSITION? IS IT A SECRET SAUCE THAT OTHERS CAN'T SEEM TO CREATE?

A few years ago, Ben Affleck and Matt Damon were no-name actors with a story to tell. They gained a huge amount of cultural influence when they won an Oscar for writing (and starring in) the movie *Good Will Hunting.* Capitalizing on that influence, they launched a program to give other scriptwriters a chance for their big break. The name was a perfect metaphor to describe their journey: Project Green Light.

We all have different talents and passions that are waiting to be unleashed—waiting to advance the vision, build the dream, or create the next thing that will change the world. How many of us sit parked at yellow? What are we waiting for? A Green Light.

GO NOW

Every story of influence has a "once upon a time." There has never been a catalytic idea that was already happening, there has never been an epic story without a beginning, and there will never be a person of influence without a starting point to the journey. This is the story of creation.

This is your story.

So, let's talk about this story of yours. To do something, you have to start somewhere. But starting isn't easy; often it's the most difficult part. Why? You don't know where or how to begin. Artists will tell you that the first word, color, or image chosen to be placed on a blank canvas is the hardest part of an entire piece. At the same time, great writers will tell you the only way to begin is to start writing whatever you think.

Then there is fear. Fear of failure—that you might take a wrong step. Yet, you must begin by taking a step—it's not hard to retrace a step or take a different step if the first one didn't work. It's only one step, forward motion. Behind every great piece of art we see hundreds of others. The masterpiece was not the first creation by the artist. It takes work and sweat to make masterpieces, but it starts with one

step. You may be paralyzed by the fear of success. What if it works? Then what? Then take the next step. Then the next and the next. I know you don't know all the steps yet, you can't know all the steps yet. You've been given a vision or a dream for a purpose. Take the steps and trust that God will guide the process. Don't let fear of the unknown taint the future of your story.

Are you waiting for a boss or mentor to give you the green light? That's a little safer, isn't it? Then you're not out there on the starting line by yourself. There's someone else to lean on, and someone else to blame if things go wrong. But is that any way to live? Always waiting on someone else? My friend Mike Metzger encouraged me with this advice: "Just do something!" The needs are so great in our fallen world that even if what you do doesn't work out, you are setting a new personal standard. You create a personal

ethos of beginning and learning in the process. A well planned out project that never happens is nothing more than a fantasy written in your journal. So what if you screw up? An idea that is acted upon and fails has its own place in your developing story. Give yourself the green light and begin a journey of influence.

Bobby Bailey, Jason Russell, and Laren Poole understand the green light. They stumbled upon injustice happening in Uganda and took that responsibility on as their own to share the story with America. They created the Invisible Children documentary that millions of people around the nation have seen. They sent 4 tour busses to every major city in America. They showed the film on Capitol Hill with the support of Congressmen. They were on Oprah. And now there are children in Uganda with lives being restored. All this from three college students learning how to make movies. How did this happen? Three guys just did something. People are drawn to people that do. The motion of stepping out and stepping forward attracts others.

BEGIN WITH THE COMMON GOOD

Now let's talk about that dream you have for a minute. Since you are putting yourself out there, taking a chance, giving yourself the green light, why not focus on the good of all mankind? If the ideas we act upon will help restore culture, our influence potential grows exponentially. The greater the cultural focus, the greater your audience. You may be thinking, "But I'm not in it to be 'big.'" I think a better word is "wide." Let me explain what I mean. You live primarily in one or more subcultures—groups of people with similar ways of living. These subcultures restrict the way you think, act, and influence. Often as Christians, we surround ourselves with other church-going people. While that may feel comfortable, it limits your ability to shine your light for all to see. To gain influence in all of culture. So I want to challenge you as you dream to stretch yourself. Pursue new ventures that are not only focused on Christians. Use your energy and your time to create solutions that serve our greater community. Find purpose in celebrating the good, the true and the beautiful, while also bringing awareness and solutions to injustice. You may be surprised at who comes alongside, what good you find, and how wide your influence will grow.

Not long ago, three friends and I started a dot-com called Gift Card Giver (**wwwgiftcardgiver.com**). We were sitting around one morning and noticed that each of us had a stack of gift cards in our wallets with a small amount of money on each one. We imagined that if we combined gift cards, others could gain from the money. So we pooled our resources, shared the idea with others, and the next thing you know we are getting gift cards sent to us from all over the nation. Everyone is drawn to the idea of helping the poor. This is a principle that not only Christians understand, it is ingrained into our human nature. Creating sustainable services and enterprises for the common good will connect with the hearts of all people, broadening your space of influence.

TRUE GREEN

Understanding the era and context that we currently live in is essential to beginning your new journey. We are moving to a new age, where authenticity is the basis for every experience. Remember back to the last intense movie that you viewed where the lead actor was acting in a studio and you could tell the backdrop was super-imposed or graphically enhanced behind them. On the surface it appeared he was accomplishing a death defying feat, when in reality he was held up with

WE ARE MOVING TO A NEW AGE, WHERE AUTHENTICITY IS THE BASIS FOR EVERY EXPERIENCE.

wires 8 inches off the floor. That's a green screen sequence. We all make fun of those scenes because they are not real. The Disneyland approach only lasts until a certain age, then it wears off. A good story impresses immediately or may even bring emotion, but a lack of authenticity will be exposed by those who take a closer look.

Every new idea that is developed must be done without selfish ambition. If you are trying to create something for selfish gain, you will not be successful. Dr. John Stott uses the phrase "the smell of hypocrisy" when referring to those who help others for personal gain or inappropriate agendas. We all know from personal experience how much a selfish persona distracts us from what is being presented. On the other side, we've all experienced people that have such a vision and calling for their work, that we can't help but be attracted and get involved.

Don't search for influence. Search yourself. Find what moves you. Look around you. Discover a place of need. Authentically pursue a vision that helps humanity. Use the gifts you have been given. Influence will follow at the moment when you can handle it.

LEADERSHIP IS INFLUENCE.

To have influence in our culture, you must begin now. Every time you put yourself out on the line and try something new, you gain influence. I've never seen a guy playing Xbox at home by himself gaining cultural influence. The product of doing something will result in a positive continuum of influence. Do Something. This is your Green Light. **C**

Jeff Shinabarger is the creative mind behind the Catalyst conference where he has been lead experience designer for the past three years. He also plays the role as Executive Editor and Creator of the *Catalyst Groupzine*. He has recently partnered with Gabe Lyons to launch the *FERMI Project* and *Q*, an exclusive boutique event designed to inform and expose church leaders to future culture. Jeff lives in Atlanta with his wife, André and dog Max. Email him at **jeff@fermiproject.com**.

© *2006 by Fermi Project. Used by permission.* **www.fermiproject.com**

REDEEMING A NEEDY NEIGHBORHOOD

AN INTERVIEW WITH REVEREND JAMES MEEKS

A CONSUMER CULTURE DOESN'T JUST AFFECT THOSE WHO HAVE TOO MUCH. IT ALSO IMPACTS THOSE WHO DON'T HAVE ENOUGH. ONE PASTOR WHO MINISTERS IN THE MIDDLE OF BOTH PLENTY AND SCARCITY IS REVEREND SENATOR JAMES MEEKS. MEEKS BEARS THAT UNUSUAL DUAL TITLE BECAUSE HE SERVES AS PASTOR OF SALEM BAPTIST CHURCH ON CHICAGO'S SOUTH SIDE (**WWW.SBCOC.ORG**), AND AS STATE SENATOR IN ILLINOIS'S 15TH DISTRICT. IN ADDITION, HE IS THE EXECUTIVE VICE PRESIDENT OF THE RAINBOWPUSH COALITION. HE ALSO IS ON THE BOARD OF DIRECTORS FOR THE CHICAGO FIRE DEPARTMENT, THE ROSELAND COMMUNITY HOSPITAL, THE KOREAN AMERICAN MERCHANT ASSOCIATION, THE OLIVE BRANCH MISSION, AND OTHERS.

EACH SUMMER, MEMBERS OF SALEM BAPTIST TAKE TO THE STREETS TO PRAY ON EVERY CORNER OF THEIR NEIGHBORHOOD. THEY PUT SHOE LEATHER TO THEIR PRAYERS BY HELPING TO TRANSFORM THE COMMUNITY IN MANY WAYS, INCLUDING COUNTERING VIOLENCE, IMPROVING EDUCATION, AND ELIMINATING CORRUPTING INFLUENCES. AS PART OF THE **CHRISTIAN VISION PROJECT**, REVEREND MEEKS SPEAKS TO THE ISSUES OF LEADING A CHURCH THAT MAKES AN IMPACT ON THE SURROUNDING CONSUMER CULTURE.

CVP: *Can peaceful people transform a violent neighborhood?*

MEEKS: We found out that there were crack houses within a block of our church. One afternoon I took 250 people, including our choir, to one of those houses. The choir sang for an hour outside that home. I knocked on the door and asked the people inside to come out and speak to me. Naturally, they hid behind the curtains for the whole hour.

But who can come and buy drugs when a choir is singing out front? It dried up the drug trade for that hour, and the next day the people left, because by then everybody knew that this place is selling drugs.

CVP: *When you were starting out, how would you have described your calling? Was it primarily to build a healthy church? To improve the community? To empower the powerless?*

MEEKS: I'm glad you asked, because you can't build a healthy church if it isn't working to improve an unhealthy community. There are many people who have built "healthy churches" while the community around them is destitute.

How can a church see a community week after week and be oblivious to what's happening in that community? That's not a healthy church!

Our mission was always to build a healthy people, and that automatically means that you are concerned about what else happens on your Jericho Road.

CVP: *How has Salem helped "light up" your Jericho Road?*

MEEKS: There was one area they called "the dirty block" in our community, known for violence, shootings, and prostitution. One Saturday a couple hundred people from our church cleaned up the whole block. We put in new storm doors. We painted every porch. We put in new sod. We cleaned the vacant lots and put in gardens. Then we installed lights in front of everybody's home.

What a joy that night to drive back through that community to see people out watering their lawns and to see children out riding their bikes. And to see all the porch lights on.

CVP: *What fears do you have to help your people overcome?*

MEEKS: Safety is everybody's first priority. Nobody wants to do anything that could put them in harm's way. I remember the first night that I said to the ladies of the church that I was taking them out to redeem prostitutes. First of all, nine had been killed with almost a Jack the Ripper style. Somebody was preying on prostitutes. But then the other thing that said to us is that if there are nine prostitutes that have been killed, our community has a heavy prostitution problem. So we decided that the women of our church should reach out to them. And so the plan was that we would take four hundred

women from midnight to three in the morning to go out and find these women. Now imagine coming home, saying to your husband, "Honey, Friday night in our church we're going to an area where they just killed nine women." Imagine being a husband hearing that.

I asked all the women of the church to wear red. We took roses with us. The first approach was to find a woman and give her a rose and to remind her of her beauty and of her value to herself, to her family, and to God. Our approach was not to be antagonistic and judgmental. We were there to give the love of Christ.

CVP: *So how did you speak to those fears?*

MEEKS: I preached a message on Rahab and the Israelite spies, entitled "Did They Save the Prostitute, or Did She Save Them?" It's such a remarkable story. The spies go into the land; Rahab saves them. They come back into the land; they save Rahab's family. But my argument is that they saved her once, but she saved them *twice.* Not only did she hide the spies, but in Rahab's family line is Jesus. Which means that through them saving Rahab, Rahab's seed saves the whole world.

I told the church, "When you save a women of the night, you don't know, you may be saving a person whose seed will cure cancer or the race problem or whatever it might be. We have to treat these women as Rahabs, as if in them is the seed of Christ."

CVP: *You've tried to bring healthy economic development into the area. Jesus says you can't serve God and Mammon. Is there a danger of a church that focuses on economic development serving Mammon?*

MEEKS: Was the feeding of the 5,000 about food? Or was it about feeding people?

When Jesus said, *"I was hungry and you fed me not; I was naked and you clothed me not?"* he's telling us that serving God involves using material resources. Using resources to meet people's needs is not serving Mammon. It's using Mammon to serve God.

If churches don't get involved in redeeming communities economically because they're scared of Mammon, that's a copout.

CVP: *When many people come to church, they assume church is about getting their own needs met. How do you transform that assumption to an attitude that a healthy church means that we will be working to renew the world around us?*

MEEKS: I have a message called, "Don't Keep the Faith." People are familiar with the saying "Keep the Faith." But I argue that faith is one of those things that cannot be kept.

CVP: *If you keep it, it dies.*

MEEKS: That's right. It's like air. You can't keep air. I tell people, "Hold your breath." Everybody holds their breath. I say, "For a week." They all exhale immediately because they know you can't keep air for a week. In order to get more you have to release what you have. It's the same when you tie a string around a finger to keep the blood there. You can't keep blood in a certain spot; it has to circulate. Faith is the same. If people just come to church and try to "keep the faith" but never put faith to work in something, we'd lose it. It dies. For our church to flourish, we have to keep finding ways to put our faith to work! **C**

For more from the Christian Vision Project and Reverend James Meeks, visit **www.christianvisionproject.com.**

© 2006 Christianity Today International. All rights reserved. Used by permission

JOSH JACKSON

EDITOR-IN-CHIEF & CO-FOUNDER, PASTE MAGAZINE
Age 34, Decatur, Georgia, www.pastemagazine.com

JOSH'S PASSION FOR MUSIC AND FILM ASSISTED IN FUELING THE LAUNCH OF PASTE MAGAZINE FOUR YEARS AGO. PASTE IS A MAGAZINE THAT SEARCHES FOR SIGNS OF LIFE IN MOVIES, MUSIC, BOOKS, TV AND WEIRD, UNCATEGORIZED STUFF THAT PEOPLE MAKE. SINCE HE AND HIS FRIEND NICK PURDY STARTED THE MAGAZINE WITH LITTLE TO NO EXPERIENCE IN NATIONAL MAGAZINE PUBLICATION OR THE MUSIC INDUSTRY, HE'S SURPRISED AND THANKFUL THAT PEOPLE SEEM TO BE PAYING ATTENTION. LOOK FOR JOSH'S TV SEGMENTS ON CNN HEADLINE NEWS WEEKLY.

SEEING LIFE

My life vision is to open myself up to the needs of people around me, something that doesn't come naturally, I'm not particularly good at, and I fail at regularly. But it's what I feel overwhelmingly called to do. My vision for *Paste* is to create a beautiful, thoughtful, engaging magazine that alerts people to art worthy of notice. Our tagline is "signs of life in music, film & culture," and I use that as the point of reference in all our coverage. We try to be discerning and critical as we celebrate the stuff that brings us joy.

ENJOYING CULTURE

As reflections of God's image, every human is a creative being, and the fruits of that creativity help us to understand truth and experience beauty. No one needs to see "engaging culture" as a burden. I get frustrated when engaging culture results in pride and arrogance (especially when it's coming from me). We don't live in a vacuum. Followers of Christ should feel the freedom to partake in the goodness of creation. Make beautiful things. Beautiful noises. Be a part of the greater cultural conversation. In doing so, you'll find yourself in places where you can love and connect with your fellow humans.

CHRISTIANS AND CULTURE

I've always been amazed at Christians who complain about the culture but think it's wrong for fellow Christians to inject their own creativity and insights into the worlds of music, film and television. Of course things are going to look screwed up to Christians if they choose to abdicate the realm of culture to every one else. At *Paste,* we try to be discerning and critical as we celebrate the stuff that brings us joy. We talk to the people creating art and media and take note of their insights, finding new ways of looking at things. And we share all of this with people who also connect with the things we love. The initial tagline of our website was "Connecting Music to the Soul." And in some ways, that's what we're still trying to do…It's actually difficult *not* to impact culture unless you actively run from it.

GOSPEL LEAVEN IN THE CULTURAL LOAF

Don't approach culture like a mechanic that's trying to fix a puttering engine. Leave any ideas that you, uniquely, have the correct vision for what culture should be at the door. You'll never be able to redeem culture, and God isn't looking to you to fix it. Just be a part of it. Be a little bit of "gospel leaven in the cultural loaf," as Nick Purdy says. Share your ideas, be creative, seek excellence in everything you do. **C**

Life is Just So Daily

By Joanna DeWolf

I have a problem. I love ideas. I love to find new concepts and theories. I love to read about them. Study them. Turn them over in my mind. Talk about them. Look for examples of them in the world around me. Contemplate how they play out in life. Consider their different facets, applications, relationships. I find great joy in the pondering and imparting of ideas. The Bible is full of these ideas. As a spiritual leader, my job is to consider these ideas. To talk about them and teach them. As a follower of Jesus, my job is to put these ideas to practice in my everyday life. So, what's the problem?

Life is just so daily.

Take for example this idea: If you want to be great in God's Kingdom, learn to be the servant of all. (See Matthew 20:26, 23:11, Luke 22:26) There's something very revolutionary (and therefore very cool) about this upside down nature of God's Kingdom. As a follower of Jesus, I live under a different set of rules and a different reward system than my American culture. It's like being an indie artist who isn't looking to be on the radio because I don't want to sell out to the system. It's fun to be an indie artist until you can't pay the bills. And it's fun to be a leader in God's Kingdom until you actually have to serve all.

As a church leader, "serving all" preaches (and it's handy for recruiting volunteers). As a follower of Jesus who is a wife and a mom, "serving all" pushes me far deeper than my natural abilities enable me to go. Serving daily in the monotonous details of life uncovers the deep roots of selfishness in my soul. Feeding, sheltering, and clothing my family translates into cooking, cleaning, and laundry EVERY day for years with no conceivable end in sight. This is no short-term missions trip. The constant demands of two young children on my time and energy sap the strength from me. This daily serving can make me downright cranky. This is when I wonder how God's idea could possibly be true. Rick Warren has led the free world to their purpose in life and is feeding Africa. I reorganized the toys today to fool the kids into thinking they are new. (*Free Parent Tip: This works!*) How am I great in God's Kingdom?

One day I was having lunch with a friend who is currently in full time ministry. Somewhere in the middle of a lengthy conversation, she said, "I want to tell you what an example it is for me that you are obeying God by staying home with your children right now. I know it is difficult for you but you still choose obedience. Your life encourages me to obey God." That's when it hit me. Well-known leaders often inspire and challenge us but it is "daily life" leaders who deeply influence us. It is our mothers and fathers, our community members, our neighbors who imprint God's Kingdom ideas in our lives. I've often preached that the key to life is not balance but obedience, but when I live it day after day those around me take notice.

"Do you want to stand out? Then step down. Be a servant…if you're content to simply be yourself, your life will count for plenty." (Matthew 23:11-12 MSG) **C**

Joanna DeWolf gets many of her ideas from reading fiction, nonfiction, the Bible, the newspaper, and food labels (but not from forwarded e-mails). She also writes and teaches regularly from her post as Mom in Lansing, Michigan.

AUTHENTIC IN INFLUENCE:

Brainstorm a list of needs you see in the people and community around you. Dream about a project (big or small) that you can do to help meet one of those needs. What is the first step? How will it help restore the culture?

Uncompromising in Integrity

Being in the world, but not of the world is my hope and the difference between me and the rest of culture. Character, conviction, discipline, and decision-making—these all make up the inner qualities and integrity of a Catalyst leader. I understand that my integrity is the guard to my soul and ultimately my life. This can't be let go or delegated. It's the foundation of who I am as a person and as a leader. It's the basis from which my moral authority is grounded. It must be nurtured, guarded, and found true under testing.

How do I live in culture, without letting the culture affect my integrity?

INTEGRITY AT RISK

RECOGNIZING THE FOUR DANGER ZONES

BY ANDY STANLEY

EVERY ONCE IN A WHILE IN A LEADER'S LIFE, AN OPPORTUNITY COMES ALONG THAT HAS "THIS IS A GOD THING" WRITTEN ALL OVER IT. IT IS INEVITABLE. YOU ARE PASSIONATE ABOUT IMPACTING THE CULTURE WITH THE TRUTH. YOU ARE PRAYING FOR RESOURCES TO ENGAGE THEM WITH EXCELLENCE; WHETHER IT'S PEOPLE OR MONEY OR EQUIPMENT OR LAND. THEN ONE DAY YOU GET THE PHONE CALL. THERE IS A MEETING, AND EVERYTHING FALLS INTO PLACE. IT COMES TOGETHER IN THE MOST OUTLANDISHLY UNEXPECTED AND CREATIVE WAYS. IT *MUST* BE A GOD THING.

I got a phone call years ago, when we were starting North Point. We had 80 acres of land under contract with no money to close, much less to build anything on it. It was clear that God was leading us, but the next steps seemed all but impossible. Then (cue the heavenly choir) the phone rang.

A local concert promoter called to set up a meeting. Our property had a natural bowl on it that would make a perfect 13,000-seat amphitheater. He wanted us to trade our property for the tract of land next to it. In exchange, his company would share the development cost for our project, we would have access to the amphitheater parking. And we could use of the amphitheater for Easter. The property we would be trading for was less expensive than the property we were trying to buy. At the end of the day, we would save several million dollars and have use of an amphitheater. The only small catch was that we would jointly own a tract of land that would be used for parking for the church and the amphitheater.

As you can imagine, I was walking around with my hands in the air saying, "God has come down!" Financially, it was a God thing. The property was a God thing. The parking was a God thing. The amphitheater was a God thing. It was amazing. So I went to our steering committee and said, "You're not going to believe this." I showed off a big color drawing of how the church and the parking and the amphitheater would look. I was still reeling, thinking, "Can you believe this? God has dropped this in our laps!"

Then it happened. I never even saw it coming. One of our committee members raised his hand and said, "I have a question. Isn't this partnership?"

Don't you hate it when that happens? One man speaks up in a meeting and everything screeches to a halt. If you're a leader, you love progress. In fact, the love of progress that God put in you, is critical to leadership. But this love of progress sets us up for some unique temptations. It sets us up to react when some annoying leader flaps his robotic arms and yells, "Danger! Danger!"

One man threatened our progress and I almost didn't listen to him. But in my heart of hearts, the minute he spoke, I knew it was over. It was over because that one man's question called me back to something more important than property or parking lots or progress: he called me back to integrity.

Compromised integrity. Usually you think of televangelists who get caught in seedy hotel rooms or youth ministers who visit porn sites on their laptops or big ministry leaders who pad their bank accounts. Those kinds of things may not be what will tempt you to forsake your integrity, but I can promise you this: *at some point in your ministry you will be tempted to compromise your integrity.* Mark my words. It will happen. And if you choose to compromise your integrity, your dream of being an influence for Christ in your culture will be compromised even more.

Why are we as leaders so prone to compromise our integrity? We've all watched great men and women fall and wondered why. Are they just stupid? Some were men and women you knew were sincere servants of God. Like them, you value

integrity. You have no desire to be blindsided by temptation in this area. You don't think you're stupid. So how do you stay out of trouble? What are the danger zones? If someone has the courage to say, "Danger! Danger!" how can you be sure you will listen?

TOO GOOD TO PASS UP

David was presented with a seemingly irresistible opportunity on his rise to leadership. This opportunity almost derailed him before he even got started. Before he was officially king, he spent most of his time and energy running away from the official king, Saul. Saul hated David because he saw him as a threat to his son Jonathan's inheritance of the throne. That, and David was a better warrior. And younger. And maybe better looking. The truth is, when David was still a kid, he had been anointed as king by Samuel. Everyone knew he was going to be king, just not yet. The soldiers who were loyal to him knew all about it too. They spent a lot of their time hiding out together, so they had plenty of time to get the message: Our guy is going to be king.

In I Samuel 24, David and his men were hiding out in a cave once again. Just then, Saul and 3,000 of his best men happened by the same cave. They had been combing the desert looking for David. They pulled over so Saul could do something that probably is not mentioned anywhere else in scripture. He dismounted and entered the cave alone to "relieve himself." He took off his clothes and assumed the most vulnerable position possible.

Ironically, "David and his men were sitting in the recesses" of that very same cave. His men took one look at the situation and said, "This is the day the Lord spoke of when he said to you, 'I will give your enemy into your hands for you to deal with as you wish.'"(Verse 4, NIV) In other words, *Is this a God thing, or what?* What are the odds of this? Only God could bring your enemy within striking range. He is alone. He is disrobed. It's like he's just waiting to die.

Then David did the unthinkable. He crept up behind Saul and cut off a corner of his robe. That's all. When you think about it, it's amazing that David pulled off that stunt undetected. But even more amazing is what David *didn't* do. He passed on an incredible opportunity. No one would have been surprised if he'd lopped off Saul's head, grabbed it by the hair, and marched out of the mouth of the cave to proclaim himself the rightful king. But David chose to weigh his actions against something other than the opportunity that presented itself. He chose integrity.

David understood an important rule: Just because it *looks* like a God thing and *feels* like a God thing doesn't necessarily mean it's a God thing.

So, how do we avoid the temptation to leverage the wrong opportunities? How do we stay out of trouble? Here are four danger zones to watch out for if, as a leader, you are serious about guarding your integrity.

FOUR DANGER ZONES

Danger Zone #1:
Your leadership ability and giftedness have the potential to take you further than your character can sustain you.

Both Saul and David were like that. They were talented military men. Their physical prowess was remarkable. We look at men like Saul and David and we automatically assume they are mature. We think a person who is really gifted must be really mature. But that just isn't the case. John C. Maxwell says,

AT SOME POINT IN YOUR MINISTRY YOU WILL BE TEMPTED TO COMPROMISE YOUR INTEGRITY

DO NOT REPLACE WHAT GOD HAS PUT IN PLACE

"There is no correlation between giftedness and maturity." And he's right.

Not only do we assume gifted leaders are mature, we assume God can use incredibly gifted people more than he can use average people with lesser gifts. We think mega musical talent, super intelligence, natural leadership ability, and good looks are the only means by which God can get a cynical culture to sit up and take notice. We make those assumptions because we don't view giftedness the way God does.

From the beginning, David understood that his role as future king was not the result of his giftedness. It's easy for us to miss this fact about David today. We talk more about his accomplishments than his shortcomings. We build him up as a superhero. We cast Richard Gere to play him in a movie. But the real David drew strength from a different kind of giftedness.

In I Samuel 16, when Samuel went to Jesse's house to anoint the next king of Israel, he took one look at Eliab, David's oldest brother, and concluded that he was the chosen one. He was tall. He was good-looking. He was the oldest. But Samuel was wrong. In verse seven God said, "Do not consider his appearance or his height for I have rejected him." The rest of this verse gives God's perspective on giftedness: "The Lord does not look at the things man looks at. Man looks at the outward appearance, but the Lord looks at the heart." (NIV) Whatever your gift—whether you're good-looking or musically talented or a gifted talker or a natural leader—it's a *gift*. It's not a *power*. Your heart—the starting place for character—is what gets God's attention. Character is what turns your giftedness into influence. Your character is what unleashes God's power.

Your talent won't guard your character. It's the other way around. And your talent isn't a guarantee that you'll impact today's culture. In fact, your giftedness can propel you into danger zones beyond your character. Just look at Saul. His progress as a leader was fueled by talent, but empty of character. That's why he could justify hurling spears at the wrong man. That's why his influence dwindled to zero. David's character, on the other hand, kept pace with his leadership gifts. That's why he couldn't justify killing Saul when it seemed perfectly opportune to do so. That's why his influence grew to staggering proportions.

Danger Zone #2:
Our commitment to integrity can be easily eroded by our love of progress.

What gets you into trouble? It is not that you are totally oblivious to temptation. It is not that you are callous to sin. You are not stupid. Most often, it is the very thing God wired into you to make you a leader: your love of progress. Your love of progress is why you probably do not enjoy counseling. Counseling is about the past and you are all about the future. For you, the future is about engaging the culture more and more effectively. Suddenly, there is an obstacle between you and this future. The most direct route around the obstacle is to compromise your integrity.

Danger Zone #3:
The excuses.

The language of compromise is spoken in excuses. We have to tell ourselves something to justify even the smallest step away from integrity. Here are the two excuses leaders are most prone to use: God promised it. I deserve it.

God promised it. You started an organization or business or ministry with a strong sense of God's calling. I mean, God gave you a verse and a sign, and you are so confident that God has called you to do what you are doing, that along with that call, there is a sense of prom-

ise. It is so easy for those of us who are in leadership to turn a blind eye to a small compromise of integrity for the sake of what God has promised us.

The other excuse is *I deserve it.* I deserve it because my wife and kids have been neglected. I deserve it because I've been serving God and working so hard, because I need a break. I deserve it because I went without a salary for the first six months. I deserve it because I need a break. Somewhere down the road you will be tempted to put some itty-bitty compromise in the context of all the sacrifices you have made and you will think, "You know, I deserve this. Maybe the average person doesn't, but me, I've been faithful and I deserve this." It may look like an opportunity, but you will know it is a compromise.

Danger Zone #4:
When our opportunities line up with our prayers and our passions, it's difficult to exercise restraint.

Opportunities must be weighed against something other than the uniqueness of the circumstances surrounding them. They must be considered in the light of something other than our passions and emotions.

Take one more look at David. The only obstacle between David and his progress toward kingship was Saul. God had promised him the throne. He certainly deserved the throne more than Saul. When he was presented with an opportunity to easily remove the obstacle, how did he know this particular opportunity was the wrong one?

David weighed the opportunity to eliminate Saul against three things. We need to put our opportunities to these three same tests if we are to maintain lives of integrity and influence: The law of God, the principles of God, and the wisdom of God.

THE LAW OF GOD

In the midst of all the emotion and the bad advice in that cave, David realized something. Regardless of the circumstances, regardless of the fact his enemy was just within his grasp, and regardless of what looked like a certain God thing, David realized it was against the law to kill the king.

Just when I thought we were on our way to a miracle, one elder brought up the law. "Isn't this kind of like a partnership?" Immediately I thought, *That's not what that verse means. That doesn't fit this situation. Do we need to pray about this? You mean to tell me, you're going to let this whole incredible deal slip away, over one verse?* One pesky leader who didn't let circumstances or emotions or the love of progress get in the way. By the grace of God, I listened. I am convinced of this: if we had moved down that road, we would have regretted it.

THE PRINCIPLES OF GOD

David's conscience was stricken over cutting off the corner of Saul's robe, much less harming Saul. He said to his men, "The Lord forbid that I should do such a thing to my Master the Lord's anointed. Or lift my hand against him for he is the anointed of the Lord." (I Samuel 24:6 NIV) In other words, not only is he the king, he is the king that God put in place.

There is a principle involved here: *Do not replace what God has put in place.* David knew better than to mess with the sovereignty of God. He knew God would make it all right in the end. When he calls out to Saul from the mouth of the cave, he says, "May the Lord judge between you and me and may the Lord avenge the wrongdoings you have done unto me. But my hand will not touch you." (verse 12)

David subordinated his love of progress—a principle that was hardwired into his makeup—to God's principles. It's the same decision you need to make every day to avoid compromising your integrity: I live for progress, I plan for progress, I invest in progress, but I am not going to sacrifice my integrity for the sake of progress.

THE WISDOM OF GOD

Finally, there is the wisdom factor. Let me ask it this way. How wise is it for a wanna-be king to murder the sitting king? While he uses the bathroom in a cave alone? Is that the story you would want to spend the rest of your life telling? That is the story of a man who trusts his own wisdom more than the wisdom of God. That is the story of an impatient leader who acts in his own power, rather than a patient leader who waits on the power of God. Which story would you want to tell your grandkids?

One day you are going to face this issue. You are going to have to choose: Do I let a compelling circumstance dictate my actions? Do I lay aside my character for the sake of progress? Do I commit this little indiscretion because, after all, I deserve it? Do I compromise my integrity to get where I believe God wants me to be? I promise you, you will be there, and in that moment, you will discover just how confident you are in the power of your God. You will find out if you want to be an influence his way or your own way. If you compromise, you will never know what he would have done and could have done on your behalf. You will never know how broad and deep your influence could have been. And you will spend the rest of your life wondering, "What if I had waited?" **C**

Andy Stanley is the lead pastor of North Point Community Church in Atlanta, Georgia. (**www.northpoint.org**) He is the bestselling author of *Visioneering, The Next Generation Leader, The Best Question Ever,* and the recent *It Came from Within.* Andy and his wife, Sandra, live in Atlanta with their two sons and daughter.

*Adapted from Andy Stanley's message at the 2005 Catalyst Conference. (***www.catalystconference.com***)*

1. How has your love of progress defined you as a leader? How has this trait helped you lead? How has it hindered your leadership?

2. When have you faced an opportunity that seemed like a "God thing" but, upon closer inspection, was not?

3. What excuses have you been tempted to use? How can you relate to the two excuses mentioned here: "I deserve it" and "God promised it"?

4. What practices can you build into your life now to ensure that you will practice restraint in your future decision making as a leader?

5. Who do you have in your life that you can count on to hold you accountable for weighing your decisions against the law of God, the principles of God, and the wisdom of God?

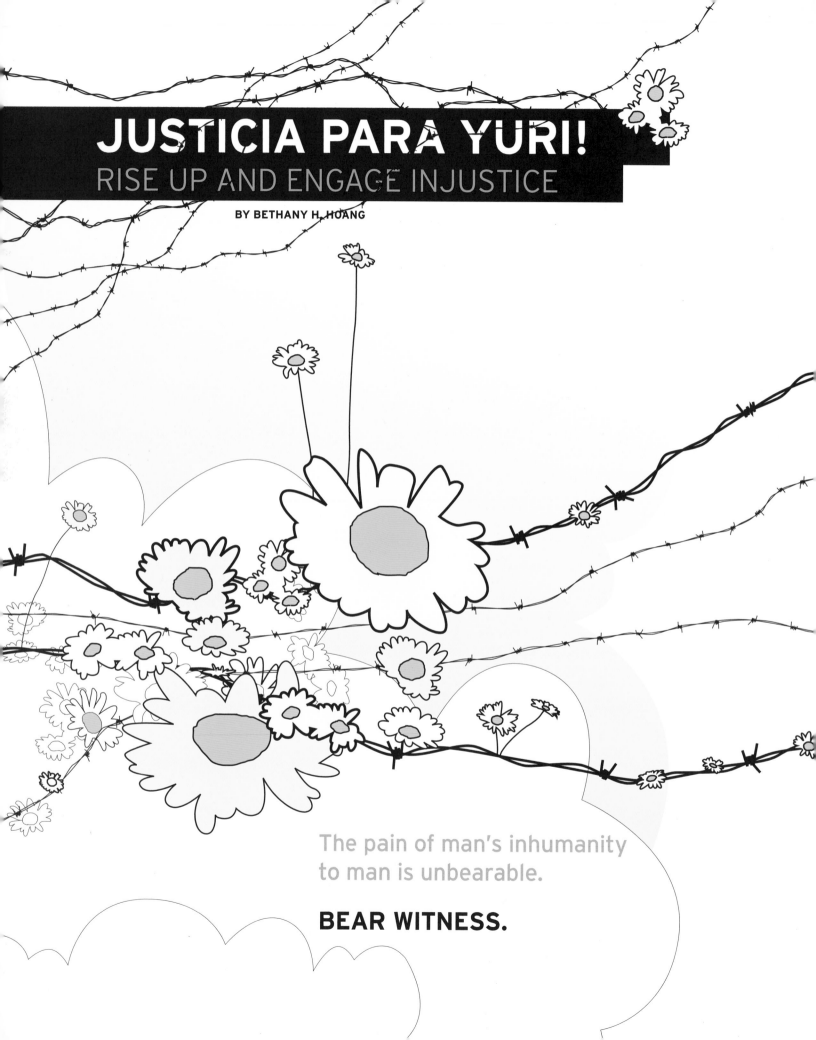

JUSTICIA PARA YURI!
RISE UP AND ENGAGE INJUSTICE

BY BETHANY H. HOANG

The pain of man's inhumanity to man is unbearable.

BEAR WITNESS.

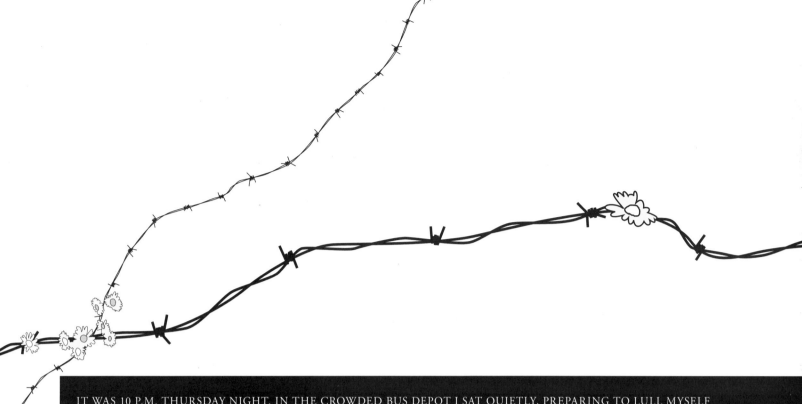

IT WAS 10 P.M. THURSDAY NIGHT. IN THE CROWDED BUS DEPOT I SAT QUIETLY, PREPARING TO LULL MYSELF TO SLEEP ONCE I BOARDED THE BUS—AN ATTEMPT THAT WOULD PROVE FUTILE. IT WOULD BE A DARK, AIRLESS, WATERLESS, 8 HOUR CLIMB UP TO 15,000 FEET AND BACK DOWN AGAIN AS WE TRAVELED FROM THE ANDEAN CITY OF HUÁNUCO, PERU BACK TO THE SPRAWLING CAPITAL OF LIMA.

As I looked into the crowd, I saw that Yuri's family had arrived. Yuri's mother would be coming with us to Lima. As I looked at Yuri's brother and father, I felt speechless. I couldn't help but stare at Yuri's father's eyes. Even as his body stood tall and strong, his eyes were so worn. His eyes carried the profound grief of life-shattering injustice.

This father's 8-year-old daughter Yuri was raped, then murdered by being thrown from a building. The police then "misplaced" basic forensic evidence and abandoned her case.

I find it hard to comprehend what it must be like to have one's life pervasively marred by injustice. Injustice is a vague term for those of us who rarely experience it in our protected lives—the machineries of power are more often on our side than against us. But injustice is a daily reality for Yuri's family. They know all too well that injustice is an abuse of power, where someone with more power takes from someone with less power. And it is not the frivolities and luxuries of life that are taken from the vulnerable, but rather the basics—freedom, dignity, and life itself.

UNBEARABLE

I could hardly sleep that week. The jarring facts of Yuri's case ... the quiet, desperate pleading of Yuri's mother as she passed around graphic photos from the scene of the rape and murder; the sunken eyes of Yuri's father, dejected in his inability to protect his defiled and dead daughter ... swirled in my heart and mind. I found myself hinging on utter despondence.

I thought back to Cambodia, and the corridors of Tou Sleng Prison. This prison once served as a holding place for torturing innocent Cambodian citizens before they were taken to the killing fields and slaughtered. As I wandered the corridors and empty cells, I came to a scribbling on the wall. Barely legible, it read, "The pain of man's inhumanity to man is unbearable." Underneath someone had taken a sharp object and literally scraped into the wall the phrase "Bear Witness."

I often think about that writing on the wall. I think about it when I get lost in the dark corridors of my mind, corridors that lead me to places of broken-hearted fear and despondency. And I think that, on one level, the writing on that wall is right on. When and if we begin to open ourselves to see inhumanity and injustice around the globe, "man's inhumanity to man" becomes crushing. Often paralyzing. And, at worst, numbing.

And yet I think that God asks us, as those made in his image, to let ourselves be drawn into the pain of suffering and violence. To let it break our hearts. Even to lead others to these places of pain. We are called to "bear witness." But our witness should not end with observation. We are called to live as those who, in the midst of the unbearableness of the pain, do not shrink back but rather rise up. We are called to rise up, engage injustice, take "the pain of man's inhumanity to man," and bring it to the foot of the cross. Jesus Himself promises that He will redeem all things, that He will make all things new.

Even rape and murder and corruption.

But I wonder if we actually believe this?

Do we believe that justice is central to the heart of God? Do we believe that God desires for justice to be one of the central focuses of the Church's identity and mission? Do we believe that justice is an essential pursuit for all those who follow Jesus? Do we believe that we personally are called to do justice? Do we believe that we are called to lead others into a lifestyle of justice? Or do we believe that justice is a niche for some to pursue and others to observe?

The truth is if our lives do not include the pursuit of justice, all of our other efforts to worship God become foul stench. We literally stink in his presence.

Jesus calls "the weightier matters of the Law." (Matthew 23:23 NIV) More specifically, they are neglecting justice. God cries out to His people, saying, "Stop doing wrong. Learn to do right." And then He immediately defines what is right in His eyes: "Seek justice, rescue the oppressed. Defend the orphan, plead for the widow."(Isaiah 1:17 NIV)

Whenever the aroma of sacrifice has not been pleasing to the Lord, it has not been a matter of neglected acts of worship, but rather a matter of the mind and heart. Isaiah laments to us, "Your whole head is injured, your whole heart afflicted. From the sole of your foot to the top of your head there is no soundness—only wounds and welts and open sores, not cleansed or bandaged or

constant intent to "learn to do right." We learn first by reading scripture with new eyes, absorbing its continual call to justice. We need to lay a firm foundation of biblical justice on which our lives and leadership can stand. While there are 39 scripture references to the pleasing aroma of burnt sacrifices, the 40th reference is to the melding of our lives with Jesus' life. Paul tells us in II Corinthians that *"we are to God the aroma of Christ"*. (2:15 NIV) Growing into a heart, mind, and whole life of justice is a matter of living our identity in Jesus. It is an issue of discipleship— "learning" from how Jesus lives.

How does Jesus live? What is his identity? His aroma? Jesus himself made it clear to us: "The Spirit of the Lord is on me, because he has anointed me to preach good news to the poor.

... persevering against injustice is a testimony to the love God Himself gives to us. It is a work of bearing witness—not to inhumanity as a final reality, but to Jesus' power to rescue, to heal, and to make all things new.

He has sent me to proclaim freedom for the prisoners and recovery of sight for the blind, to release the oppressed." (Luke 4:18 NIV)

In descriptions of sacrificial offering in the Hebrew scriptures, the Law states that the burning will create "an aroma pleasing to the Lord." Thirty-nine times this phrase appears in the scriptures. But there are two scenarios when the sacrificial aroma becomes an abhorrence to the Lord. In Leviticus 26, this is due to the people's unrelenting idol worship. In Isaiah, it is from the absence of justice.

Throughout Isaiah it is clear that even as God's people are worshipping according to the Law, they are neglecting what

soothed with oil. … Wash and make yourselves clean."(Isaiah 1:5-6, 16 NIV)

How do we come before the Lord with a pure heart and a healed mind that desires justice, that lives a life of bringing justice to others? How do we escape from understanding justice as a niche ministry to be done by the brave and marginal few and bring it into our whole heads, our whole hearts, our whole lives?

The pursuit of justice involves first a

Learning also comes simply and necessarily by diving in, by going to places where systems of justice are broken, and by spending time with the people who lives are broken as a result. We need only ask God to open our eyes and lead us where He wants us to go. Is there a place in your community or in the world you've always wondered about? Go to that place. Protect the vulnerable. Look for ways to intervene in the abuses of power. Go with the intent to lead others in mapping territory for the work of justice. Figure out how justice systems are broken, listen to those who are victimized by injustice, and ask God for a plan to make an impact.

If this feels daunting, think of the brilliant victories of history. There may be 27 million slaves in the world today, but 150 years ago slavery was abolished in our own country. In the past year IJM has seen hundreds of slaves rescued in other nations. Hundreds quickly turn to millions and finally to total abolition as perpetrators begin to see that they are being held accountable. There may be a million women and girls newly trafficked into forced prostitution each year, but in the past few weeks dozens of these women and children were rescued; their brothel owners and traffickers prosecuted, ending the cycle of oppression. Red-light districts are shrinking and sex tourist towns disappearing as accountability rises.

The Church needs only to live her identity—to show up and see how God will work through us.

As we grow in conviction that justice is central to our calling as followers of Jesus, we

detention, slavery or sex trafficking among the millions, the scales of injustice begin to recalibrate. Those who assumed they had no accountability begin to realize that others are paying attention. Corruption becomes more costly. And so Roberto took Yuri's case, and the entire staff threw themselves into seeking *"justicia para Yuri … justicia para Yuri"* (the chanting of the crowd still rings in my head). They plastered the town with the details of the injustice done to Yuri. They made the vague clear. They brought words to the unspeakable.

Yuri's perpetrators were finally brought to trial. In a pre-meeting with the supreme court judges, we were told that the poor rarely receive justice. The trial resulted in the full acquittal of the two men who had the most influence and means and the conviction of a boy who had no means, no influence and little evidence against him. Leaving the jail

Our small band of lawyers, social workers, Yuri's mother, and volunteers from various churches arrived in Lima at 6 a.m., showered, drank some coffee, put on our best suits, and mounted the steps of the Peruvian National Congress. Press conferences, meetings with congressmen and news broadcasting that day would bring Yuri's case out of the shadows of a small city and into the Peruvian limelight. Unprecedented defense of the poor would gain attention throughout the nation, setting a mark, laying the claim that the voiceless will be given a voice.

Yuri may be gone, and her trial still in appeals, but persevering against injustice is a testimony to the love God Himself gives to us. It is a work of

bearing witness—not to inhumanity as a final reality, but to Jesus' power to rescue, to heal, and to make all things new.

will need to increasingly understand justice itself as a spiritual discipline. Justice work can all too easily look like a firecracker—even if we explode with conviction, excitement quickly dies, and with it, commitment. We must daily ask God for the perseverance to move forward. We must continue to stare injustice in the face, get up under it and carry it forward to the foot of the cross. It is a work that can be carried as we ourselves are carried by the Holy Spirit.

RECALIBRATING THE SCALES
International Justice Mission's (IJM) casework partner in Peru has an attorney named Roberto.* Roberto knows that when cases such as Yuri's are overlooked and forgotten on the individual scale, injustice on the systemic scale flourishes. But if you pursue even one case of unprosecuted rape, land seizure, illegal

compound, we found ourselves driving alongside a red truck carrying not only the supreme court justices, but also the "defense" attorney. Two days later, Yuri's mother said goodbye to her husband and son and boarded a bus with us to make the long overnight trip to Lima.

May we cleanse ourselves of broken-hearted fear and daily ask God to make us His people who are marked and moved instead by broken-hearted courage. May we be an aroma pleasing to the Lord. **C**

Bethany H. Hoang travels globally, speaking and teaching to thousands on behalf of IJM at churches, conferences, and universities. As Director of the IJM Institute, Mrs. Hoang is responsible for creating and implementing a variety of cutting-edge initiatives that are designed to engage the worldwide church and academic communities in a deeper level of understanding, passion, and commitment to seeking justice on behalf of those who suffer abuse and oppression in our world.

©2006 by Bethany Hoang. Used by permission of IJM.

To conceal their identities and safeguard ongoing IJM casework, we have used pseudonyms for particular individuals mentioned here, though the stories themselves are real. Actual names and casework are on file with IJM.

International Justice Mission is a human rights agency that rescues victims of violence, sexual exploitation, slavery, and oppression. For more information and to mobilize, go to **www.ijm.org**.

HOW TO PAY FOR A FREE CELL PHONE

BY DONALD MILLER

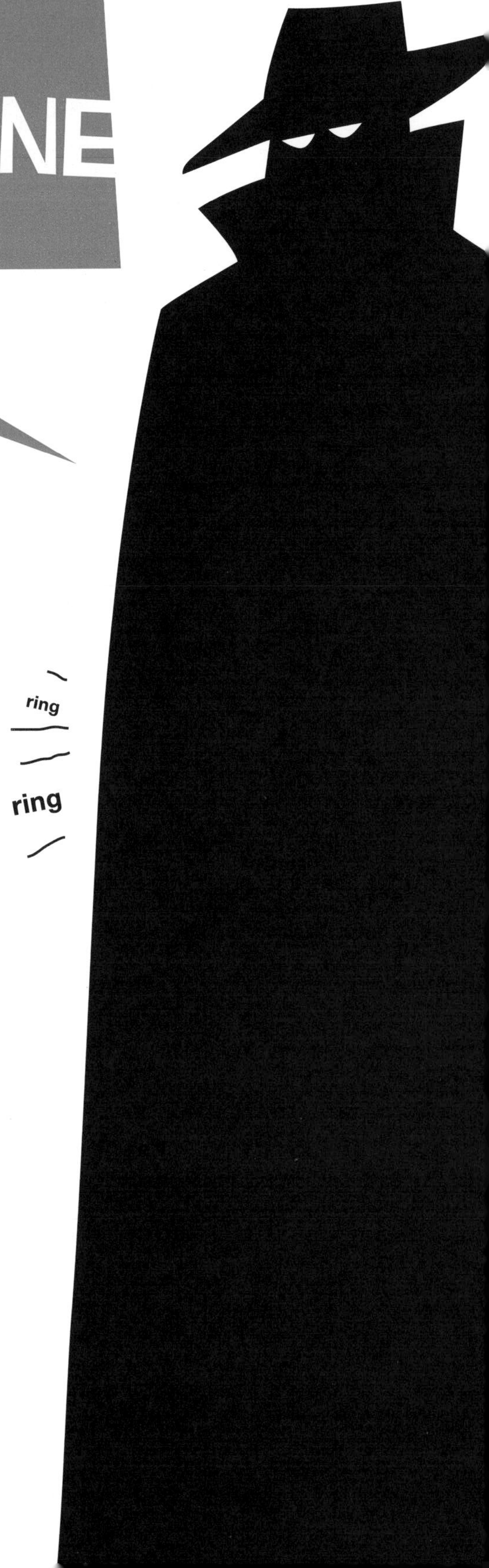

I LIVED WITH MY FRIEND AND MENTOR JOHN MACMURRY AND HIS FAMILY FOR FOUR YEARS AND LEARNED A GREAT DEAL WHILE I WAS THERE. THE FIRST AND FOREMOST RULE IN THE MACMURRAY HOME, AND I'VE PERSONALLY OBSERVED THIS, IS ALWAYS TELL THE TRUTH. JOHN SAYS IT'S THE BASIS FOR ALL HEALTHY RELATIONSHIPS. TRUTH CAN'T EXIST WITHOUT THIS RULE WORKING. WHICH REMINDS ME OF A STORY ...

John and I were sitting in the family room one night watching Sports Center when he asked about my new cell phone. I had set it down on the armrest, and he picked it up, wondering out loud about how small it was.

"I got it free," I told him.

"How did you get it for free?" he asked.

"Well, my other one broke, so I took it in to see if they could replace it. They had this new computer system at the Sprint store downtown, and they didn't have their records. They didn't know whether mine was still under warranty. It wasn't, I knew, because I had looked at the receipt before I brought it in. It was more than a year old. The guy asked me about it, and I told him I didn't know, but it was right around a year. Just a white lie, you know. Anyway, the phone was so messed up they replaced it with a newer model. So, I got a free phone."

John kept looking at the phone for a minute, then handed it back to me and went into the kitchen to get an apple. He came back and sat down, and we talked about the Seahawks for a while, wondering between ourselves if Holmgren could get them to the Superbowl.

"Did you ever see that movie *The Family Man* with Nicolas Cage?" John asked while taking a bite of his apple, leaving the conversation about football.

"I think I did see it, yeah. It's like *Scrooge* or something, right?" I asked.

"Something like that," John continued. "There's this scene in the movie where Nicolas Cage walks into a convenience store to get a cup of coffee or something, I don't remember. And Don Cheadle plays the guy working at the counter. Turns out there's a girl in line before Nicolas Cage, and she's buying something for ninety-

ring

ring

> THE BIBLE TALKS ABOUT HAVING A CALLOUSED HEART. THAT'S WHEN SIN, AFTER A PERIOD OF TIME, HAS SO DECEIVED US WE NO LONGER CARE WHETHER OUR THOUGHTS AND ACTIONS ARE RIGHT OR WRONG. AND WE HAVE TO GUARD AGAINST THAT.

nine cents, and she hands Cheadle a dollar. Cheadle takes nine dollars out of the till and counts it out to the girl, giving her way too much change, right?"

"Right," I say.

"And the girl doesn't correct him. She sees that he is handing her way too much money—change for a ten—yet she picks it up and puts it in her pocket without saying a word. And as she is walking out the door, Cheadle stops her, you know, to give her another chance. He asks her if there is anything else she needs. She shakes her head *no* and walks out."

"I see what you're getting at, John," I say, knowing he is trying to make me feel guilty about the phone.

"Let me finish," he says. "So Cheadle looks over at Nicolas Cage, and he says, *Did you see that? She was willing to sell her character for nine dollars. Nine dollars!*" After John says this, he looks back at the television. He picks up the remote and turns up the volume. After a little while I speak up.

"Do you think that is what I am doing?" I asked. "... with the phone and all? Do you think I am selling my character or something?" And to be honest, I said this with a smirk.

"I do," John said, not being judgmental, just stating a fact. "I don't mean to be a holy roller, Don," he continued, "but the Bible talks about having a calloused heart. That's when sin, after a period of time, has so deceived us we no longer care whether our thoughts and actions are right or wrong. And we have to guard against that. Our hearts will go there easily, and often over what looks like little things—little white lies. All I am saying to you, as your friend, is, Watch for this kind of thing."

"I see," I told him. We didn't talk about it after that. We talked more about the Seahawks, then about an old rerun of The *X-Files* that came on. John went to bed soon after that, and I surfed the channels and watched an interview with Richard Nixon from back in the day. He looked tired but also relatively innocent. I am not saying he didn't do anything wrong, I just mean by today's standards, he looked innocent. Basically, he cheated to get ahead in politics. That's hardly a crime today. It's almost like people don't even respect a politician who can't get away with distorting the truth. I didn't like that he looked so innocent. And I wondered why he didn't just admit he did something wrong. I went back to the Sprint store the next day. It cost me more than nine dollars, but I got my character back. **C**

Donald Miller is a frequent speaker, focusing on the merit of Christian spirituality as an explanation for beauty, meaning, and the human struggle. His other books include *Blue Like Jazz* (Nelson Books, 2003), *Through Painted Deserts* (Nelson Books, 2005) and the upcoming *A Map of Eden*. For more information and updates visit **www.donaldmillerwords.com**.

Reprinted from To Own a Dragon *© 2006 by Donald Miller and John MacMurry. Used by permission of Nav Press.* (**www.navpress.com**) *All rights reserved.*

A New Integrity
MEASURING YOUR LIFE BY LOVE

By Leonard Sweet

NOTICING THE DOMINANCE OF THE RAIN THEME IN THE ART AND MUSIC OF THE HOPI PEOPLE, AN ANTHRO-POLOGIST ASKED A HOPI TRIBAL LEADER WHY SO MANY OF HIS PEOPLE'S SONGS DEALT WITH RAIN. THE HOPI REPLIED THAT IT WAS BECAUSE WATER IS SO SCARCE IN THE LAND WHERE THEY LIVE. HE THEN ASKED THE ANTHROPOLOGIST: "IS THAT WHY SO MANY OF YOUR SONGS ARE ABOUT LOVE?"[1]

We live in a world that is awash in love songs and love stories but where love that looks beyond the I is as rare as windows and clocks in casinos. How are we to love and be loved? This is the hardest of questions being asked today.

In his development of the metaphor of the church as the body of Christ, Paul encouraged the Ephesian Christians to think of themselves as a new temple, a temple of God. (Ephesians 2:21; 1 Corinthians 3: 16) The Temple was a symbol of The Presence, the divine presence in the midst of the people. (Exodus 25:21-22) But with the death of Stephen, early Christians began to realize that a temple "made with hands" was no longer necessary, because an organic, living temple was present in the "body" of the church, and decentralized temples were present in the individual "living stones" that made up the church. Paul then admits that the "love of Christ" defies description, but drawing from the Temple imagery he offers a multidimensional metaphor to help us know the unknowable: "I pray that you may have the power to comprehend, with all the saints, what is the breadth and length and height and depth, and to know the love of Christ that surpasses knowledge, so that you may be filled with all the fullness of God." (Ephesians 3:18-19)

THREE DIMENSIONS OF LOVE
The temple of love is built on the following measurements:

1. LOVE CUBED BY LENGTH
The love that leads to golden anniversaries has integrity of length. And length is not simply the passage of time, marked in years and anniversary cards, but also the trouble loves goes to. You could think of it as long-suffering. When you consider how far love will go, it doesn't make sense.

In the modern world, we learned to say, "Come, let us reason together." But in the

PART OF THE INTEGRITY OF THE LIFE OF LOVE IS THAT LOVE ITSELF IS INTEGRAL TO ALL OF LIFE.

world that is being born, we must learn to say, "Come, let us love together." Or in more theological words, "I am loved, therefore I am."

Notice that the lifestyle of love—the life that is lived in The Presence—is not based on "I love, therefore I am" but "I am loved, therefore I am."[2] Or in more biblically resonant words, "We love because he first loved us." (1 John 4:19) The difference is crucial. We are not self-empowering, autonomous individuals with a capacity to love. Our ability to love right is itself a gift, one that does not come from within but from a God who loves us in spite of our unloveliness. This gift from God makes us lovely and able to love like God loves.

All love is relational. The notion that we can give love without receiving love

violates the biblical understanding, where "Love is from God; everyone who loves is born of God and knows God. Whoever does not love does not know God, for God is love." (1 John 4:7-8) For us to experience love, we must receive the love offered to us. "God's love was revealed among us in this way: God sent his only Son into the world so that we might live through him. In this is love, not that we loved God but that he loved us and sent his Son to be the atoning sacrifice for our sins."(1 John 4:9-10)

2. LOVE CUBED BY BREADTH

Love is all-encompassing. Nothing is left out of the equation. Nothing and no one is out of bounds for love. The whole world is God's "love place."[3] So it's not hard to figure out whom to love. Everyone.

The Temple was God's dwelling place, the habitation of The Presence. But it was a limited and misleading metaphor, for the prophets were constantly reminding Israel that God is not confined to the Temple box: "Thus says the Lord: Heaven is my throne and the earth is my footstool; what is the house that you would build for me, and what is my resting place?" (Isaiah 66:1)

When you are in relationship with someone, little things mean a lot. Like that watch fob of your great-grandfather's; or that sweater of your mother's that she was always trying to put on you when she got cold. These "worthless" things become your life's greatest treasures, your love icons. When you are in relationship with the Creator of the universe, little things mean a lot. Like that sparrow that falls from the sky. Or that lily in the field. Or that "little one" whom no one else will talk to.

What are your love icons? Do they represent the helpless, the weak, and those who are "worthless" in the eyes of the world? Or are they people and things that have the power to position you to gain a personal advantage?

"My beloved friends, let us continue to love each other since love comes from God."(1 John 4:7 MSG) Or as Jesus put it, if you only love those who love you, what's the big deal?[4] And if, through the power of the Spirit, you can find it in your heart to love those who reject you and revile you, how much more so God? You can't out-love the Lord. The needle of our inner compass needs to point in the direction of true north: Jesus the Christ. But if you look closely at any needle that's pointing true north, it trembles. Love trembles because intimacy hurts. Love is painful. The preciousness of love is matched by the precariousness of love. Love can't be controlled, only cultivated. There is no love without loss of self and loss of control. Love is the hardest thing in the world to get right, because when you give up control you consent to uncertainty and unpredictable outcomes. Yet losing yourself to find yourself is the way of love.

The life integrity that love delivers is not only about what happens on the outside; it's a thoroughgoing life—a new, transformed life—that is integral from the inside out. Love is the wound that breaks open the heart, so that a new heart can be born and a whole soul can be awakened. In the Christian meta-narrative, everyone with a new identity, integrity, and intimacy functions from a broken heart. The testimony of the Scriptures is this: if you love, your heart will break. The only question is: What kind of love will break your heart?

The cross is the ultimate symbol of a broken heart. For on the cross, God's heart broke. The mixture of blood and water that flowed from Jesus' side reveals what really killed Jesus—a broken heart. Today there is a medical event called "broken heart syndrome." A broken heart can kill you, or it can birth in you a new heart. Jesus' broken heart birthed a new humanity. The promise of The Presence is that it takes a heart broken by love to birth God's love and make the heart beat in sync with God's heart. That's the breadth of love—love without measure.

3. LOVE CUBED BY DEPTH

The deeper you go, the holier love gets. The Temple was a place of holiness. The deeper one got into it, the more it became a place of communication, a place where God speaks. The deeper a person went into the Temple, the more holy it got. The problem with the church today is less that it is out of date than it is out of depth.

Part of the integrity of the life of love is that love itself is integral to all of life. Love coheres our existence; it integrates our life. Without the verb of love, life loses cohesion, falls apart. When you're "in love," everything in the world looks different.

Exactly. Love exceeds and reverses the tried and true. Love is a high standard, depth-sounding word. To believe what is unbelievable, to live what is unlivable, to see what is unseeable, to do what is undoable—these are the deep ways of love. It's time we rise to the occasion and explore love's depths. Only through love do we become more like God.

We've made love into a low-standard word. "Making love" means one-night stands and sex-to-excess. We now fall in and out of love like one falls in and out of bed. We ask, "What's your love interest?" as if love is not a commitment or a passion but merely a passing interest. Our problem is not that people aren't using condoms; our problem is that we treat people like condoms: we use them once and then throw them away.

Our current notion of love—an "emotional" state that seizes one's being—is a consequence of modernity.[5] The old-fashioned way of love was to choose your love,

THE LIFE INTEGRITY THAT LOVE DELIVERS IS NOT ONLY ABOUT WHAT HAPPENS ON THE OUTSIDE; IT'S A THOROUGHGOING LIFE—A NEW, TRANSFORMED LIFE—THAT IS INTEGRAL FROM THE INSIDE OUT.

then love your choice. Or in non-Western cultures, where arranged marriages are still widespread, "have your love chosen for you, then choose to love the one who has been chosen." Likewise, God chooses whom we are to love; then it is up to us to choose to love God's choice for us. And the choice is unlimited—it includes everyone. Remember, the dimensions of love are immeasurable.

Postmodern culture can make it harder to love than ever before. In fact, love is made more difficult as the world brings the "yous" closer and closer together. There is far greater and wider proximity of "others" to love, but much less of what it takes to enable us to love those in close proximity. Ironically, as we have access to greater material wealth, which enables us to help others, our commitments to one another diminish. The greater our mediated exposure to distant pain and suffering in the world, the smaller our personal investments in ameliorating pain and suffering. The more we see pictures of distant misery and anguish, the more we distance ourselves from misery and anguish.

We've never cared so much. We've never done so little. In the Jewish tradition, the heart had two chambers, "love like water" and "love like fire." We are "saved" by both water and fire, but prefer the water. With "love like water," love soothes and satisfies. It makes everything grow. But with "love like fire," love burns and sears. Or in the words of the Scriptures, "Love is a flame of the Lord." (Song of Solomon 8:6) God's

love is white-hot love...not lukewarm love, not ice cold love, not even "cool" love or "candle" love. The fire of love is the fire of God, and to fire up love is to be fired up and to participate in the beating heart that is at the center of the universe.

"Our God is a consuming fire," the writer of Hebrews declared. (Hebrews 12: 29) Does that "consuming fire" dwell in you—the fire that burned on Mount Sinai, the fire that burned the bush but did not consume it? Fire burns away that which is not pure. The fire is not to be feared; the evil is to be feared. God will not burn us more than we can bear. But we will be burned. Are you inviting the burning of God? Has the fire invaded your darkness and possessed your soul? Do you keep the sacred fires burning?

Fire shows itself as light, the creative energy of God we know as love. Are you on fire with that consuming fire of love? Do lightning strikes of The Presence thunder from your presence? **C**

Leonard Sweet, PhD, serves as the E. Stanley Jones Professor of Evangelism at Drew Theological School in Madison, New Jersey. He is also a Distinguished Visiting Professor at George Fox University in Newberg, Oregon, and founder and president of SpiritVenture Ministries. He is the author of *The Three Hardest Words* published by WaterBrook Press. He has also written *Out of the Question...Into the Mystery* and the trilogy *SoulTsunami, Aqua-Church*, and *SoulSalsa*. Check out Len's newest project, **www.wikiletics.com**, the first wiki preaching resource on the web.

All Scripture, unless otherwise noted, are taken from the New Revised Standard Version *of the Bible. Adapted from* The Three Hardest Words in the World to Get Right. *Copyright 2006 by Leonard Sweet (**www.leonardsweet.com**). Used by permission of WaterBrook Press, Colorado Springs, CO. All Rights Reserved.*

SOME THINGS ARE AGELESS

AN INTERVIEW WITH FREDERICA MATHEWES-GREEN

AS A WRITER AND CULTURE CRITIC, FREDERICA MATHEWES-GREEN HAS LANDED STORIES ON NATIONAL PUBLIC RADIO, IN THE PAGES OF MAJOR MAGAZINES AND NEWSPAPERS, AND IN BESTSELLING BOOKS ON CULTURE AND CHRISTIAN SPIRITUALITY. LIKE ALL PUBLIC FIGURES WHO CHALLENGE THE ASSUMPTIONS OF MAINSTREAM CULTURE, SHE HAS HAD TO LEARN HOW TO STAY FOCUSED AND HUMBLE IN THE MIDST OF BOTH SUCCESS AND HOSTILITY. THERE ARE FEW CHRISTIANS WHO MODEL GRACE AND CREATIVITY BETTER THAN THIS GRANDMOTHER OF EIGHT. IN THIS INTERVIEW FOR THE **CHRISTIAN VISION PROJECT** SHE DESCRIBES TWO BASIC SPIRITUAL DISCIPLINES THAT LEAD TO A LIFE OF INTEGRITY IN A FRAGMENTED CULTURE.

CVP: *How would you diagnose our culture?*

MATHEWES-GREEN: I find that when I'm speaking, to any kind of audience, there's one word that consistently produces a response. The word is *loneliness.*

You might not think that loneliness is such a big problem. But the extreme individualism of our age has made people focus more and more on their atomized single self: defining themselves as the unique person separate from everyone else.

Our forebears defined themselves by what they produced. Now people define themselves by what they consume. And this undermines our sense of effectiveness in the world. No matter how much you define yourself as this important, significant individual, there's a feeling that nothing you do is going to make any difference.

This is even harder for Christians. We have the mandate to go out and bring the gospel to the world. And yet it often seems like nobody's listening. So we are tempted to try things we shouldn't get into, because we think nobody will find out. That's the path to disintegration—when we are so isolated, lonely, and ineffective that we start to think our lives don't matter.

CVP: *What's the remedy?*

MATHEWES-GREEN: I believe that the path to integrity requires going back as far as we can to the beginnings of Christian history, and adopting those spiritual disciplines that were used in the first few centuries.

Saint Paul says that the life of a Christian is like an athlete's. Well, from the outside, I sure don't look like an athlete. But as I've learned the spiritual disciplines, especially the most basic ones of prayer and fasting, I can see the change. I feel a bit more of the presence of the Lord. But that hasn't happened just by cultivating sentimental gooey feelings about the Lord! I've had to learn to follow explicit disciplines rooted deep in history.

CVP: *So what does a spiritual discipline of prayer look like?*

MATHEWES-GREEN: The most significant form of prayer to me is the simplest and the most difficult. It's called the Jesus prayer, and it's very short: "Lord Jesus Christ, have mercy on me." Ever since the fourth or fifth century, Christians have been using this prayer, repeated continuously, as a way of practicing what Saint Paul calls us to do: "pray without ceasing." Most of the time, our minds are just dawdling around, thinking about trivialities, but if you can keep focused on the Lord all the time, it brings your whole life into coherence.

The point of the prayer is to encounter Jesus, in our hearts. The more you can look into your heart and address this prayer simply to him in humility, in simplicity of heart, you begin to sense that connection there.

People get discouraged at first. You think you're going to sit down and do the Jesus prayer for five minutes and you do three or four of them—and you're thinking about your grocery list or a phone call you have to make. Don't beat yourself up about it. Don't stop saying the prayer because you do it badly. Just pick yourself up and start in again.

CVP: *Fasting—what does that mean as a spiritual discipline?*

MATHEWES-GREEN: The early Christians fasted on Wednesday and Friday. Many Christians have continued that Wednes-day-Friday fast from the first century, and our whole family is among them. But we don't go totally without food. Instead we follow what the early writer Tertullian called the "Daniel fast." We eat the same kinds of foods that Daniel ate in the king's palace—essentially a vegan diet. No meat, no dairy products, no fish.

CVP: *So what do you eat on Wednesdays and Fridays?*

MATHEWES-GREEN: Well, at first you eat a lot of peanut butter sandwiches! Then you discover this whole other world of cooking you never thought about before. Indian food, Chinese food, hummus and pita—there are vegan dishes from all over the world.

As with the Jesus prayer, the point isn't the discipline itself but what it cultivates in us. If I'm able to turn down a jelly doughnut a couple times a week, I can also resist getting angry at the person driving in front of me. I can learn to control my anger, my greed, my selfishness, because I've been weight-lifting with jelly doughnuts! I've been weight-lifting with these elements of the fast. Fasting strengthens self-control.

CVP: *How have you seen these disciplines bear fruit?*

MATHEWES-GREEN: A number of years ago I was invited to give a speech for a group with an odd name: the Pro-Life Association of Gays and Lesbians. Towards the end of my speech, a group of thirty or forty women came in with protest signs and trailed by television cameras. They clearly weren't there to hear what I had to say: they just wanted to challenge me during the question and answer period. They were angry; they were mocking me; they were antagonistic. My heart was pounding, my stomach was clenching, my mouth was dry.

But about halfway through this tense exchange I found this incredible peace spreading all through me. I was suddenly able to see each one of these hostile questioners as a beloved child of God, as somebody who was hurting and in pain. When I left that evening, I felt so much joy in the Lord, in what had really been one of the most terrifying experiences of my life. I thought, this must be what it's like for the martyrs—my little tiny experience, as much as I could bear, of martyrdom. I discovered that there is so much joy in loving our enemies—just as Christ loved us when we were his enemies.

The spiritual disciplines enable us to be more than we could be on our own. If I had tried to approach that situation by memorizing a list of snappy answers, I could have won the debate, but I wouldn't have won any hearts.

The spiritual disciplines equip us, they build us up, and they put us in an eternal community. And they equip us even to love our enemies. We discover that we are never alone in this world—that nobody has to be our enemy, that we are always able to reach out in love. There is nothing that anybody could ultimately take away from us, because we have everything in the Lord Christ. And when we live that kind of life, we become the presence of Christ, the fragrance of Christ, and begin to change our world. **C**

For more from the Christian Vision Project and Frederica Mathewes-Green, visit **www.christianvisionproject.com**.

© 2006 Christianity Today International. All rights reserved. Used by permission.

DANIEL HOMRICH
FOUNDER, THE PASSPORT
Age 25, Atlanta, Georgia, www.thepassport.org

5 CONTINENTS. 20 COUNTRIES. 90 DAYS. DANIEL HOMRICH HAS SEEN THE WORLD THIS YEAR. THROUGH DIGITAL MEDIA HE HAS CAPTURED THE SIGHTS, SOUNDS AND COLORS OF INDIVIDUALS AND ORGANIZATIONS HELPING THE POOR, ANGUISHED AND HURT. HIS ORGANIZATION, THE PASSPORT, SEEKS TO EDUCATE, ENGAGE, AND EMPOWER INDIVIDUALS AND ORGANIZATIONS TOWARD INVOLVEMENT ON ISSUES OF SOCIAL JUSTICE.

FAMILY MATTER

I was raised with a praying mother and alcoholic father who got divorced when I was 8 years old. Although there was difficulty early in my life, I decided to follow the Lord because of the prayers of my mother and the strong example my siblings set for me. During my pursuit of the Lord I fought hard to follow my dreams even if it seemed to be unconventional.

THE GOOD AND THE HARD

Making connections around the world allows me to witness firsthand people inspired to take action in investing in the lives of the oppressed. One of the best parts of our journey is meeting individuals that give of themselves to justice whether they think anyone is watching or not. These are people whose motives are the purest—who serve with genuine conviction. Those who can't go to sleep at night without making a difference for people and their environment. These are people I aspire to become like. I must also, however, personally wrestle with grasping the shear expansiveness of the suffering.

CANDID LEADERSHIP

I tend to lead in an unorthodox style. Unorthodox in the sense that it is more candid leadership; I try to identify and pull out people's true ambitions and give them an outlet to reach these ambitions. Over the years I have developed a network of friends in many areas of society. For example, this last trip I had everyone from professional athletes to single parents to multimillionaire businessmen on board with my project. With the diversity in who I deal with the objectives have to be genuine and transcend social or cultural walls. I try to draw out desires in people's hearts that are innately inside of them by showing them that they are truly part of a bigger picture.

SEEING REAL LIFE

I have endeavored to build an international community of relationships. Their insights have given me a deeper understanding of the world in which I live. My work requires me to travel a lot and along those journeys, I have gained a grass roots perspective on politico-socio situations that may be quite different from what mainstream media purports. As a result, I have seen people in my sphere of influence desire to look deeper at global issues rather than believing hook, line, and sinker what they see on their local news network. This continually creates stimulating conversations about the circumstances people live in day to day beyond what statistics show.

INFLUENCE THROUGH INTEGRITY

Uncompromising integrity means staying true to your calling and values even when it does not seem practical or advantageous. Find what you are passionate about and you feel is written into your destiny and pursue it. Using your education and your experience, consider how to do this is in the most effective form possible. Many allow their emotion or the person they may be standing next to dictate their actions. I have seen in my limited 25 years that if you live consistent integrity you will find a greater sphere of influence. People will open up to people they can trust. ◉

Pedro's Question

By Sarah Raymond Cunningham

My fellow students and I, who were studying urban life in Chicago, gladly slumped into chairs provided to us by a neighborhood non-profit agency. Clearly, we were still scathed by our most recent ride on the city bus—a bus that, unfortunately, always seemed to be on the brink of a ten-car accident and a definitive loss in its battle against the Windy City winter. Unfortunately, thanks to our pending frostbite and pneumonia-in-the-making, we were far more interested in the hot chocolate being distributed by the speaker, community leader Pedro Windsor Garcia, than the speech he had prepared for us. Nevertheless, when Pedro asked us to "close our eyes," I complied.

"Close your eyes and think about this." Pedro instructed, "What, in this life, are you willing to die for?" As the dark silence surrounded me, I played along, internally rattling off the standard Christian college student answers: *I would die for ... my faith in God ... my little brothers ... defenseless children ..*With my answers nailed down, I sat in silence—eyes clamped shut—waiting for Pedro to bring an end to the uncomfortable quiet. Finally, a voice cut in. Without warning, Pedro demanded, "Now, open your eyes, and tell me what are you willing to *live* for?"

As I struggled to form a response to this second question, I was stunned by the irony of my answer: *Ultimately, if I have any integrity at all,* I realized, *the two answers—what I would die for and what I would live for–have to be exactly the same.* It is relatively easy to express commitment to our ideals on life's special occasions—church conferences or family holiday dinners or, maybe, even at gunpoint—but it is in many ways, much more challenging to stay aligned to our values in our standard daily routines. However, as seventeenth century philosopher, Blaise Pascal, pointed out, "The power of man's virtue should not be measured by his special efforts, but by his ordinary doings."

If I want people to see the intensity and convictions behind my beliefs, I have to somehow translate this willingness to "take a bullet" for them into ordinary, day to day behavior. I have made it a life habit to assess my integrity with a similar two-question heart check. For example, does the way I lived God's ideals today suggest that I would be willing to die for them? Or does the way I interacted with my brothers (or other loved ones) imply that I love them enough to give up my life for them? By breaking up the life we've pledged to Christ into daily installments, we help manage our investment. We invite the Holy Spirit to show us when our day to day actions may undermine our ideals, and eventually strip our investment—the integrity of our testimony —of its long-term worth.

Today, I will focus on giving one day to Him, and tomorrow, I will give another. The days will become weeks; weeks will become months; and months will become years. And eventually, whether I ever have to face bullets (or Pedro's questions again for that matter), I will be able to look back and know that I gave my life to Christ one day at a time. **C**

Sarah Cunningham is a high school teacher and speaker who lives in Jackson, Michigan with her husband Chuck. She is the author of *Dear Church: Letters From A Disillusioned Generation* (Zondervan, 2006). Check out **www.dearchurch.com**.

UNCOMPROMISING IN INTEGRITY:

Set aside some time to review how well your words match your actions. Try to think over the last week. Were there things you promised that went unfulfilled? Have you taught one thing and lived another? Were you more gracious and patient at church or at a restaurant than you were at home? Spend a day intentionally trying to think before you speak. At the end of the day, tell someone how you did and how it felt.

SESSION 04
Passionate about God

I must be aware of my small role in God's big, developing story. I am just a piece of the culture I live in, which is only part of all humanity. This is critical to my humility, faith, and trust in Him as the definer of how He will use me and my calling. To increase my awareness, I must connect with God without ceasing through all of life, whether in study, music, art, film, vocation or relationships. My passion for God to receive Glory must be bigger than my desire for Glory.

How do I practically live out my faith in culture? How do I demonstrate passion for God in all areas of my life?

THE END OF THE SPEAR...

The Beginning of the Lesson for Church Leaders

How one Stone Age church finally found its passion.

BY BEN ORTLIP
BASED ON AN INTERVIEW WITH STEVE SAINT

A CATALYST LEADER IS PASSIONATE ABOUT GOD. AND THAT MEANS BEING PASSIONATE ABOUT THE SAME THINGS GOD IS PASSIONATE ABOUT. WHEN I WAS A YOUNG BOY, MY PARENTS' PASSION FOR GOD ENGENDERED A PASSION TO ENGAGE A CULTURE CALLED THE WAODANI, OR AUCAS, IN THE JUNGLES OF ECUADOR. THERE, IN 1956, MY FATHER AND FOUR OF HIS MISSIONARY FRIENDS WERE SPEARED TO DEATH ON THE BANKS OF THE EHUENGUNO RIVER BY SIX WAODANI WARRIORS. THOSE WERE THE VERY PEOPLE WE HAD COME TO SERVE AND TO SHARE THE GOSPEL OF JESUS CHRIST WITH MILLIONS OF PEOPLE ALL OVER THE WORLD HAVE FOLLOWED THE STORY OF JIM ELLIOT, ROGER YOUDERIAN, ED MCCULLY, PETE FLEMING, AND MY DAD, NATE SAINT.

As portrayed in the film, *End of the Spear*, God then opened a door for Elisabeth Elliot and my aunt, Rachel Saint, to go live with the Waodani. Fittingly, when they saw the gospel of Jesus modeled out through the unrelenting love of my aunt and others, many of those same warriors began to "walk God's trail." My Dad's passion for God prompted a willingness to die, which was an undeniable testimony to the Waodani who killed him. Later, when my sister and I were baptized by two of the men who had speared our Dad to death, the church worldwide seems to

have been inspired by the transforming and reconciling power of the gospel. I spent part of my childhood among the Waodani people and watched as a first generation church took root in their culture. But as I would learn later, the "end of the spear" was just the beginning of the lesson for church leaders.

THE RISE AND FALL OF PASSION
Many years passed, and in 1994 I returned to those jungles hoping to find a flourishing and thriving church. I recalled the great care with which the church had been

planted, the presence of the Holy Spirit, and the passion of the Waodani people. With twentieth century resources, equipment, and training behind them, I couldn't wait to see how far they had come.

But what I saw instead was a church that was far less functional than it had been in my mid-teens. Instead of a self-propagating, self-governing and self-supporting church among the Waodani, there was just a collection of individual believers. I was both saddened and perplexed. What had happened?

One snapshot explains it all. I noticed that the Waodani elders weren't baptizing new converts. My sister Kathy and I had been baptized by two men named Kimo and Dyuwi. I asked them, "You were elders when you took Tamaya and me into the water; are you still taking new God followers into the water?"

They answered, "The Cowodi (foreigners) take the people into the water." Not only that, but the foreigners were flying the planes for the Waodani, installing and fixing their two-way radios, distributing medicines to them, taking care of their sick, building their schools, and teaching their children to read and write. To top it off, foreigners, including missionaries were paying for all of it.

Meanwhile, a state of spiritual lethargy had gradually fallen over the Waodani church. In a tragic irony, the generosity of well-meaning missionaries almost destroyed the church they were working so hard to serve. As a result, the Waodani people were not reaching their culture as they had at first. They were not encouraged to do much of anything for the kingdom. As far as they knew, being a Christian meant sitting in the pew while the professionals took care of everything. In essence, their natural passion for God was being stifled.

LESSONS FROM A STONE AGE CHURCH

The Waodani culture offers a microcosm of the culture at large. It shows us what can happen when church leaders fail to grasp what it means to be passionate about God. God's passion is not simply that leaders pursue their passion to reach a culture. The leader's ultimate job is to incite the peoples' passion for God—one they can call their own.

Why is it we can lead someone in our own culture to Christ, assimilate them into the church, and then five years later find that person has become a nice, churchy guy, but nothing more? Why aren't our churches penetrating the culture more pervasively? Why are our leaders often ineffective? What happened to the Waodani church provides part of the answer. I believe that people, with the best of intentions, committed what I have come to call "The Great Omission." That is, they effectively eliminated the contribution of indigenous believers to the fulfillment of the Great Commission.

I'm convinced the same tragedy is happening in the American church today. Instead of growing healthy churches, many leaders are making the same mistakes missionaries have made in other countries. The result is churches that are ill-prepared to do the very thing they were made to do: fulfill the Great Commission. That's why I believe the "missions principles" I have to share with you translate into "ministry principles." They are relevant for any leader who is about the work of the kingdom in any part of the world today. These principles are vital for church leaders whose calling is to cultivate a self-propagating, self-governing and self-supporting passion for God in the hearts of believers.

STONE AGE MINISTRY PRINCIPLES: 1. THE THOUGHT DOESN'T COUNT

First, we must bravely and honestly face the fact that good intentions are not an excuse for poor execution. Passion isn't

Steve Saint was born and raised in Ecuador where his parents were missionaries. His father, Nate Saint, was one of five young men killed in 1956 by the Waodani Indians (also known as Aucas) whom they were trying to reach with the Gospel. Miraculously, two years after the killings, Steve's Aunt Rachel (along with Elisabeth Elliot) was invited by the tribe to live with them where she remained until her death in 1994. Steve's mother Marj moved with her three children to Quito, where Steve attended school, visiting his aunt and the Waodani during school vacations. He grew up knowing the men who had killed his father and came to love them, to regard them as family, to be baptized by their hands, and to be embraced as a son.

enough. When, in the name of Christ's commission, we do for other believers what they can and should do for themselves, we undermine the very church that God has called us to create. Instead of investing in future leaders, we divest them of the power and passion it takes to lead.

When I asked the Waodani Christians why they weren't building "God's houses," they simply told me they didn't know how. This was odd because when I was a kid, these same people built their own church building. The next time I was in the community where we had buried my Aunt Rachel, I took a look at the one remaining Waodani church building.

It was rustic but very nice by jungle standards. It was built on concrete posts, with a board floor and siding, covered by a tin roof. I noticed that the floor was rotten in one corner where frequent rains blew in through the chain link windows.

I asked several Waodani men why they didn't fix the floor. They seemed perplexed. When they finally gave me an answer, it was this: "God's house, who does it belong to? We don't know." They weren't fixing the floor because they didn't have permission. They had not built it, and they had not paid for it; so they reasonably concluded it wasn't theirs. I began to understand why they had not been building church buildings in the other communities.

When kind Christians with good intentions decided to help the Waodani by building them a "nice" church building, it sent a message to the Waodani that the church buildings they knew how to build, with split bamboo floors and thatched roofs, were not acceptable. They concluded that only foreigners are able to build proper God's houses. So foreigners should build all of them. They expected that when outsiders figured the Waodani needed more God's houses, they would

come build more. Their wrong thinking wasn't their fault. They simply made logical assumptions given the strategy of the well-meaning outsiders.

2. YOU'RE NOT THE ONLY EXPERT

If you're gifted in ministry, your competence can actually intimidate and dissuade future leaders. In fact, the more competent, the more intimidating. It can send this message: "Step aside. The experts are here. You don't have what it takes, but we do." All too often the average church member feels disenfranchised or unnecessary. The experts have taken over.

The church in North America is blessed with top notch training, resources, and innovative ministries. But with all that excellence surrounding us, it's easy to make the mistake of thinking that only the best is acceptable. Without even realizing it, our manner begins to carry overtones of arrogance. Instead of encouraging others in their passion to serve Christ, we suggest a standard that is unreachable by the average church member. We don't mean to. But that's how it comes across.

Never let your superior education, superior technology, or superior resources become a mirage of arrogance for your brothers and sisters. The more competent you are, the more humility you must convey.

According to Paul, the passion of every believer plays a vital role in the body. Each of us is given "expert status" in the body. That means each member has everything it takes to fill his or her role. Interestingly, he cautions us of the tendency to think we're more significant than we really are: "I say to every man among you not to think more highly of himself than he ought to think; but to think so as to have sound judgment, as God has allotted to each a measure of faith. For just as we have many members in one body and all the members do not have the same function, so we who are many are one body in

Christ, and individually members one of another." (Romans 12:3-4 NASB)

3. DEPENDENCY DESTROYS. INTER-DEPENDENCY STRENGTHENS.

There's a fine line between dependency and inter-dependency. But dependency is dangerous and potentially fatal to any church—whether in the jungle or the city. Giving to others has always been an effective way to engage a culture. We give to the "have-nots" in the hope of gaining influence with them. But if we're not careful, our habit of serving can lead to a dependency that encourages a welfare mentality and debilitates the local church. In the case of the Waodani, it was full-blown economic welfare. But the most common threat for American churches is spiritual welfare.

The Waodani told me they wanted to have a clinic of their own with their own equipment to do their own dental work. They wanted their own plane to fly patients and medicines from place to place as they saw fit. My initial reaction to these requests was a mixture of elation and fear. I was excited that they wanted to take responsibility for their own people's needs, but helping them do it seemed like an overwhelming task. Unfortunately, friends back in the States offered to help by paying for the things the Waodani needed. I say "unfortunately" because I knew that the Waodani needed to pay for these things themselves, but the offer to have outsiders foot the bill was extremely tempting.

I tried to convince myself that designing all the necessary equipment was a big enough undertaking. Learning to use that equipment and then teaching the Waodani to do it too added another huge challenge. Developing an economy for them so that they could pay for all of it was too big to even contemplate. But then I began to think through the process. If the Waodani couldn't buy the equipment, they couldn't afford to maintain it. And if they

WHEN WE DO FOR OTHER BELIEVERS
WHAT THEY CAN AND SHOULD DO FOR
THEMSELVES, WE UNDERMINE THE CHURCH.

THE END OF THE SPEAR WAS JUST THE BEGINNING OF THE LESSON FOR CHURCH LEADERS.

couldn't buy it or maintain it, then the equipment wouldn't last very long. When they needed replacement equipment and when other tribes saw what the Waodani had and wanted some of their own, would our benefactors give to everyone else what they had given us?

It was difficult to resist the temptation to go the easier route, which would have added the Waodani's dependencey on me to all their other dependencies. We struggled together so that the Waodani God-followers would be empowered to become the people God intended them to be. Not too many years ago, the first Waodani aircraft in history made its maiden flight over Waodani territory with a Waodani at the controls. The Waodani have proven the can use portable dental chairs with solar-powered drills that can be carried in a backpack. Such innovations are tools the Waodani can master if they have the sufficient "want to." But make no mistake, it is easier to get the disease than cure it. "An ounce of prevention is better than a pound of cure" is never more true than it is in regard to the insidious, debilitating, demeaning and disillusioning subject of dependency.

There's a lesson here about spiritual welfare too. Every believer needs to experience what it's like to step out in ministry depending solely on the Holy Spirit for support. Our interaction with God at this level is what fuels our passion for Him. If church leaders step in too often, it cultivates dependency rather than inter-dependency.

ENGAGING THE CULTURE IS NOT A SPECTATOR SPORT

Christ has commissioned us, his church, to distribute his free offer of a remedy for the fatal sin disease that has infected everyone everywhere. The Christian church has been working at this task for twenty centuries. We have done better in some of those centuries than in others. In the twentieth century we made a crucial mistake that debilitated what was otherwise a great effort. We left most of the combatants out of the conflict. That great omission hurt us.

Reaching the world with God's offer of salvation is not a marathon for a few; it is a relay race that should involve all believers. Paul made it clear that for the body to be whole, every joint and every part needs to work together, which "causes the growth of the body for the building up of itself in love." (Ephesians 4:16 NASB) God has commissioned every one of his followers, and through the Holy Spirit, we all have what it takes. But we can only get the job done if we work together as one body—putting what we have to offer into one pot under the united leadership of Jesus Christ.

In the summer of 2000, Tementa and Mincaye and I stood together on the main stage at Amsterdam 2000, a conference sponsored by the Billy Graham Association. When I explained to Tementa and Mincaye that everyone of the thousands of people in attendance was a "God follower" who had came from countries all over the "dirt" (world) to share and learn ideas for taking God's "carvings" (the Bible) to other people, they were obviously excited.

I introduced Mincaye. In 1956, Mincaye killed my father before he learned to walk God's trail. As I translated, he explained how he lived "badly, badly, hating and killing, that is how I lived," before he started walking God's trail. Then he went on to briefly explain how much better life was since he started following God and how he wanted to tell the rest of his people how to follow God too.

He concluded by saying, "Now I see you God followers from all over the world very well. Leaving here and going back to our own places, I will still see you again when we live together in God's place." As he spoke, Mincaye's words were translated so that delegates from 209 nations could understand. His last comments are relevant for every one of us who walks God's trail, wherever we walk it: "Now I say to all of you, each of us going to our own place, we should speak God's carving very clearly so that going to God's place we will take many people with us!"

Being passionate about God means making His passion yours. And God's passion is for each disciple under your care to discover their own passion for Him. The leader's job is not simply to engage the culture; nor is it to live spiritually *for* that culture. It is to encourage them to cultivate passion for God as they pursue the call to make disciples themselves and experience the power of the Holy Spirit along the way. **C**

Steve Saint was born and raised in South America by North American parents. He is a businessman, missionary pilot, builder, designer, Certified Financial Planner, speaker, and writer. Son of a missionary martyr Nate Saint, Steve has become "family" to the tribe who killed his father. His unique life has given him a different perspective on the Great Commission.

Adapted in part from The Great Omission: Fulfilling Christ's Commission Completely by Steve Saint, ©2001, YWAM Publishing. Used by permission.

1. **What factors most influence your own passion for God?**

2. **How are you helping others in your church to experience the same thing?**

3. **In what ways is your church like the Waodani church?**

4. **How have good intentions caused you to get off track?**

5. **How can you foster a relationship of interdependency with the people you lead?**

Green-Thumbed Gardener

By Jarrett Stevens

MY FORAY INTO LAWN CARE WAS NOTHING SHORT OF A DISASTER. I WAS THIRTEEN AND MY FAMILY HAD JUST MOVED INTO A NEW HOUSE IN A BRAND NEW HOUSING DEVELOPMENT. THE HOUSE WAS GREAT, WITH A BEAUTIFUL VIEW OF THE SAN FRANCISCO BAY. EVERYTHING ABOUT THE HOUSE WAS NEW, EXCEPT FOR THE BACKYARD. IN BETWEEN OUR BEAUTIFUL NEW HOUSE AND OUR BEAUTIFUL NEW VIEW, LAY A QUARTER-ACRE OF DESOLATE DESERT. IT WAS NOTHING BUT DIRT AND WEEDS. ROUND ABOUT THE TIME I BEGAN TO FEEL SORRY FOR THE POOR LANDSCAPER WHO WOULD HAVE TO FACE THIS CHALLENGE, MY DAD INFORMED ME THAT I WOULD BE THE ONE THE FAMILY WAS SENDING INTO THAT WIL-DERNESS WASTELAND WE CALLED A BACKYARD.

I spent days in that yard attempting to remove three-foot-tall weeds that had been waiting for me their entire lives. It was hard work. Those weeds were willful and the soil was utterly uncooperative. I would spend the rest of the summer engaging in hand-to-hand combat with the weeds on their turf and on their terms. It only took one summer for me to learn just how much I hate gardening.

But my adventures in gardening were far from over. After buying our first house, I was informed by my wife Jeanne about my new role as the unpaid groundskeeper of our family. It was a role I relished at first. Mowing, edging, trimming, weeding when necessary. I was proud of my little yard, until I looked over the fence and noticed my neighbor's yard—so clean, so creative, so much better than mine. Everywhere I went I saw yards that put mine to shame. In an attempt to keep my yard not only looking good, but better than everyone else's, I resorted to cupboards full of chemicals, sprays, and special tools used at just the right time. It's a never-ending battle that only

further enforces what I knew during that wilderness wasteland of my youth—the secret to a good garden is a great gardener.

Ever the contextualist, Jesus pulls from the soil of our story an image that everyone could understand. He speaks of gardening. An image that casts himself as the vine, us as the branches, and his Father as the gardener. The power of the image must be explored if we are to understand and trust our green-thumbed gardener God. After all, it was in a garden that it all began, where humanity was hand-planted by God and rose from the fresh soil of creation. It is there in the garden that God tended to Adam and Eve, not only nurturing them with his love, but inviting them into the metaphor as they cared for the garden themselves. God caring for them, them caring for the garden. This is where the image begins, this is what Jesus is taking us back to.

"I am the true vine, and my Father is the gardener" (John 15:1 NIV).

Jesus uses the image of a vine, most likely a grapevine typical to the ones found in Middle Eastern vineyards. Unlike the beautiful roaming vineyards of the Napa Valley, vineyards in Jesus' day were smaller and lower to the ground. Vines did not grow up, but out, atop the soil. They were planted far enough apart so the gardener could walk in between them, inspecting them, correcting them, and after three years of being planted, harvesting them. All of it was done by hand. The soil tested and prepared, the seeds planted and watered, the branches properly placed and pruned for maximum growth.

Jesus is not speaking here of the macro-managed crop fields of "fly-over" states. Crops that are planted and harvested not by hand, but by machines. Out of necessity we have perfected the art of harvesting to a science of large-scale proportions. Human contact all but diminished. A far cry from my little backyard masterpieces. A far cry from the dirty fingernails and hands

of God. Hands that plant and water and weed and prune. Hands that are intimately familiar and unafraid of the dirty soil of this world. Hands that reach in deep, that hold up straight, that carefully inspect, that provide for every need. God cannot garden from a distance. It is in the trusting intimacy of the presence of God that we can grow.

"He cuts off every branch in me that bears no fruit, while every branch that does bear fruit he prunes so that it will be even more fruitful"

John 15:2 NIV

This then is what the Good Gardener does—watching and working, cutting and pruning. The image, while slightly foreign, is not an easy one. Cutting and pruning involves pain and blades and loss, none of which get anyone excited. Pruning is a critically misunderstood aspect of gardening. It involves cutting back or cutting off any branches that are fruitless or dead on the vine. It seems kind of cruel or careless, but it is essential. Without pruning, fruitless branches will continue to draw the water and nutrients that the rest of the plant needs. In essence, these "dead" branches starve the rest of the plant, taking life and giving back nothing in return.

That's all fine and good—God is a gardener, he prunes. Great. Lovely concept.

But what does that have to do with us? What are we supposed to do?

"Remain in me, as I also remain in you. No branch can bear fruit by itself; it must remain in the vine. Neither can you bear fruit unless you remain in me."

John 15:4 NIV

His command couldn't be any simpler. Jesus is telling his disciples to do what he has always told them to do. They are to stay connected to the life vine of Jesus. Stay. Before you go, you stay. Before you grow, you stay. The Vine knows exactly what it must do. The Gardener knows exactly what he must do. All the branch needs to do is stay. It is when we stay that we know.

"I am the vine; you are the branches. If you remain in me and I in you, you will bear much fruit; apart from me you can do nothing."

John 15:5 NIV

Our job couldn't be any simpler: All we have to do is stay. It's amazing how I struggle and strive and stray when all I've ever been asked to do is stay. The promise is clear—stay with me, connect to me, drawing your life from me, and you will not only grow, but you will bear fruit. You are supposed to bear fruit. You were created to grow and bear fruit. You have something of worth and wonder to give

> IT WAS WITH THE MOTIVE AND ATTITUDE OF THE HEART, I.E. THE EMOTIONAL CENTER, THAT [CHRIST] WAS CONCERNED. IT WAS THIS THAT HE CALLED ON MEN TO CHANGE, FOR IT IS PLAIN THAT ONCE THE INNER AFFECTIONS ARE ALIGNED WITH GOD, THE OUTWARD EXPRESSION OF THE LIFE WILL LOOK AFTER ITSELF.
>
> —J.B. PHILIPS

to this world. You are not supposed to be the same yesterday, today, and tomorrow—that's God's job. Your job is to grow and give of yourself the life that has been given to you.

Round about the time I thought I knew what I was doing in my yard, I had to go and introduce a foreign element—our ever inquisitive and perpetually peeing yellow Labrador, Molly. Molly is not a respecter of gardens. And that's to say nothing for what she's done to the lawn. She is an artist of sorts, adding splashes of yellow burnt out grass to an otherwise green lawn. I have spent the better part of this summer raking, fertilizing, planting, watering, replanting, and eventually sodding over the damage she has done. It seems as though my work in the yard is never done.

How true this is of our Gardener God, whose work is never done. Just when things begin to grow and bring life, disease enters in, weeds sprout up, rain doesn't come, and to top it all off, a dog comes along and pees all over us. His work is never done, not only because of the elements of the environment we live in, but also because (if not chiefly because) we refuse to stay still. We refuse to grow. We refuse to remain. We refuse to trust the gardener.

Contrary to popular belief and unspoken suspicion, we do not find God as the puppet master we might have imagined—manipulating, controlling, void of freedom, life, and

will. Instead, Jesus introduces us to a God who walks through the garden of this world lovingly cultivating and crafting a space for us to do what we were created to do—to grow. This gardener knows and cares for every branch. He never stops. He knows when and where to water, to weed, to prune. He is the one who does the work. A branch cannot see the whole of the garden. A branch cannot control a single one of the elements. A branch cannot will its way to grow. A branch cannot survive on its own. It lives and grows and bears fruit only by the hand of the gardener.

Why then are we so intent on taking care of ourselves? Why do we work so hard to create and protect a life for ourselves on our own terms and by our own efforts? Why are we so preoccupied with seeing a mighty forest through the little branches of our lives? Why do we feel like we have so little to offer this world? Why do words like love, joy, peace, patience, kindness, goodness, faithfulness, gentleness, and self-control seem more like good ideas, than actual realities that flow from our lives? Why do we find it so hard to trust the one who planted us and knows us, and who longs for us to grow? Why won't we just stay?

Could it be that we have missed the God of green thumbs? The God that Jesus trusted to guide, to guard, and to shape his every decision, his every relationship, his every day, his very life? Could it be that all your striving and struggling to craft and create a life for yourself in the shallow soil of self-will and determination has left you more empty and lifeless than ever? Maybe God is inviting you right now to stop, to sit, to stay, to trust, to plant yourself deeply and wait and watch as he does in your life what he has been doing throughout human history. Maybe it's time for you to come to your Gardener God and offer back to him the life he promised could be yours. Will you do just about the only thing you can do … will you stay? **C**

Jarrett Stevens is director of the college and singles ministry, and teacher for 7|22 at North Point Church in Alpharetta, Georgia. (**www.722.org**) Previously, he served for 10 years as the Next-Gen Teaching Pastor at Willow Creek Community Church. He lives with his wife, Jeannie, their ridiculously handsome son, Elijah (whom Jarrett dresses) and an emotionally needy Yellow Labrador Retriever named Molly.

Taken from The Deity Formerly Known as God, *copyright © 2006 by Jarrett Stevens. Used by permission of* Zondervan. (**www.zondervan.com**)

sabbath
shabbat
by lauren f. winner

RECENTLY, AT A USED BOOKSTORE, I CAME ACROSS NAN FINK'S MEMOIR STRANGER IN THE MIDST, THE STORY OF HER CONVERSION TO JUDAISM. SHE DESCRIBES THE PREPARATIONS SHE AND HER SOON-TO-BE-HUSBAND MADE FOR SHABBAT:

On Friday afternoon, at the very last minute, we'd rush home, stopping at the grocery to pick up supplies. Flying into the kitchen we'd cook ahead for the next twenty-four hours. Soup and salad, baked chicken, yams and applesauce for dinner, and vegetable cholent or lasagna for the next day's lunch. Sometimes I'd think how strange it was to be in such a frenzy to get ready for a day of rest.

Shabbat preparations had their own rhythm, and once the table was set and the house straightened, the pace began to slow. "It's your turn first in the shower," I'd call to Michael. "Okay, but it's getting late," he'd answer, concerned about starting Shabbat at sunset.

In the bathroom I'd linger at the mirror, examining myself, stroking the little lines on my face, taking as much time as I could to settle into a mood of quietness. When I joined Michael and his son for the lighting of the candles, the whole house seemed transformed. Papers and books were neatly piled, flowers stood in a vase on the table, and the golden light of the setting sun filled the room . . .

Shabbat is like nothing else. Time as we know it does not exist for these twenty-four hours, and the worries of the week soon fall away. A feeling of joy appears. The smallest object, a leaf or a spoon, shimmers in a soft light, and the heart opens. Shabbat is a meditation of unbelievable beauty.[1]

I was sitting with a cup of hot chai in a red velvet chair at the Mudhouse, a coffee shop in Charlottesville, when I read that passage. It was a Sunday afternoon. I had attended church in the morning, then cleaned out my car, then read *Those Can-Do Pigs* with my friend's two-year-old twins, and eventually wended my way down to the Mudhouse for chai and a half hour with a good book. It

was not an ordinary workday, and I did feel somewhat more relaxed than I would on Monday morning. But it was not Shabbat. Nan Fink nailed it: Shabbat is like nothing else. And Shabbat is, without question, the piece of Judaism I miss the most.

It is also the piece I should most easily be able to keep. A yearning to, say, observe the Jewish new year, or a desire to hear the Torah chanted in Hebrew: Those things might be harder to incorporate into a Christian life. But the Sabbath! The Sabbath is a basic unit of Christian time, a day the Church, too, tries to devote to reverence of God and rest from toil. And yet here a Sunday afternoon finds me sitting in a coffee shop, spending money, scribbling in the margins of my book, very much in "time as we know it," not at all sure that I have opened my heart in any particular way.

God first commands the Sabbath to the Jewish people in Exodus, with the initial revelation of the Ten Commandments, and then again in Deuteronomy. The two iterations are similar, though not identical. In Exodus God says, "*Remember* the Sabbath day and keep it holy," whereas in Deuteronomy He enjoins us to "*observe* the Sabbath day and keep it holy." Elsewhere in the Hebrew Bible, God elaborates upon this simple instruction, noting in Exodus 35, for example, that no fire should be kindled on Shabbat, and in Isaiah 66 that on the Sabbath, the faithful should "come to worship before me."

There are, in Judaism, two types of commandments (*mitzvot*): the *mitzvot asei*, or the "Thou shalts," and the *mitzvot lo ta'aseh*, or the "Thou shalt nots." Sabbath observance comprises both. You are commanded, principally, to be joyful and restful on Shabbat, to hold great feasts, sing happy hymns,

In failing to live a Sabbath truly distinct from weekly time, I had violated a most basic command: to keep the Sabbath holy.

dress in your finest. Married couples even get rabbinical brownie points for having sex on the Sabbath.

And then, of course, are the *mitzvot lo ta'aseh*. The cornerstone of Jewish Sabbath observance is the prohibition of work in Exodus 20 and Deuteronomy 5: "You shall not do any work, you or your son or your daughter, your male or female servant or your cattle or your sojourner who stays with you." Over time, the rabbis teased out of the text just what the prohibition on work meant, first identifying thirty-nine categories of activities to be avoided on Shabbat, and then fleshing out the implications of those thirty-nine (if one is not to light a fire, for example, one also ought not handle matches or kindling).

It's easy to look at the Jewish Sabbath as a long list of thou shalt nots: Don't turn on lights; don't drive; don't cook; don't carry a pair of scissors anywhere at all (for if you carry them you might be tempted to use them, and cutting is also forbidden on Shabbat); it's okay to carry a stone or a sweater or a scarf, but only inside your own house, not out onto the street and then into the house of another; don't plan for the week ahead; don't write a sonnet or a sestina or a haiku; don't even copy down a recipe; and while you are allowed to sing, you shouldn't play a musical instrument, and of course you mustn't turn on a radio or a record player. What all this boils down to (and boiling is another thing you cannot do on Shabbat) is *do not create*. Do not create a casserole or a Valentine card or a symphony or a pot of coffee. Do not create anything at all, for one of the things the Sabbath reprises is God's rest after He finished creating.

One of the finest explanations I know of the Orthodox Sabbath comes from Lis Harris's *Holy Days*, a journalistic ethnography of a Hasidic family in Crown Heights, New York. Harris, a secular Jew, has come to Crown Heights to spend Shabbat with the Konigsbergs. She is perplexed, and a little annoyed, by all the restrictions. Over dinner, she asks her hosts why God cares whether or not she microwaves a frozen dinner on Friday night. "What happens when we stop working and controlling nature?" Moishe Konigsberg responds. "When we don't operate machines, or pick flowers, or pluck fish from the sea? . . . When we cease interfering in the world we are acknowledging that it is God's world."

I remember, from my Jewish days, the language we used to name the Sabbath. We spoke of the day as *Shabbat haMalka*, the Sabbath Queen, and we sang hymns of praise on Friday night that welcomed the Sabbath as a bride. It is something of this reverence, and this celebration, that is missing from my Sabbaths now.

I remember the end of Shabbat, Saturday night. By the time Saturday night rolls around, part of you is eager to hop in your car and race to a movie, go out dancing, sip a late-night espresso. But still, even after a full day of Shabbat rest and even Shabbat toe-tapping boredom (because, let's face it, occasionally Shabbat gets dull), even then you are sad to see Shabbat go. You mark the end of Shabbat with a ceremony called *havdalah*, which comes from the Hebrew verb meaning "to separate," in this case separating Shabbat from the week. *havdalah* involves a number of ritual objects–wine for tasting, and a braided candle for lighting, and a box of fragrant spices

(cloves, often, and cinnamon), and you pass around the spice box because smelling the sweet spices comforts you a little, you who are sad that Shabbat has ended. One of the reasons you are sad is this: Judaism speaks of a *neshamah yeteirah*, an extra soul that comes to dwell in you on the Sabbath but departs once the week begins.

I remember that, for Jews, the Sabbath shapes all the rhythms of calendar and time; the entire week points toward Shabbat. The rabbis, who are always interested in the subtleties of Torah prose, puzzled over the two different versions of the Sabbath commandment. Why, in Exodus, does God tell us to *remember* the Sabbath, whereas in Deuteronomy He instructs *observance* of the Sabbath? One story the rabbis tell about the difference between remembrance and observance has to do with ordering time. Sunday, Monday, and Tuesday are caught up in remembering the preceding Shabbat, while Wednesday through Friday are devoted to preparing for the next Shabbat.

What, really, was wrong with my Mudhouse Sabbath? After all, I did spend Sunday morning in church. And I wasn't *working* that afternoon, not exactly. A fine few hours, except that my Sunday was more an afternoon off than a Sabbath. It was an add-on to a busy week, not the fundamental unit around which I organized my life. The Hebrew word for *holy* means, literally, "set apart." In failing to live a Sabbath truly distinct from weekly time, I had violated a most basic command: to keep the Sabbath holy.

I am not suggesting that Christians embrace the strict regulations of the Orthodox Jewish Sabbath. Indeed, the New Testament unambiguously inaugurates a new understanding of Shabbat. In his epistles, Paul makes clear that the Sabbath, like other external signs of piety, is insufficient for salvation. As he writes in his letter to the Colossians, "Therefore do not let anyone judge you ... with regard to a religious festival, a New Moon celebration or a Sabbath day. These are a shadow of the things that were to come; the reality, however, is found in Christ." And Jesus, when rebuked by the Pharisees for plucking grain from a field on Shabbat, criticizes those who would make a fetish of Sabbath observance, insisting that "the Sabbath was made for man, not man for the Sabbath."

But there is something, in the Jewish Sabbath that is absent from most Christian Sundays: a true cessation from the rhythms of work and world, a time wholly set apart, and, perhaps above all, a sense that the point of Shabbat, the orientation of Shabbat, is toward God.

Pick up any glossy women's magazine from the last few years and you'll see what I mean. The Sabbath has come back into fashion, even among the most secular Americans, but the Sabbath we now embrace is a curious one. Articles abound extolling the virtues of treating yourself to a day of rest, a relaxing and leisurely visit to the spa, an extra-long bubble bath, and a glass of Chardonnay. *Take a day off*, the magazines urge their harried readers. *Rest*.

There might be something to celebrate in this revival of Sabbath, but it seems to me that there are at least two flaws in the reasoning. First is what we might call capitalism's justification for Sabbath rest: resting one day a week makes you more productive during the other six. Or, as my father has often told me,

I'll get more done working eleven months a year than twelve. And while that may be true, rest for the sake of future productivity is at odds with the spirit of Shabbat.

We could call the second problem with the current Sabbath vogue the fallacy of the direct object. Whom is the contemporary Sabbath designed to honor? Whom does it benefit? Why, the bubble-bath taker herself, of course! The Bible suggests something different. In observing the Sabbath, one is both giving a gift to God and imitating Him. Exodus and Deuteronomy make this clear when they say, "Six days shall you labor and do all your work. But the seventh day is a sabbath to the Lord your God." *To the Lord your God*.

Christianity, of course, has a long tradition of Sabbath observance, so a revitalized Sabbath is more a reclaiming of the Christian birthright than the self-conscious adoption of something Jewish. Jesus observed Shabbat, even as He challenged the specifics of Mosaic Sabbath law; and since at least the year 321, when Constantine declared Sunday as Sabbath for all his empire, Christians have understood the Sabbath as a day for rest, communal worship, and celebration. New England Puritans summed up their thoughts about Sunday thus: "Good Sabbaths make good Christians."

For Christians, the Sabbath has an added dimension: It commemorates not only God's resting from Creation, but also God's Resurrection. As eighteenth-century Pietist Johann Friedrich Starck put it, "Under the New Testament, Christians also consecrate one day out of seven, Sunday, to God, that being the day on which Christ rose from the dead, and the Holy Spirit was poured out." (Starck encouraged readers even to begin their Sabbath practices on Saturday evening, urging the Christian to "disentangle his mind from worldly cares and troubles ... Prepare himself for the coming Sunday with prayer, ... [and] Retire to rest betimes," so as to be punctual and sprightly at church the next morning.) As for me, I am starting small. I have joined a Bible study that meets Sundays at five, a bookend to my day that helps me live into Shabbat–there's not enough time between church and Bible study to pull out my laptop and start working, so instead I try to have a leisurely lunch with friends from church. I have forsworn Sunday shopping (a bigger sacrifice than you may realize), and I sometimes join my friend Ginger on her afternoon visits to church shut-ins. Sometimes before Bible study, you will find me with the twins and the can-do pigs, and sometimes still you will find me at the Mudhouse. Not much, when compared to the dramatic cessations of the Orthodox Shabbat; but still, the first arcs of a return to Sabbath. **C**

Lauren Winner is completing a Ph.D. in American religious history from Columbia University while both teaching and studying at Duke Divinity School. She travels widely speaking to audiences in the wake of her book *Real Sex*. She is also the author of the acclaimed memoir, *Girl Meets God*.

Reprinted from Mudhouse Sabbath, © *2003 by Lauren F. Winner. Used by Permission of Paraclete Press,* **www.paracletepress.com**.

THE REST OF TIME
STOPPING TO NUMBER OUR DAYS ARIGHT

BY MARK BUCHANAN

SABBATH-KEEPING IS MORE THAN TIME-MANAGEMENT. IT IS A FRESH ORIENTATION TO TIME, WHERE WE THINK WITH HOLY IMAGINATION ABOUT HOW THE ARC OF OUR MOMENTS AND HOURS AND DAYS INTERSECTS ETERNITY. "TEACH US TO NUMBER OUR DAYS ARIGHT," MOSES ASKED GOD, "THAT WE MAY GAIN A HEART OF WISDOM."(PSALM 90:12 NIV) TEACH US THAT THIS IS NOT JUST ANOTHER DAY OF THE WEEK, BUT THE DAY THAT THE LORD HAS MADE.

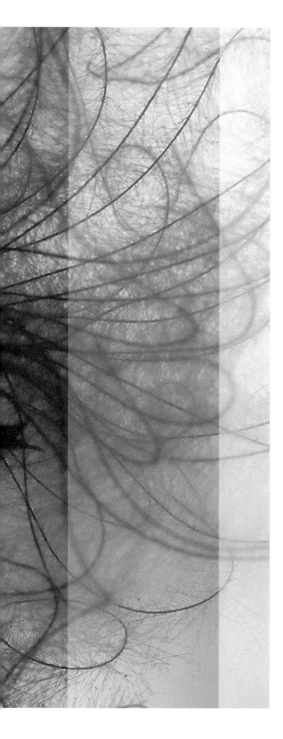

This is God's time-management technique. There is a right way to tally up days. There's an arithmetic of time-keeping, and God must tutor us in it. Wisdom is not the precondition for learning this arithmetic. It's the fruit of it. Wisdom comes from learning to number our days aright. You don't need to be wise to sign up for God's school. But if you're diligent, attentive, inquisitive in his classes, you'll emerge that way.

It's easy to get this wrong. God's school is not like most. It's not regimented, age-adjusted, fixed in its curriculum. The classroom is life itself, the curriculum all life's demands and interruptions and tedium, its surprises and disappointments. In the midst of this, through these things themselves, God hands us an abacus and tells us to tally it all up.

Meaning? Meaning, work out where time and eternity meet. Pay attention to how God is afoot in the mystery of each moment, in its mad rush or maddening plod. He is present in all that. But too often we are so time-obsessed we take no time to really notice.

I write this at a time when the church talks much about being purpose-driven. This is a good thing, but we ought to practice a bit of holy cynicism about it. We should be a little uneasy about the pairing of purposefulness with drivenness. Something's out of kilter there.

Drivenness may awaken or be a catalyst for purpose, but it rarely fulfils it: more often it jettisons it. A common characteristic of driven people is that, at some point, they forget the purpose. They lose the point. The very reason they began something—embarked on a journey, undertook a project, waged a war, entered a profession, married a girl—erodes under the weight of their striving. Their original inspiration may be noble. But driven too hard, it gets supplanted by greed for more, dread of setback, force of habit.

Drivenness erodes purposefulness. The difference between living on purpose and being driven surfaces most clearly in what we do with time. The driven are fanatical time-managers—time-mongers, time-herders, time-hoarders. Living on purpose requires skilful time management, true, but not the kind that turns brittle, that attempts to quarantine most of what makes life itself—the mess, the surprise, the breakdowns, the breakthroughs. Too much rigidity stifles purpose. I find that the more I try to manage time the more anxious I get about it.

And the more prone I am to lose my purpose. The truly purposeful have an ironic secret: they manage time less and pay attention more. The most purposeful people I know rarely over-manage time, and when they do it's usually because they're lapsing into drivenness, into a loss of purpose for which they overcompensate with mere busyness. No, the distinguishing mark of the purposeful is not time-management.

It's that they notice. They're fully awake. Jesus, for example. He lived life with the clearest and highest purpose. Yet he veered and strayed from one interruption to the next, with no apparent plan in hand other than his single overarching one: get to Jerusalem, and die. Otherwise, his days, as far as we can figure, were a series of zigzags and detours, apparent whims and second-thoughts, interruptions and delays, off-the-cuff plans, spur-of-the moment decisions, leisurely meals, serendipitous rounds of storytelling.

Who touched me?
You give them something to eat.
Let's go to the other side.

Jesus was available—or not—according to some oblique logic all his own. He had an inner ear for the Father's whispers, a third eye for the Spirit's motions. One minute he's not going to the temple, the next he is. One minute he refuses to help a wedding host solve his wine drought, the next he's all over it. He's ready to drop everything and rush over to a complete stranger's house to heal his servant, but dawdles four days while Lazarus—"the one he loves"—writhes in his death throes, or fails to come at all when John—"the greatest in the Kingdom of heaven"—languishes on Death Row. The closest we get to what dictated Jesus' schedule is his own statement in John's gospel: "The wind blows wherever it pleases. You hear its sound, but you cannot tell where it comes from or where it is going. So it is with everyone born of the Spirit." (John 3:8 NIV)

The Apostle Peter, after declaring that Jesus is "Lord of all," describes the supreme sovereign's *modus operandi*: "God anointed Jesus of Nazareth with the Holy Spirit and power, *and . . . he went around doing good . . .*"(Acts 10:36 NIV) So that's it, the sum of Christ's earthly vocation: he wandered and he blessed. He was a physician vagabond. He was the original doctor without borders. His purpose was crystallized, but his method almost scattershot.

No, Jesus didn't seem to keep time. But he *noticed*. So many people along the way—blind men, lame men, wild men, fishermen, tax men, weeping whores, pleading fathers, grieving mothers, dying children, singing children, *anyone*—captured his attention. He stopped to tell a lot of stories, many which arose out of, well, more interruptions—"Teacher, tell my brother to divide the inheritance with me ... (Luke 12:13 NIV) Teacher, what must I do to inherit eternal life? (Luke 10:25 NIV) Son of David, have mercy on me . . ." (Matthew 15:22 NIV) What's more, he invited others to go and do likewise. Those driven to get and spend, to judge and exclude, he called to attention.

Look at the birds!
Do you see this woman?
Why do you call me good?
Who do you say I am?

Life does not consist in the abundance of our possessions, Jesus warned. And then he told a story, about a rich fool who noticed all the trivial things and was oblivious to all the important ones. What matters, Jesus concluded, isn't being rich in stuff: it's being rich toward God. He explained the essence of such richness elsewhere: it's having eyes to see, ears to hear.

It's to notice, to pay attention to the time of God's visitation. Purposefulness requires we pay attention, and paying attention means—almost by definition—that we make room for surprise. We become hospitable to interruption. I doubt we can *notice* for long without this. And to sustain it we need theological touchstones for it—a conviction in our bones that God is Lord of our days and years, and that *his* purposes and his presence often come disguised as interruptions, detours, messes, defeats.

I came to you naked, Jesus says. *I came to you thirsty.*

"When, Lord?" we ask, startled.

When he wore the disguise of an interruption. Think a moment of all the events and encounters that have shaped you most deeply and lastingly. How many did you see coming? How many did you engineer, manufacture, chase down?

And how many were interruptions? Children? You might have planned that as meticulously, as a NASA rocket launch, but did you have any idea, really, what it would be like, who this child in your arms really was, who you would become because of him or her? The span between life as we intend it and life as we receive

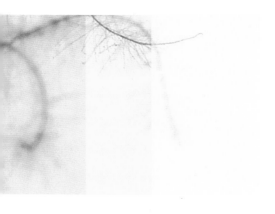

it is vast. Our true purpose is worked out in that gap. It is fashioned in the crucible of interruptions.

Mr. Holland's Opus is the story of a man with a magnificent ambition. He wants to be a great composer. But he still has to pay the bills, so he and his young wife move to a small town where he teaches high school music, strictly for the money. All the while, he works on his masterpiece, his opus, laying the ground for his real calling. The plan is to teach for a few years, and then step into his destiny.

But life keeps intruding. It keeps interrupting. One year folds into two, into five, into fifteen. And then one day, Mr. Holland is old, and the school board shuffles him out for early retirement. He packs his desk. His wife and grown son come to fetch him. Walking down the school's wide empty hallways, he hears a sound in the auditorium. He goes to see what it is.

It's a surprise Hundreds of his students from his years of teaching—many now old themselves—dozens of his colleagues, both current and former, hundred of friends, fans, well-wishers: the room is packed. All have gathered to say thank you. An orchestra is there, made up of Mr. Holland's students through the years. They've been preparing to perform Mr. Holland's Opus—the composition that, over 4 decades, he hammered out and tinkered with, polished, discarded, recovered, reworked, never finished.

They play it now But of course, he knows, everyone knows: his opus isn't the composition. His real opus, his true life's masterpiece, stands before him, here, now. It's not the music. It is all these lives—men and women, young and old—which his life has touched. It is all these people who his passions and convictions have helped, and shaped, and changed. It's all that's being formed in the crucible of interruptions.

This is his work. This is his purpose.

Finally, after all these years, he's learned to number his days.

In 1973, the comedian Johnny Carson nearly caused a national crisis with a single wisecrack. That was the year North America's long flight of post-war prosperity, fell to earth like a shot goose in one ungainly plummet. There was runaway inflation. There were oil and food shortages. All the abundance that Americans had come to see as their due, their birthright, suddenly seemed in jeopardy.

And so on December 19, 1973, at 11:35 PM, when Johnny Carson walked on the live studio set of The Tonight Show and quipped, "There's an acute shortage of toilet paper in the United States," it wasn't funny. The joke had a toehold in reality: earlier in the day, Congressman Harold Froehlich from Wisconsin had warned that if the federal bureaucracy didn't get its act together soon and catch up on its sup-

ply bids, government agencies would run out of toilet tissue within a month or two. Carson took this shard of trivia and played it for a laugh. Then, as was his trademark, he took a swing at an invisible golf ball, took a commercial break, and got on with the show.

Not so the nation. Twenty million viewers flew into panic. The next morning, hundreds of thousands of frantic shoppers lined up outside the supermarkets of America, poised to dash to the paper aisles and stockpile roles, fighting over bundles of 2-ply and 4-ply. There were brawls in aisle ways and scrums at the checkout. Some store managers tried to limit sales—4 roles per customer—but they had no way of monitoring how many times a customer came back, and most came back repeatedly. By noon on December 20—mere hours after Johnny's flippant remark—America was sold out.

Johnny Carson's one offhand gag-line had sparked a national run (no pun intended) on toilet tissue.

We're generally gullible about news of scarcity. We have, it seems, an in built skittishness about shortfall. This has been with us a long while, since the garden, by my reckoning.

Most of us live afraid that we're almost out of time. But you and I, we're heirs of eternity. We're not short of days.

We just need to number them aright. **C**

Mark Buchanan lives on Vancouver Island, Canada, with his wife three children. He is a pastor and the author of three other books, *Your God is Too Safe*, *Things Unseen*, and *The Holy Wild*. Some days he is restful or playful, without shame. Check out his blog at **www.markbuchanan.net**.

Reprinted by permission from The Rest of God: Restoring Your Soul by Restoring Sabbath *by Mark Buchanan, © 2006, W Publishing, a division of Thomas Nelson, Inc., Nashville, Tennessee. All Rights Reserved.*

Candid with Eugene Peterson

CATALYST: *Eugene, we understand that at one time you were a pastor. Could you tell us about what kind of a pastor you were and what kind of advice you might have for today's church leaders?*

PETERSON: First of all, I never intended to be a pastor. I was going to be a professor and was preparing for that. I got a part time job in a congregation just to help with the finances. And I realized this is what I wanted to do all my life. So over a period of three years, I changed my vocational direction and became a pastor and had a chance to start a new congregation.

In some ways, I was totally unprepared. I learned on the job. I soon found that the prevailing idea of what pastors are in America was something I didn't care to imitate. In nearly 30 years at Christ our King Church, we tried to discover the roots of pastoral vocation in America, but in continuity with what's been going on for 2,000 years.

CATALYST: *Historically, what did you find was the vocation of a pastor?*

PETERSON: There are a lot of different ways to serve the Lord: evangelism, missionary work, organizational work, etc. A pastor has a unique place in all of this. I realized I needed to stick to what I was called to do. The way I understood the uniqueness of the pastoral vocation is that it is insistently personal. You cannot do pastoral work in a programmatic, or impersonal, or organizational way.

You've got to know the names of these people, know their lives, be in their homes. The unique vocation of pastor is to know those people. And at the same time, to know the scriptures, the whole world of scripture, so that stories of those people get integrated to the stories of scripture.

CATALYST: *Most of the books you've written tend to focus on pastors. Why is that?*

PETERSON: When I became a pastor, I found that a lot of pastors hated what they were doing. They were cynical. They were disillusioned. A lot of them quit. They still do. The fallout in the pastoral vocation is enormous. I was finding being a pastor was the most exciting thing I'd ever done. You're right in the middle of all this sin, and salvation, and death, and birth, and it's all so local, and it's all so personal. If I hadn't been writing the kind of stuff I've been writing, I'd have been a

Eugene Peterson on Sabbath

"Most of us find it's the most radical thing we have ever done and the most creative."

novelist because the congregation is a rich source of human relationships, and God relationships, and spiritual relationships.

CATALYST: *Most people know your name because of* The Message, *can you talk about why you felt the need to write this very unique paraphrase of the Bible?*

PETERSON: Well, it wasn't my idea. I would never have dreamed of doing it, to tell you the truth. It would be too daunting. I was asked to do it. It started with a Bible study which wasn't going very well on Galatians. I shifted my approach and translated Galatians into the language I thought those people were speaking. And it worked really well. I did it for a whole year with this group of 14 or 15 adults.

Then I put it into a book. A few years later, an editor from NavPress Publishers called me up and said, "I've been reading this translation that you made of Galatians and I've been carrying it around. I photo copied it. I've been reading it to my friends, reading it myself, and we're all just getting really tired of Galatians. Why don't you do the New Testament?"

That's how it started. I was reluctant to do it. I didn't think I could, and I said "no" three years. Then I left my congregation intending to write. That's

when the editor called again and I said, "I can give it a try, I guess." That's how it started.

CATALYST: *Was it daunting to consider the idea that you would be writing a translation of the Bible?*

PETERSON: To tell you the truth, I never thought I would because I didn't think anybody would buy it. So I wasn't intimidated by being counted in the company of Kenneth Taylor, or J.B. Phillips, or James Moffett. I just was doing my work. What happened as I was doing this is I realized I'd been doing it all my life.

This is the way I've been thinking and talking with my congregation. This is my style of preaching, my teaching. I started out as a teacher of biblical languages. I always read my Bible in Greek and Hebrew. It had been kind of composting in me all those years. And now here it was coming together in a way I never expected it to come together. It seemed pretty natural, to tell you the truth. It was an integration of everything I'd been doing for 50 years.

CATALYST: *Storytelling is a lost art in today's culture. Do you think that's part of the reason for the success of* The Message?

PETERSON: I think so ... the Bible is basically a story. Most of it started out not as written but spoken. I tried to recapture

Candid with Eugene Peterson

the orality of what was written. Originally, there were no verse numbers. People were reading this as a story. You wouldn't read a page or a paragraph of a novel and quit. There's a whole story to be known there. I successfully kept verse numbers out of the text for several years, but finally had to give that up.

CATALYST: *Let's talk a little bit now about the topic of rhythm. I know that you like to refer to a balanced life as a life in rhythm. And the balance of living by rhythm versus living by schedule is a pretty tough thing to practice. Can you give us some insight on how you practice that and how to implement that in our lives?*

PETERSON: Let me qualify this by saying that rhythm is very individual. You can't impose a rhythm on someone, you have to enter into a rhythm. And people don't have to have the same rhythm. Some people can walk in three-quarter time and some in four-four time. You don't have to do it the same ... you can't do it the same. You've got to find the rhythm of your own body, your own life, your own history. Having rhythm means that you live out of who you are in relationship to who God is, who Jesus is. So it's more like a dance.

One of the hard things in America is to escape this scheduled world that we're living in—where things are so disconnected from the seasons, from the night and day, the rhythms that are around us and that are within us, our heartbeat, our pulse, our breathing. So if we just let the culture determine the way we live, we're going to live pretty jerky lives. I think for me, and for many I've worked with and talked to around this, the place to begin is the Sabbath. The Sabbath is the one interruption into the life of jerky fragmentation that is still possible. You can take a day off.

CATALYST: *What should a Sabbath look like in my life? What does it look like in yours?*

PETERSON: A day of unplugging. That's a good way to put it. When I was a pastor, the Sabbath was on Monday, because Sunday was a workday for me. My wife and I didn't practice Sabbath when we had small children, because it took us a few years to figure out our rhythm.

But typically on a Monday we would pack a lunch and we would go to the woods. We'd hike for three or four hours in silence. Then we prayed, had lunch, talked, and worked our way back home.

We'd get home by the time the kids were home. Interesting, they loved this. We weren't uptight about anything because it was the Lord's day. We played and we prayed and didn't do anything that was necessary. Unplugged everything.

It transformed our lives, our family life, our personal lives, and our congregational life. Not everybody did it, but they saw us doing it. Somehow that gave them a sense that they don't have to do what the world's telling them to do. It really does take effort and determination. Those of us who want to keep the Sabbath are going to have to be pretty intentional about it.

I've been doing this for at least 40 years consistently and I've had dozens of students and parishioners who have also adopted this practice. Most of us find it's the most radical thing we've ever done— and the most creative. **C**

Eugene Peterson was for many years the James M. Houston Professor of Spiritual Theology at Regent College. He also served as founding pastor of Christ Our King Presbyterian Church in Bel Air, Maryland. A prolific author, he is probably most well known for *The Message*, his translation of the Bible in the language of today. (**www.navpress.com**) Now retired from full-time teaching, Peterson and his wife Jan live in the Big Sky Country of rural Montana.

Adapted from the Catalyst Podcast, Episode 5. *Download and listen to the entire interview at* www.catalystspace.com.

RADICAL RECONCILIATION
AN INTERVIEW WITH BRENDA SALTER MCNEIL

BRENDA SALTER MCNEIL EXUDES PASSION, AS ANYONE KNOWS WHO
HAS PRAYED WITH HER, HEARD HER SPEAK, OR SIMPLY SAT IN THE
SAME ROOM WITH HER. SHE COMBINES BOUNDLESS ENERGY AND A
THOUSAND-WATT SMILE WITH A QUIET CENTER THAT MAKES YOU WANT
TO SLOW DOWN AND LISTEN. BRENDA IS A CONSULTANT TO CHURCHES
AND CHRISTIAN ORGANIZATIONS THAT WANT TO TAKE THE NEXT STEP
TOWARD RACIAL AND ETHNIC RECONCILIATION. IN HER CONSULTING
WORK AND IN HER BOOK *THE HEART OF RACIAL JUSTICE* (CO-AUTHORED
WITH RICK RICHARDSON), SHE BRINGS BOTH PROFESSIONAL INSIGHT
AND SPIRITUAL DEPTH TO ONE OF THE MOST CHALLENGING ISSUES
FACING NORTH AMERICAN CHRISTIANITY. IN THIS INTERVIEW FOR THE
CHRISTIAN VISION PROJECT, SHE SPOKE ABOUT WHAT CAN SUSTAIN
THE PASSION OF AN AGENT FOR RADICAL CHANGE.

CVP: *What is your passion as a Christian leader?*

MCNEIL: Racial reconciliation. Christians talk about racial reconciliation a lot,
and people want to do it, but often they're
talking about a kingdom value without
even really knowing what it looks like. We
help them understand what it looks like.

CVP: *Nearly all Christians would affirm
the value of racial reconciliation, but why
are so few passionate about it?*

MCNEIL: Generally something has to
push us from where we're stuck to where
we want to go. In the early church, the disciples were told that they were going to go
to the ends of the earth. They were going
to Judea, they were going to Samaria—to
be with people they didn't like at all. But
they didn't move at all! They stayed right
there in Jerusalem.

And that's generally what we do. We stay
right where we are. First Baptist might
invite Second Baptist for a service, our
church might go have a reconciliation
service with another church, but for the
most part we stay the way we were, unless
something shakes us up and moves us.

For the early church, that catalytic
event was persecution, in the form of
a man named Saul. They didn't like it
one bit, and generally catalytic events
aren't things that we like one bit either.
They shake us, they make the ground
under us unstable, and they make us
cry out for God. But they move us from
where we are to where we say we want
to go.

CVP: *Many people have experienced emotional events about racial reconciliation,
but then somehow the momentum dies.*

MCNEIL: There are times that people hear a wonderful speaker or go to a conference or read a book, and it's the flavor of the month, and they're fired up, and they feel like, "Oh, we should do something about this!" But often those efforts are short-lived. For a person to stay in the long haul, there needs to be a mandate that comes from the heart of God, that makes that person stick with it long after the glamour has worn off. It's like marriage. People stay married not because they feel like staying married all the time, they stay married because they covenanted together before God that they would.

Many people also lose interest in reconciliation because they haven't identified their need for other people. They say, "We want to do racial reconciliation! We want our church to be more diverse!" Why? What's the need for that diversity? Why would your church be better if you had more Filipino people, more Korean people, more African-American people, more Hispanic people? Often people don't have an answer to that question. So we do it because we think it would be nice, but not because it's necessary. When their culture begins to change our institution, then we want them gone. Because we wanted to have them with us in a very nice way, but we really didn't want them to reorganize our church or our institution.

CVP: *That kind of change can be hard work.*

MCNEIL: The Bible says we've been entrusted with the ministry of reconciliation, and I believe it is a precious ministry. However, it is a weighty ministry. This is a spiritual battle, and if we try to attempt this in our own strength, or just with the weapons of the world, we will fail. We need to tap into the strength of God.

That requires prayer, and not just prayer that talks to God, but prayer that gets our marching orders from God: "God, we don't know what to do, but our eyes are watching you. And if you tell us, we'll do it." That takes courage, and generally a whole lot of faith, knee-knocking faith, because God is not always going to tell us things that make us comfortable. We've got to be ready for the unconventional voice of God, for the power of God.

Now that's the passionate activist Brenda talking, but let me tell you something else. I'm learning to take a weekly Sabbath, and it's probably the hardest thing I've ever tried to do. We live in such a busy, work-driven, achievement-oriented society that it's killing us. We can't think a clear thought. What's on the inside of our spirits can hardly surface sometimes, because we're driven at such a pace. So the Scripture that God is using to change me is, "Don't be conformed any longer to this world"—this world driven by success, and numbers, and activity to prove your worth—"but be transformed by the renewing of your mind."

I grew up with old folks, black folk, who believed in keeping the Sabbath day holy. They didn't cook on the Sabbath, they didn't iron on the Sabbath, they basically made it a day of worship. So I go to a place where I can enjoy the presence of God, where I'm not a celebrity and no one knows me. I don't want to be called Reverend Brenda or Doctor anybody! Often I spend the day at a convent. The nuns and I eat lunch in silence. Then I

walk outside and I notice things that I haven't seen in years. Sometimes I meditate on the Stations of the Cross—quite unusual for a Pentecostal girl, but I'm learning. Sometimes I'll do something just for fun. Sometimes I sleep.

For many of us, Sunday can't be our Sabbath, because we do church for a living. I'm a person who preaches a lot on Sundays, and though it is my act of worship, I generally work hard on the days I preach. So I've taken Thursdays as my Sabbath day. I ask my secretary to clear my calendar, I do not take appointments—sometimes she has to prevent even me from putting an appointment on that day!

CVP: *What else can rob us of passion when ministry gets difficult?*

MCNEIL: I am concerned by a spirit of fear that has gripped our culture. September 11, 2001, changed everything for us. I've become very aware of how much people do and say things based upon fear. We're sold products based upon fear—insurance, medicine, home improvement systems—to keep us safe. So people, Christians included, feel justified in making sure that they keep the "other" away, because that person could be dangerous somehow. That spirit of fear is causing great damage to our faith and our passion. Jesus asked his disciples, "O ye of little faith, why were ye afraid?" God has not given us a spirit of fear—when we take on huge challenges in Jesus' name and in his power, we find that there is truly nothing we need to fear. **C**

For more from the Christian Vision Project and Brenda Salter McNeil, visit **www.christianvisionproject.com**.

© 2006 Christianity Today International. All rights reserved. Used by permission.

NAOMI ZACHARIAS

DIRECTOR, WELLSPRING INTERNATIONAL

Age 28, www.wellspringinternational.org

FROM COCA-COLA TO THE WHITE HOUSE, NAOMI HAS WORKED MANY PEOPLE'S DREAM JOBS. ANSWERING GOD'S CALL, HOWEVER, BROUGHT HER BACK TO HER FATHER'S ORGANIZATION TO LAUNCH A HUMANITAR-IAN OUTREACH MINISTRY. NAOMI NOW TRAVELS THE WORLD TO SERVE WOMEN AND CHILDREN AT RISK. PEOPLE OFTEN ASK IF IT IS HARD TO RELATE TO WOMEN WHO HAVE BEEN TRAFFICKED, IMPRISONED, OR ABUSED AND FROM SO MANY DIFFERENT CULTURES. HER ANSWER? IT IS WHERE SHE FEELS MOST ACCEPTED AND AT HOME.

PRICELESS PEARLS

My friend was traveling overseas, look-ing for jewelry to bring back as a gift for a few of us who have grown close as we stumble through life. She found these unique, black pearl pendants. They were not round, but oval, and not smooth, but a little rough around the edges. She asked the lady behind the counter about them, who smiled and said, "Some people see them as flawed. Others see them as spe-cial." I now wear that pendant proudly. For some reason, God sees me as special, even with my flaws. He has drawn me to that "special-ness" in others too. I see His reflection most clearly in the eyes of those whom society wrongly discards. My call-ing is to honor and serve God by reaching out to those who are broken and hurting.

SOMETIMES AN EMPTY THRONE

My relationship with God is one that has become more raw. Faith for me is not easy. But at its base is an absolute confidence in God that keeps me fight-ing for what I know to be true. There are moments where I feel, as C.S. Lewis described, that I approach the throne only to find it empty. There are other moments where I am certain He is sitting right there. I connect with him by surrounding myself with real people who help me sift through the masks and the superficial. By reading things that pull me deeper into understanding the complexities of life and accepting His mystery. By involving myself in things that remind me of His beauty, His grace, His healing power. His transcendent beauty is found in the beautiful and non-beautiful parts of life, and I love that.

THE FILTER

God is the filter in me that everything travels through. It's the voice inside that reminds me of why I can't make one choice, and it's the peace inside that helps me rest in another. His word is not a rulebook, it's more like a survival guide. When I go to Him in my brokenness, I don't forget where I've been. I remember, and suddenly it has a purpose and is beautiful.

CONVERSATIONS

We have recently had the opportunity to help a family in need from a very differ-ent religious background. They have been so gracious, and asked, "Why would you do this for us?" Medical facilities we have worked with for this family want to sit down and understand why we are doing what we are doing. It is an opportunity to live the love of Christ. And it also cre-ates this whole trail of dialogue between all the people involved. We have donors supporting these efforts who are not from a Christian worldview and would not nor-mally be giving to a ministry. But we share a common desire to help someone in need, and suddenly the relationship begins. On all sides, it has opened dialogue and built relationships on what Christ lived. **C**

Art Surrendered

By Ted Vaughn

Artists are some of the most passionate people you will ever meet. Artists can speak out against injustice and hypocrisy. Artists look at life and respond to life differently than non-artists. King David was such an artist and wrote this about the evening sky: "When I look at the night sky and see the work of your fingers—the moon and the stars you have set in place—what are mortals that you should think of us, mere humans that you should care for us?" (Psalm 8:3-4 NLT) Long before these words were canonized and used for study and reflection, they were the natural and passionate words of an artist seeking, yearning, and discovering God.

I lead artists. It's a strange gig and I love it. Mobilizing this artistic temperament and raw passion so that it communicates God's message of hope, truth, and redemption has been a remarkable journey. Learning how to shepherd and care for the unique needs of artists has sometimes stretched my leadership near its breaking point. At the same time, however, I've learned that God uses artists to awaken us to truth, to change lives, and to have a powerful impact in places that intellect alone cannot take us.

Our hearts were designed by God to fathom more than our minds could ever handle. For this reason, art often seems irrational, because the heart is reaching out beyond the rational mind, trying to find the meaning of its existence. This helps me understand artists. Their guts drive them beyond rational thinking. Their passion is overwhelming and compelling, pulling them in directions that the mind questions and seeks to mitigate. This art and artistic passion can easily become an idol that we ascribe God's name to. For this reason, artists must continually surrender their passion to God and hold their "artistic guts" in check. They must verify their connection to God and often recalibrate their heart and mind heavenward.

God is the original artist—the author and designer of the creative process. Consider Paul's words from Ephesians 2:10: "For we are God's workmanship, created in Christ Jesus to do good works, which God prepared in advance for us to do." (NIV) Workmanship can be translated to mean "work of art." Paul is saying that from design, we are God's work of art. We were in His mind's eye long before we were flesh and blood. Before we ever created anything, we were His creation: a work of art uniquely cherished and known by its Creator. The passion that went into Bach's symphonies or Picasso's masterpieces is nothing compared to the passion God has for each of us, His beloved creation, his work of art created long ago.

This is the invitation God extends to artists: Connect with the original, ultimate, and unending source of creative energy. Create art humanity has only dreamed of, art that screams of God's glory, redemption, and hope; art that reflects the loving heart of the author and finisher of all of creation. Celebrate the good, the true and the beautiful. **C**

Ted Vaughn is the Director of Contemporary Worship Arts at Solana Beach Presbyterian Church (**www.solonapres.org**). He and his wife Licia have two children, Bethany (10) and Emilia (2) and live in Carlsbad, California. Contact Ted at **vaughn@solanapres.org**.

PASSIONATE ABOUT GOD:

Practice a Sabbath. Set aside one day this week to completely unplug from work, technology, entertainment, and parties. Spend the day in rest and reflection. Worship God through written word. Create a poem, a song, or journal a prayer that expresses your passion and love for God. Reflect on the ways you demonstrate your passion for God in culture. If you feel comfortable, share your creation with a friend or your learning community.

SESSION 05
Intentional about Community

People are in my life at all levels. Close personal friends that keep me accountable, question my deepest motives, and help me stay true to the wisdom God has imprinted on my heart. I value the people that work for and alongside me, recognizing that I am fulfilling an influential role with people God has entrusted to my care. I value the wisdom of those more experienced than me and seek out counsel in all things of importance.

Do I value those God has placed around me enough to be vulnerable with them? Does my community encompass all aspects of the greater culture?

THE COMING LONELINESS

EPIDEMIC
What's at stake with our internal struggle
between privacy and community

By Ben Ortlip

PEOPLE. YOU CAN'T LIVE WITH THEM. YOU CAN'T LIVE WITHOUT THEM. THAT'S THE PREMISE OF WHAT IS RAPIDLY EMERGING AS NEXT YEAR'S HOT TOPIC: SOCIAL ISOLATION. IT'S ALREADY BEGINNING TO SHOW UP IN THE MAJOR PRESS OUTLETS. IT'S BEING TALKED ABOUT ON NPR, IN ACADEMIC CIRCLES, AND EVEN AT CAMP DAVID. EARLIER THIS YEAR, A MAJOR STUDY BY DUKE UNIVERSITY AND THE UNIVERSITY OF ARIZONA SHOOK THE MARBLE WALLS OF THE AMERICAN SOCIOLOGICAL REVIEW. THE TWENTY-YEAR PROJECT CONCLUDED THAT AMERICANS ARE BECOMING ISOLATED AT AN ALARMING RATE. IN A PAPER BLUNTLY TITLED SOCIAL ISOLATION IN AMERICA, RESEARCHERS STATED, "THE NUMBER OF PEOPLE WHO HAVE SOMEONE TO TALK TO ABOUT MATTERS THAT ARE IMPORTANT TO THEM HAS DECLINED DRAMATICALLY. [FROM 1985 TO 2004] ... WE [WENT] FROM A QUARTER OF THE AMERICAN POPULATION BEING ISOLATED ... TO ALMOST HALF OF THE POPULATION [NOW] FALLING INTO THAT CATEGORY."[1]

At first glance, the report may seem to be stating the obvious. It's no secret that America is sprawling with garage door communities. We live among neighbors we've never met. We choose television over social events. And many of our most influential role models are fictional characters or the celebrities who portray them. The decline of authentic relationships is changing the very fabric of our culture.

But a closer evaluation shows that this is more than just a social narrative. It's an issue that's gaining momentum. And it's changing the way American culture will function fifty years from now. Whether you're talking global warming or social cooling, major topics like this usually take decades to establish mainstream credibility. And the isolation discussion is already starting to achieve such notoriety. In the future, you can expect to hear more about this issue, not less. That's because there are some very important statistics riding on the culture's ability to stay connected. Just as a shift of a few degrees in the earth's temperature causes a dramatic change in the climate, a shift in the way we interact can result in a cultural landscape that's barely recognizable.

For starters, social isolation is equal to smoking as an independent risk factor for death. Companionship has long been recognized as a psychological factor that also impacts us physically. One study compared elderly heart-attack victims and found that those with two or more close companions experienced twice the one-year survival rate versus those who faced it alone.

Isolation is also linked to a wide variety of pathological disorders. In some cases, it is considered a direct factor in the development of mental illness. Crime is also impacted by isolation. Even where it's not a direct causal factor, seclusion often serves as an important incubator in which criminal ideas are allowed to develop. Think Columbine, the Unabomber, Eric Rudolph, or the D.C. Beltway sniper. In each case, the perpetrators' distorted thinking required isolation to reach the boiling point. There is an important element of social alignment that is maintained when we are in contact with others. Isolation eliminates those guardrails and cuts people off from natural sources of accountability.

SAFETY IN NUMBERS
On a practical level, social isolation threatens our basic functionality in everyday life. Close relationships multiply our resources when we're looking for a job, keeping abreast of trends in technology, or looking for the best deal on a digital camera. A good social network acts as a support system that enables our overall progress. It also forms a safety net in a crisis. "That image of people on roofs after Katrina resonates with me, because those people did not know someone with a car," explains Lynn Smith-Lovin, a Duke University sociologist and one of the authors of the twenty year study. She adds, "Whether it's picking up a child in day care or finding someone to help you out of the city in a hurricane, these are people we depend on."

Harvard professor Robert Putnam calls these benefits "Social Capital." According to his model, our personal networks have collective value that manifests itself in four ways: environments of trust; shared information; cooperative action; and "norms of reciprocity," or the inclination to do things for each other. Putnam's book, *Bowling Alone: The Collapse and Revival of American Community*, traces the roots of our isolation back to the 1960s with the rise of television, two-career families, and suburban decentralization. As a thematic word picture, he observes that although more Americans are bowling today than in the 60s, membership in bowling leagues has evaporated, leaving a lot of people to bowl alone.

Ironically, Smith-Lovin and the other authors of the twenty year study originally set out to disprove Putnam. But their findings quickly turned them into converts instead. "Shifts in work, geographic, and recreational patterns may have combined to create a larger demarcation between a smaller core of very close confidant ties and a much larger array of less interconnected, more geographically dispersed, more unidimensional relationships," they conceded. "Whatever the reason, it appears that Americans are connected far less tightly now than they were 19 years ago."[2]

BASIC INSTINCTS
While Americans are growing apart, the concept of community is alive and well in many third world nations. When Smith-Lovin's twenty year study was being

released in the U.S. last Spring, representatives of Catalyst were in Rwanda to observe the progress of Catalyst's Rwandan Wells project. Instead of disintegrating people groups, the Catalyst delegation found tightly knit communities of interdependent villagers. The Rwandan people rely on each other for basic necessities. And that foundation results in overlapping networks of close relationships that eventually envelope everyone.

"In Rwanda, they know how to live in community," remarks Jeff Shinabarger, one of the Catalyst delegates. "They are dependant on each other for ultimate survival. They do everything in community, everyone has a role to play; starting as a three year old, you work and take part in the family. We have so much to learn from a pre-modern society in understanding the idea of community to redeem that in our culture."

Clearly, humans gravitate into social groups. Yet in the right conditions, we will begin to gravitate away from them. We will pursue privacy and individuality at the risk of alienating ourselves from vital, life-sustaining relationships. What causes this shift in our core human behavior? What's at stake for the culture either way? And what should Catalyst Leaders do to equip themselves for the coming isolation epidemic?

THE NEED FOR CONNECTION
At the root of our internal struggle is a fascinating paradox—an epic face-off in which two of our most basic human needs battle for control. While both of these core needs are innate and valid, they are also in direct conflict with each other. And the tension between them leads to mixed motives when it comes to community. The first is our need for connection.

Few would argue with the idea that people need each other. As John Donne articulated during the Renaissance period, "No man is an island, entire of itself ... because I am involved in mankind." Even if we attempt to disconnect, the impact of our disconnection sends ripples throughout the rest of the population. When a father separates from his wife and children, the void unleashes a social firestorm that first ravages the family, and eventually encumbers the culture at large. In the same way, when the average citizen withdraws from the local community, their lawns are soon overtaken by weeds—both literally and figuratively. Somehow, we have been created not for *in*dependence, but for *inter*dependence. And those groups who have thrived throughout history are those who have understood the difference between the two, and have mastered the art of balancing them.

The need for connection is first practical. On the surface, prosperous Americans live in large homes and enjoy fine food because of things like hard work, education, and intelligence. But even the most independent of self-made achievers depends on others, such as those who build houses, sustain the food supply, and comprise the economic system that enables them to earn their fortunes. So even when we pursue individuality and privacy, we do so within the context of a culture that is—and will always be—our very lifeline. Without the support of others, individual Americans would literally starve or at least be reduced to subsistence.

The need for connection is also spiritual and emotional. Even if we could achieve complete autonomy for our physical needs, our existence would be incomplete. In her book on the topic, Jennifer Hillman, Professor of Psychology at Penn State University, writes, "[The] psychological sense of community provides a sense of belonging, identity, emotional connection, and wellbeing. There are many positives that result from people experiencing and perceiving a sense of community."[3]

Psychiatrists have observed that when children are deprived of key social interaction, it actually inhibits emotional and cognitive development. Conversely, healthy interaction can have therapeutic and restorative benefits that enhance a person's well-being. Dr. Bruce Perry, a San Diego, CA psychiatrist who works with high-risk children, explains, "One of the most important things that we try to do for children who have experienced some form of trauma is make sure that they're living in an environment where they have opportunities for wealth of relationships, where they have neighbors, and extended family, and family members who can be supportive and present and invested in their lives."

And these metaphysical effects aren't just for children. A study by Human Communication Research examined the connection between loneliness and local television news viewing. Their research on 329 adults found that loneliness resulted in ritualized news viewing as a form of "parasocial interaction" to compensate for unmet social interactivity.[4] When deprived of adequate social contact with friends and neighbors, we will seek solutions to this need another way. We need connections.

THE NEED FOR PRIVACY

In competition with our innate need for connection is our persistent desire for privacy. But understanding this need is even more difficult because of the way it is distorted and blown out of proportion in the media. For example, solitude is often portrayed as a symbol of accomplishment in our culture. "Escaping the crowd" is a perk reserved for those who achieve status. Ads for investment firms entice us with scenes of private beaches and vast estate homes in which human interaction is reduced or eliminated altogether. Recognizing our exhaustion from an unrelenting lifestyle, marketers dangle the promise of isolation as an ultimate reward. Over time, we have been conditioned to view withdrawal as a source of pleasure.

But even though most people could use a moment to think, it's not likely that we would actually benefit from additional solitude. If anything, we are epidemically deprived of the holistic benefits that come from deep, authentic connections to our communities. Detached from this support system, we are prone to fatigue, depression, anxiety, and malaise. And in the clutter of messages, we mistake our need for restoration as a need for isolation.

Nevertheless, privacy is an authentic need. Before we can present ourselves as a functional member of the community, we must have a clear sense of who we are apart from the community. We must understand our unique identity. If our only picture is of our interaction with others, we can't fully understand our unique purposes in life. Only in isolation are we totally free to explore the deepest levels of honesty with ourselves. In solitude, we come face to face with our character, our true strengths, and our chronic weaknesses.

But in our first-world nation, privacy is not typically used as a checkpoint; it is often an indulgence or an obsession. These days, virtually all our physical needs can be satisfied at Wal-Mart or the corner grocery store. There's no need to engage with others for the purpose of daily survival. Forming communities is no longer a natural tendency. In fact, socializing can be downright inconvenient. After a hard day at the office, or with the kids, who wants to put on a social mask for the neighbors? It's much more appealing to read a book or watch TV.

Another reason to avoid community is the fear of rejection. Most of us have experienced community before. And instead of finding support and affirmation, we felt estranged, rejected, and unacceptable. As a result, we respond to those negative experiences accordingly: we withdraw. After all, it's easier. Why take a chance on getting hurt emotionally?

A MILE WIDE, AN INCH DEEP

More and more today, relationships are not forged from the crucibles of hardship and survival. In generations past, as in primitive cultures, people were more likely to experience their struggles together, out in the open. The idea of "sharing" a personal concern was irrelevant, because most issues were literally shared by the whole community in the form of tangible burdens. Deep, supportive relationships were a natural by-product of those survival communities. Notably, wherever people are fully known, they experience the therapeutic, supportive benefits that come from belonging to a deep-rooted community. Today, our friendships are more likely to be the random by-product of social curiosity or amusement. As a result, they tend to be disposable, superficial, and less reliable than those born out of necessity. Our social networks include more people and cover more geography than ever before, but the depth of relationships within those networks has decreased. We may be widely known, but fewer of us are fully known.

This changing social landscape is rewriting the definition of community, as well as the way people interact in groups. To make matters worse, technology like chat rooms and instant messaging has turbocharged the evolution. The ratio of surface relationships to deep ones is higher than ever.

The term "civil inattention," coined by sociologist Erving Goffman, refers to the mutual recognition of people in public places engaging in non-committal interaction. Traditionally, this basic form of socialization took place on street corners or at the water cooler. But as recently as the last decade, it is rapidly shifting to venues like MySpace. In a paper entitled, "Social Interaction Design Case Study: MySpace," Adrian Chan notes, "MySpace is a kind of 'presencing' system: personal presence within a social context. Members present themselves on it through their profiles, and engage in a form of online socializing that works by creating local scenes around members rather than places, events, or discussions. People are the site's content, each member's profile standing in for him or her 24/7. MySpace occupies a strange zone between public and private—as the online world is a public space not in the present tense, but in the archived tense. Similarly, one's presence online is not real in the physical present, but becomes real and valid as it attracts attention and participation. If there is such a thing as social capital, then it is earned and spent as social currency at MySpace."[5]

But Princeton sociologist Robert Wuthnow expresses his concern about the ability of these alternatives to substitute for the need for deep relationships. "The kind of community [bloggers] create is quite different from the communities in which people have lived in the past.

THE DECLINE OF AUTHENTIC RELATIONSHIPS IS CHANGING THE VERY FABRIC OF OUR CULTURE.

These communities are more fluid and more concerned with the [interests of] of the individual. ... Some [blogs] merely provide occasions for individuals to focus on themselves in the presence of others. The social contract binding members together asserts only the weakest of obligations. Come if you have time. Talk if you feel like it. Respect everyone's opinion. Never criticize. Leave quietly if you become dissatisfied. We can imagine that [bloggers] really substitute for families, neighborhoods, and broader community attachments that may demand lifelong commitments, when, in fact, they do not."

In the emerging social model, people are less inclined to advance beyond the level of intimacy found in Goffman's description of civil inattention: "I see you, you exist, and though I can't say that I want to talk, I'm not ignoring you, either."

A JONATHAN AND A NATHAN

King David was a man who wrestled between privacy and community. He was both intensely private (as evidenced by his intimate solitude with God) and passionately social (leading public worship in the streets). Moreover, he was a leader. And from his experiences we can glean suggestions about how a Catalyst Leader should pursue and preserve community.

First, David engaged with the community. Even before he was king, David was interested in the affairs of the community. His natural concern for important events led to his curiosity about the situation with Goliath and his eventual showdown with the war-

rior. As a young shepherd, he learned the concept of caring for a community as a whole. By the time he became the leader of Israel, David's mindset was to ensure their well-being like a flock. This community mindset served as a backdrop for his other relationships, and no doubt influenced all of them.

At the personal level, two of David's relationships exemplify the kind of depth that results in guidance and support. The first is David's friendship with his peer, Jonathan. Jonathan's assistance proved vital to David when Saul (Jonathan's father, no less) sought to kill him. Clearly, Jonathan was someone with whom David could share his deepest concerns. As 1 Samuel records, "Jonathan made a covenant with David because he loved him as himself. Jonathan took off the robe he was wearing and gave it to David, along with his tunic, and even his sword, his bow and his belt." (1 Samuel 18:3-4 NIV)

The second is David's relationship with his advisor, Nathan. As the local prophet, Nathan already played a key role in the community. But beyond that, David and Nathan appear to share a deep friendship. Perhaps it's no coincidence that David named his son Nathan; or that David first shared his desire to build a temple with Nathan; or that Nathan named another of David's children; or that Nathan was loyal to David when

Adonijah tried to usurp the throne. Most familiar, Nathan was close enough to David to provide accountability when he fell into sin over Bathsheba.

As Catalyst Leaders, we can apply these cues to guard against the coming isolation epidemic. First, be intentional about engaging with your community. In the workplace, in the neighborhood, and in the nation. Wherever you share mutual interests with others, there is your community. Second, pursue deep, meaningful relationships with peers. Everyone needs a Jonathan—someone close enough to know, and concerned enough to help. Third, find your Nathan—a spiritual adviser with whom you can disclose your spiritual needs.

THE FUTURE OF COMMUNITY

The concept of community is vanishing daily. More and more, we are surrounded by people who don't know what it looks like to be fully known and outrageously supported by another. The future of community depends on those Catalyst Leaders who understand not only the value of deep relationships, but also the importance of mutual support. It is our nature to run from community because it reveals the ugly truth about us. But we must run to community because God intended for us to need each other. And this need is a social foreshadowing of our need for Him. **C**

Ben Ortlip writes books and study curriculum for several prominent Christian authors and oversees creative projects for trend-setting ministries like Campus Crusade for Christ, Injoy, FamilyLife, Walk Thru the Bible, and Northpoint Ministries. Ben is co-author of the breakout small group study *Blueprint for Life*. He and his wife, Lisa, live in Cumming, Georgia with their six children.

1. **What evidence have you seen that communities are failing in America?**

2. **What encouragement have you seen that suggests there's hope for our communities?**

3. **Who is your Jonathan?**

4. **Who is your Nathan?**

5. **What would it look like to be engaged with your community?**

An Experiment in Truth

COMING OUT OF COLLEGE, MY FRIENDS AND I HAD A HUNCH THAT THERE IS MORE TO LIFE THAN WHAT WE HAD BEEN TOLD TO PURSUE. WE KNEW THAT THE WORLD CANNOT AFFORD THE AMERICAN DREAM AND THAT THE GOOD NEWS IS THAT THERE IS ANOTHER DREAM. WE LOOKED TO THE EARLY CHURCH AND TO THE SCRIPTURES AND TO THE POOR TO FIND IT.

So about thirty of us from Eastern College continued dreaming together about another way of doing life. Most of us were getting tired of talking and were ready to live. We went to the ghetto. We narrowed our vision to this: love God, love people, and follow Jesus. And we began calling our little experiment The Simple Way. In January 1997, six of us moved into a little row house in Kensington, one of Pennsylvania's poorest neighborhoods, just minutes from old St. Edward's cathedral. It felt like we were reinventing the early church for the first time in two thousand years. (We were quite ignorant.)

We had no idea what we were getting into. We had no big vision for programs or community development. We wanted only to be passionate lovers of God and people and to take the gospel way of life seriously. People sometimes ask us what we do all day on an "average day" at the Simple Way. It gets a little crazy since our lives are full of surprises and interruptions. I'll do my best to describe it to you.

We hang out with kids and help them with homework in our living room, and jump in open fire hydrants on hot summer days. We share food with folks who need it, and eat the beans and rice our neighbor Ms. Sunshine makes for us. Folks drop in all day to say hi, have a safe place to cry, or get some water or a blanket. We run a community store out of our house. We reclaim abandoned lots and make gardens amid the concrete wreckage around us. We plant flowers inside old TV screens and computer monitors on our roof. We see our friends waste away from drug addiction, and on a good day, someone is set free. We try to make ugly things beautiful and to make murals. Instead of violence, we learn imagination and sharing. We share life with our neighbors and try to take care of each other.

We preach, prophesy, and dream together about how to awaken the church from her violent slumber. Sometimes we speak to change the world; other times we speak to keep the world from changing us. We are about ending poverty, not simply managing it. We give people fish. We teach them to fish. We tear down the walls that have been built up around the fish pond. And we figure out who polluted it.

We spend our lives actively resisting everything that destroys life, whether that be terrorism or the war on terrorism. We believe in another way of life—the kingdom of God—which stands in opposition to the principalities, powers, and rulers of this dark world (Ephesians 6:12).

Since those early days, we've made plenty of mistakes and have never learned the secret to not hurting each other. We have described the layers of our common life as an onion, at the core of which are the partners who covenant to love and cherish each other (the hardest and most beautiful thing we do), and each of us shares healthy responsibilities and expectations. We've hashed out our nonnegotiables and tried to understand those we do not agree with.

New folks have brought energy and imagination, and we've seen new visions born. Our programs revolve around the needs and gifts in our community and are always changing. They never define us, for we set out not to start programs but simply to be good neighbors.

We now have so many partner communities and organizations that it really feels like a movement much bigger than the Simple Way. And we are just one little cell within the Body, very full of life but only a small part of the whole. Cells are born and cells die, but the Body lives forever.

Wanderers and Sympathizers

One of the things that has fascinated me about the days of the early church is how those who abandoned homes and possessions to follow Jesus lived in such union with those who opened their homes to them and the poor. The wanderers were traveling apostles and relied on the support of the sympathizers. Both shaped the early church. They did not look down on each other. The sympathizers did not write the wanderers off as radicals or freaks, and the wanderers did not judge the sympathizers as sellouts. They loved and supported one another. From

WE RECLAIM ABANDONED LOTS AND MAKE GARDENS AMID THE CONCRETE WRECKAGE ... WE PLANT FLOWERS INSIDE OLD TV SCREENS ... WE TRY TO MAKE UGLY THINGS BEAUTIFUL...

our earliest days, we have seen the importance of that partnership as we have commissioned wanderers and nomads who travel like the apostles did, or like the later circuit riders of the church (who traveled on horseback, which is a little harder nowadays). These new pilgrims help to cross-pollinate our communities and lives. We have had folks travel the country by bike, by car, on foot, using biodiesel, and by RV, seeking to intersect our lives in the Christian underground.

Despectacularizing Things

Again, it's easy to see these things as spectacular, but I really believe that's only because we live in a world that has lost its imagination. These things were normal in the early church. It's just what conversion looked like. We must be careful not to allow ourselves to be written off as radicals when church history and the contemporary Christian landscape are filled with ordinary radicals. But today people crave the spectacular. People are drawn to lights and celebrities, to arenas and mega-churches. In the desert, Jesus was tempted by the spectacular—to throw himself from the temple so that people

might believe—to shock and awe people, if you will. Today the church is tempted by the spectacular, to do big, miraculous things so people might believe, but Jesus has called us to littleness and compares our revolution to the little mustard seed, to yeast making its way through dough, slowly infecting this dark world with love. Many of us who find ourselves living differently from the dominant culture end up needing to "despectacularize" things a little so that the simple way is made as accessible as possible to other ordinary radicals.

Sometimes people call folks here at the Simple Way saints. Usually they either want to applaud our lives and live vicariously through us, or they want to write us off as superhuman and create a safe distance. One of my favorite quotes, written on my wall here in bold black marker, is from Dorothy Day: "Don't call us saints; we don't want to be dismissed that easily."

The truth is that when people look at us like we are sacrificial servants, I have to laugh. We've just fallen in love with

God and our neighbors, and that is transforming our lives. Besides, I think if most other folks knew Adrienne and the kids, a beautiful family that has been living with us after coming out of the shelter system, they'd do the same things we are doing. It just makes sense not to have families on the street or in abandoned houses, especially when we have a spare bedroom. Honestly, the way of life we have chosen often seems more natural than the alternative. The alternative—moving out and living in the suburbs—seems terribly sacrificial (or painfully empty). What must it be like not to have block parties or not to actually know the people around us? There are times when I have been very frustrated with wealthy folks for hoarding their stuff. But now I know enough rich folks to know the loneliness that is all too familiar to many of them. I read a study comparing the health of a society with its economics, and one of the things it revealed is that wealthy countries like ours have the highest rates of depression, suicide, and loneliness. We are the richest and most miserable people in the world.

I feel sorry that so many of us have settled for a lonely world of independence and riches when we could all experience the fullness of life in community and interdependence. Why would I want a fancy car when I can ride a bike, or a TV when I can play outside with sidewalk chalk? Okay, sometimes I still want the hot tub on the roof, but the rest I can live without. And I mean live without. Patting Mother Teresa on the back, someone said to her, "I wouldn't do what you do for a million dollars." She said with a grin, "Me neither." I almost feel selfish sometimes, for the gift of community. The beautiful thing is that there is enough to go around.

Not Easy But Good

Once we get past the rebellious or reactive countercultural paradigm and muster up the courage to try living in new ways, most of us find that community is very natural and makes a lot of sense, and that it is not as foreign to most of the world's population as it is to us. Community is what we are created for. We are made in the image of a God who is community, a plurality of oneness. When the first human was made, things were not good until there were two, helping one another. The biblical story is the story of community, from beginning to end. Jesus lived and modeled community with his little band of disciples. He always sent them out in pairs, and the early church is the story of a people who were together and were of one heart and mind, sharing all in common. The story ends with a vision of the new community in the book of Revelation, where the city of God is dressed beautifully for her lover, this community called the New Jerusalem, where heaven visits earth and people are fully reconciled to God and each other, the lion lays down with the lamb, mourning turns to dancing, and the garden takes over the concrete world!

But that doesn't mean community is easy. For everything in this world tries to pull us away from community, pushes us to choose ourselves over others, to choose independence over interdependence, to choose great things over small things, to choose going fast alone over going far together. The simple way is not the easy way. No one ever promised us that community or Christian discipleship would be easy. There's a commonly mistranslated verse where Jesus tells the disciples, "Come to me, all you who are weary and burdened, and I will give you rest. Take my yoke upon you and learn from Me. … For My yoke is easy and My burden is light." (Matthew 11:28-30 NASB) People take that to mean that if we come to Jesus, everything will be easy. (The word good is often mistranslated as "easy"). Ha, that's funny. My life was pretty easy before I met Jesus. In one sense, the load is lighter because we carry the burdens of the world together. But he is still telling us to pick up a yoke. Yoke had a lot of different meanings. It was the tool used for harnessing animals for farming. It was the word used for taking on a rabbi's teaching (as Jesus seems to use it here). Yoke was also the word used for the brutal weight of slavery and oppression that the prophets call us to break (Isaiah 58, among other passages). One of the things I think Jesus is doing is setting us free from the heavy yoke of an oppressive way of life. I know plenty of people, both rich and poor, who are suffocating from the weight of the American dream, who find themselves heavily burdened by the lifeless toil and consumption we put upon ourselves. This is the yoke we are being set free from. The new yoke is still not easy (it's a cross, for heaven's sake), but we carry it together, and it is good and leads us to rest, especially for the weariest traveler.

In fact, if our lives are easy, we must be doing something wrong. Momma T also used to say, "Following Jesus is simple, but not easy. Love until it hurts, and then love more." This love is not sentimental but heartwrenching, the most difficult and the most beautiful thing in the world. **C**

Shane Claiborne is a prominent activist and sought after speaker. He is one of the founding members of The Simple Way, a community in inner city Philadelphia that has helped birth and connect radical faith communities around the world. (**www.thesimpleway.org**) Shane serves on the board of directors for the Christian Community Development Association and in his down-time is quite a dynamic circus performer.

Adapted from The Irresistible Revolution: Living as an Ordinary Radical, *© 2006 by The Simple Way. Used by permission of Zondervan.* (**www.zondervan.com**)

SOMETIMES WE SPEAK TO CHANGE THE WORLD; OTHER TIMES WE SPEAK TO KEEP THE WORLD FROM CHANGING US.

THE CULTURE-SHAPING CHURCH

THE BEACH, THE GOSPEL, AND FIVE BIG ROCKS

BY GABE LYONS

CLINT KEMP IS HIS NAME. HE'S AN ENTREPRENEUR, LITTLE KNOWN PASTOR AND THIRTEENTH GENERATION NATIVE OF THE BAHAMAS. MAYBE YOU HAVEN'T HEARD OF HIM YET, BUT HE IS CHANGING THE FACE OF CHRISTIANITY IN THE BAHAMIAN CULTURE. HIS STORY SHEDS NEW LIGHT ON HOW THE CHURCH CAN ONCE AGAIN REGAIN INFLUENCE IN CULTURE. THE STORY OF THIS COMMUNITY BEING THE CHURCH PROVIDES AN ENTIRELY NEW PARADIGM TO CONSIDER FOR THOSE EXPERIMENTING WITH PRESSING THE GOSPEL FORWARD IN THE CONTEXT OF AMERICAN CULTURE.

My wife and I took a detour during our recent vacation in the Bahamas to spend a day with our new friend. We met Clint at our hotel in Nassau, jumped into his eco-friendly car and off we went across the island.

Our first conversation turned to the effects major resort hotels are having on the Nassau culture and environment. This topic struck a cord with Clint. It was obvious that for all the good these massive resort hotels brought to the island's

economy, it was creating environmental challenges for the beaches, wildlife, and people it employed. His unique perspective on this topic foreshadowed his unique way of being a *Christian* in his culture.

As we drove through the city streets, he began telling us his story. His church used to be more of a seeker-friendly style, attracting the unchurched with a great Sunday service and environment. Over time though, he recognized that this model of church was not creating the kind of

Christ-followers that could revolutionize the island. He wanted more for his people and this sent him on a journey to discover the deeper life and experience Christ was calling their church to become.

As we pulled into the parking lot of his church, I couldn't help but notice the sign reading in large letters: NEW PROVIDENCE COMMUNITY CENTER. At the bottom of the sign in very small letters it read, "Where New Providence Community Church meets." This small sign spoke volumes. It starts with the simple fact that Clint understands and is committed to true community. I had heard about Clint from several other influential leaders in the U.S. church. He has made a habit of convening thoughtful leaders around the concept of creating a holistic church. As we discussed the far-reaching influence of their church community, he carefully credited any success to a rigorous commitment to a community of friends that have helped shape the church's philosophy and expressions. Clint is far from a one man show.

This sign also illustrates the way their church sees their role in culture. They had created a "community center" that could serve their neighbors in tangible ways while also being a place to have spiritual conversations about life. As we walked through the halls of the center, we saw walls displaying works of art by the island's leading artists. There were many ways that children and families could interact with the center. From after-school training in Taekwando and gymnastics, to formal art lessons and pottery creation, it was obvious that their view of the "church" is a place that serves the community, rather than a place the community serves. In many ways, their church was at the center of the community – painting a vivid picture of how the church can shape and influence society and culture at large.

Clint showed us an art studio, designed for children to learn how to create art and pottery on Sunday mornings during the adult teaching time. It is an interesting concept. They desire to connect a child's creative intuition with spirituality, helping them understand how God, as creator, has instilled His likeness into each of them. Every week they work on creating a piece of art and are instructed on the relationship of the art to its maker.

Next, we walked outside and visited their gardens. Within a greenhouse complex, they have constructed gardens that are tended by the children and teenagers that participate in their church. On Sunday mornings, these children work in the gardens with their parents and experience reflection and solitude. They put their hands in the dirt and help plants grow through careful tending, watering, pruning and nurturing. They develop a spiritual understanding of God's creation, the environment and how it symbolizes so much about their relationship to God's design.

As we left the gardens, I noticed five large, 20-ton, boulders surrounding a reflective pool, each with its own walkway to approach it. This is an art installation several artists in the community created representing the five main areas of focus for their church. The first rock, painted entirely red, represents their battle against AIDS and the service to those affected by it. (Nassau has one of the highest concentrated areas of AIDS cases in the first world. The church is a part of piloting programs to cut occurrences in half.) Three additional boulders represent

Economic Justice, Grace, and Reconciliation. The fifth rock, which represents Environmental Justice, was covered with shards of glass and trash collected from a beach clean up.

We learned how the people of the church are working to restore a dune destroyed by a recent hurricane. By working at this site monthly alongside public and private sector advocates, they are helping ensure the environmental and personal safety of an important portion of the island. They also lead the way in partnership with other local churches to bring reconciliation and justice to Haitians suffering from mistreatment in their community.

Finally, Clint took us to a location called "Sacred Space." Forty feet below us we saw the crystal clear waters of the Atlantic Ocean crashing against the cliffs. This area used to be an environmental wasteland, serving for years as the unofficial island dump. Littered with trash, appliances, old tires, furniture and garbage—the entire location had become overgrown. Interestingly, the space happened to sit above the site where slave ships would dock over 160 years ago. (The Bahamas played an active role in the slave trade between Africa and America.)

New Providence Community Church decided to adopt this place and began restoring it. They believed that as followers of Christ, they had a responsibility to redeem this hideous, corrupted area of the island. For two years, their people spent days and weekends removing the trash and cleaning the entire space. Many of the island's artists and environmentalists caught wind of this and became interested in the project. One world renowned artist created 12 carvings of Jesus' disciples from the fallen trees. Another hung custom designed wind chimes throughout the area, while others cleared away the brush. Today, the space is a favorite spot to visit for local Bahamians, tourists and even celebrities. The breathtaking sunset views create an

amazing spiritual experience – but more than that, it's a testimony to the leaders of the Island of how a community can be a significant part of the restoration of all things within their society.

As we were standing at the edge of the cliffs in this beautiful space, Clint shared with me that over the past six months, his spiritual discipline had been to watch the sunset three nights a week. He recalled that the first couple of months felt like staring into space; but then, in a moment, it all changed. It was the deepest soul connection he had ever experienced with the Father.

Then Clint made one of the most profound statements I have heard in relation to the church in western society. He said, *"Gabe, over the next decade, the two most effective expressions of the Gospel will be through social justice and environmental justice."*

This is deeply insightful. The culture at large has become intrigued with both social injustice and environmental concerns. To understand that the essence of the Gospel has everything to do with these two mainstream obsessions should be stirring to all leaders in the church. Both research and trends show that culture at large, especially the younger generation, is naturally drawn to these

two global issues. Recognizing that the expressed Gospel seeks to overcome the injustices in the world for both humankind and God's creation, should bring encouragement and renewal to the work of Christians throughout the West, providing an insight into what God might be up to in our generation.

New Providence Community Church is shaping the culture of the Bahamas because they have approached their mission with the belief that they are called to be the Gospel in the context of their community. By deciding not to make their church a place for people to come and see, they have pushed their people to go and do. And they clearly illustrate the influence one church can have when it takes this mission seriously.

As a result...
- Their church is included on the major plans related to community development for the island.
- They have been platformed as the premiere example of how the government should work to environmentally protect areas of the island and provide restored space for locals to enjoy.
- Parliamentarians include Clint and the leaders of their church, on major policy decisions and matters that effect the majority population.

- They are working to build more Community Centers throughout the island.
- They are partnering with the U.S. Embassy in a festival and print campaign to raise AIDS awareness.
- The National Emergency Management Administration partners with the church to host educational and awareness seminars in their center.
- Their Community Center is the main Hurricane shelter for the entire area.
- Their influence has spread into the arts community where they host benefits and art auctions.

This church has earned a seat at the table with the arts community, business and political leaders, and the socialites

... providing an opportunity to influence the future of the island itself.

Because their work takes place in an island environment—a controlled study so to speak—it is the perfect, measurable, proving ground for the positive cultural influence Christians can have when they are engaged in promoting justice, doing good and being a force for renewal and restoration in their local context. It is my prediction that in Western culture, this approach will likely lead the next phase of church missiology. When adopted, it will be the pre-cursor to the church regaining its place as a culture-shaping institution for the common good of all mankind throughout society. ⒞

Gabe Lyons co-founded Catalyst and has provided vision to this growing movement. In 2003 he launched his own organization, Relevate, which convenes and mobilizes societal leaders to create and celebrate good culture. They have recently created the FERMI Project, a joint effort by leading voices in the church to create seismic change in how the church views its role in shaping mainstream culture (**www.fermiproject.com**). In 2007, he will launch Q, an exclusive boutique event, designed to inform and expose church leaders to future culture. Gabe lives in Atlanta with his wife, Rebekah, and their three children. Email him at **glyons@fermiproject.com**

©2006 by Fermi Project. Used by Permission

THIS BEAUTIFUL MESS
Practicing the Presence of the Kingdom of God

BY RICK MCKINLEY

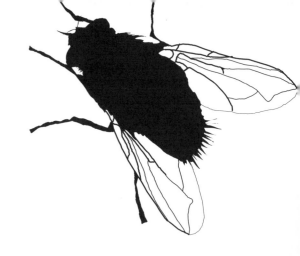

"THIS BEAUTIFUL MESS ... " A WEIRD, BUT INTRIGUING STATEMENT. WHAT CAN BE BEAUTIFUL ABOUT A MESS?

I remember as a kid going to the dump on Saturdays with my Dad. I used to love everything about it (I know, scary). I loved pulling on leather work gloves. I loved packing the truck with all the busted junk and smelly garbage we wanted to get rid of. I loved jumping up in the cab with Dad and driving away with our load, off for another adventure into the steamy lands of Middle Earth.

I loved everything about going to the dump until we got there and opened the truck door. Then love turned to morbid fascination. Piles of junk, moldering yard debris, decaying garbage, solids turning to goo and oozing out all over the place. The stench of ruin and rot hit you hard, like a fist in the gut. It coated the back of your throat with acid and smoke. If you've never been a young boy, well, it's hard to explain the appeal. Maybe it's because you come back with another

gross-out story of something you saw or smelled or stepped in. One time we saw a family there eating lunch on a rickety picnic table right in the middle of all that stink. We laughed about that for years.

Looking back though, I find beauty in the experience. Not in the dump itself—I'm mostly out of the 'gross is cool' stage—but in the whole "going" there experience with Dad. I was with him. I was being useful. Dad and I were working and sweating and together doing a man's work. I see now that going to the dump was beautiful *and* it was gross and messy.

So why would I use "beautiful mess" to define the Kingdom of God? God is perfect. God is not messy. Could his Kingdom be messy?

Perhaps in this way: Think of mess as real and apparent complexity, as absolute resistance to the tidy, easy, or

manageable. Think of mysterious new life growing inexplicably out of loss and decay. Think of richness in what the world casts off. Think of a boy finding family and purpose and goodness in a desolate place—right smack in the overwhelming stink of it.

MESS LIKE THAT.

Jesus said, "Blessed are the poor in spirit." Happy are the forlorn. Favored are the forgotten. Beautiful is the mess.

What could he have meant? How could both ends of the statement be true? All we know is that inside the dynamic of that paradox is a God-sized idea, and to accept one truth without the other would be to miss it completely.

Christians don't like mess much—not in our world, but especially not in ourselves or our churches. Somewhere along the line, we embraced the picture that Jesus

BLESSED ARE THE POOR IN SPIRIT FOR THEIRS IS THE KINGDOM OF HEAVEN.

would turn us into perfect people unpolluted by the world or our own sin. But he didn't. In him, we are new creations; in ourselves, we are dump dwellers. Longing for our full redemption, we strive to please him, and groan in our fallenness, and bask in his beauty. For whatever reason, Jesus didn't choose to instantly sanitize the whole germy bunch of us. We often think he did, though, so we spend a lot of time running around with mops and buckets getting ready for bunk inspection. In our kingdoms we begin to believe that we can fix all our messes. In Jesus' Kingdom he alone can start with our messes and accomplish something we could never have imagined. And he does.

WHICH BRINGS US TO BEAUTY.

The Kingdom of God is the living, breathing presence and purpose and reign of God on our planet. It's beautiful *and* irreducible. To reduce it to a seven-point outline might help you on the quiz, but it won't get you any closer to the experience. Like cutting up a corpse to figure out what it means to be human—sure, you'd end up with identifiable body parts in formaldehyde, and maybe a micron photograph of a neurotransmitter, but the wonder of throbbing human life would elude you. Do you think in some piece of

brain you'd find clues to friendship and falling in love, or learn why beach sand feels good between your toes, or what it means to be a child of God who also happens to like football, cigars, and the taste of a great Cabernet?

To be human is to live with loose ends, with people and in a world of loose ends, knowing you've been made for perfection. Knowing that you've been placed here to bring a taste of something beautiful and blessed. Theology though has little tolerance for loose ends. As the study of God, it mostly uses human tools like logic and interpretation and systems to define him and how he works in our lives. Countless brilliant women and men have written penetrating works that help us to think more clearly about God. They give us a rich literary heritage, and I encourage you to read them. But be careful. You can study God expertly in his parts and miss him entirely as a Being, a Whole. Sometimes I think today's evangelicals have pinned God to a cork board, labeled all his parts, and then breathed a sigh of relief. *Whew! Job done,* they gasp. *At least now we have no more confusion about God. At least now we have a brand we can market. At least now we can be excruciatingly confident that we are right.*

RIGHT AS BODY PARTS IN FORMALDEHYDE.

I've found that theology, especially of the systematic kind, becomes more helpful when you think of it as grammar. Grammar helps us read and write, but it can't on its own give us one memorable sentence. That's because grammar is a tool, not an end in itself. Meaningful communication is the end. Communication like, say, poetry. Yes, your grammar helps you to understand and experience a poem. But right when you're getting comfortable, a good poet will break a rule of language, turn an image inside out, give you the slip, send you falling.

And there's nothing you can say in response but, *Hmm, good poem. I felt those words.*

To help us encounter truths that would die if pinned to a cork board, Jesus showed us his Kingdom in a gallery of poems, or word pictures, called parables. Each parable showed another facet of what he wanted to teach. What he did not do was give us *one* picture of his Kingdom, much less a short dictionary definition. Of course, he could have. He could have pinned it up there—defined and dead—for all to inspect.

Instead he gave us a multifaceted picture that is full of shape and contour and texture and tension and beauty and mess. It is a both three dimensional and experiential. To be known, it must be desired, received, and lived over and over again. In the genius of Jesus we find ourselves grasping aspects of the Kingdom through a *living* definition that is growing and changing all the time. Not neat (that's dogma). Not reduced (that's formula). Not disassembled (that's dead).

BUT BEAUTIFUL.

In high school my friends and I became friends with one of the school employees. She was a gruff, middle-aged woman. Her stern exterior was meant to scare us into good behavior, I suppose. But inside she was very cool. Like your friend's mom who was really cool, that's how she was. She made sure no one left campus at lunch or smoked behind the backstops. For some reason that I still can't figure out, she really liked *us* though. We called her Mom.

Mom would go into the janitor's office and call the school for us and pretend to be our mom and get us a permission slip out of school. Yes, the dreaded "cutting school." I'm passing on a little personal history here, not making a recommendation (although if you didn't cut class even once, you know you wish you did). Mom would make calls for three or four of us. How she pulled it off I don't know, but sure enough, while we were sitting in class the phone would ring and the teacher would send us on our way.

Oh, freedom. We'd pile into my car and make our escape. Gone, away, free. Everyone else was back there grinding it out in class, watching the clock. But we were flying, no longer prisoners of any program, rule or schedule.

I hope that this feels like a permission slip from Mom for you. Get out of religion free. Get out of the American Republican Christian church parking lot free. You see, Someone knows and really likes *you.* Someone understands your struggles and trusts your intentions, can see into your future and isn't worried about you at all. Someone *wants* you to find that larger, freer experience of being that you sense is out there just waiting for you to live it.

PERMISSION GRANTED.

I realize that seeking the King with mostly pictures and stories to go by may feel dangerous or rebellious to you. But I encourage you to receive this, not as the last theological word on anything, but as a well-intentioned, God-loving invitation to go and grow and be where you haven't before.

Listen to the teachings of Jesus. Puzzle over his pictures and stories. Then look for his redemptive reign at work in the mess of your day. It's there, I promise. You may not end up with a perfect argument for every question about Jesus our King. But by the end you'll know what it means to say, maybe for the first time, *Hmmm. I felt his beauty.* **C**

Rick McKinley is the lead pastor at Imago Dei Community Church (**www.imagodeicommunity.com**). He is also the author of *Jesus In the Margins* (Multnomah, 2005).

Excerpted from This Beautiful Mess © *2006 by Rick McKinley. Used by permission of Multnomah Publishers, Inc.* (**www.multnomahpublishers.com**)

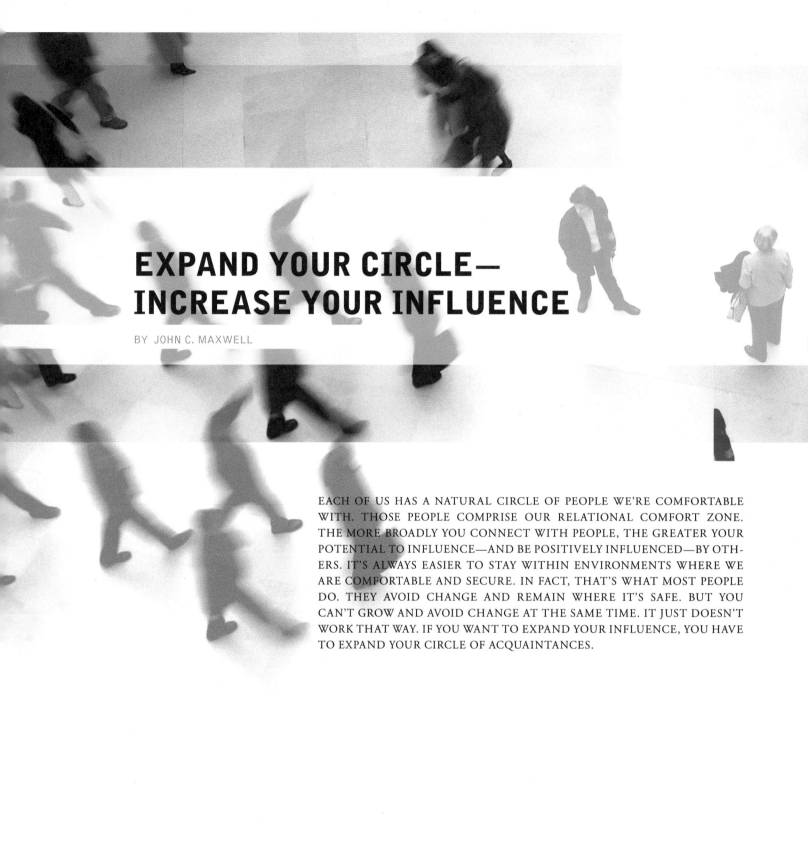

EXPAND YOUR CIRCLE— INCREASE YOUR INFLUENCE

BY JOHN C. MAXWELL

EACH OF US HAS A NATURAL CIRCLE OF PEOPLE WE'RE COMFORTABLE WITH. THOSE PEOPLE COMPRISE OUR RELATIONAL COMFORT ZONE. THE MORE BROADLY YOU CONNECT WITH PEOPLE, THE GREATER YOUR POTENTIAL TO INFLUENCE—AND BE POSITIVELY INFLUENCED—BY OTHERS. IT'S ALWAYS EASIER TO STAY WITHIN ENVIRONMENTS WHERE WE ARE COMFORTABLE AND SECURE. IN FACT, THAT'S WHAT MOST PEOPLE DO. THEY AVOID CHANGE AND REMAIN WHERE IT'S SAFE. BUT YOU CAN'T GROW AND AVOID CHANGE AT THE SAME TIME. IT JUST DOESN'T WORK THAT WAY. IF YOU WANT TO EXPAND YOUR INFLUENCE, YOU HAVE TO EXPAND YOUR CIRCLE OF ACQUAINTANCES.

Expanding your circle of acquaintances may be uncomfortable, but it can do a lot for you. First, it helps you improve. Expanding your circle will expose you to new ideas. It will prompt you to see things from a different point of view, which will help you generate new ideas of your own. It will help you to learn new working methods and pick up additional skills. And it will help you to become more innovative. Expanding your circle also expands your network, putting you in contact with more people and giving you potential access to their networks.

HOW TO EXPAND YOUR CIRCLE

If you are not inclined to stretch yourself relationally, then think about this. People are like rubber bands. They are most valuable when they are stretched, not when they are at rest. Your value as a leader will increase as you stretch and get out of your comfort zone relationships, which are usually comprised of:

- People you've known for a long time,
- People with whom you have common experiences,
- People that you know like you.

What would happen if the number of people in your circle expanded from five to fifty or from a dozen to more than a hundred? When you had a question your coworkers and you couldn't answer, how quickly do you think you could get it from someone you know? If a friend were looking for a job, how much more likely would it be for you to help her connect with someone who might be looking for help? If you were trying to break into a new market, wouldn't it be likely that you could call an acquaintance and get a quick overview of that industry—or at least call someone who has a friend in that industry? You would even have quicker access to information on the best restaurants in town, the best vacation spots, or where to buy a car. And with every quick connection you are able to make or share with a colleague, the more value you would have—and more influence you would gain—with your peers.

If you desire to expand your circle of acquaintances, all you need are a strategy and will to do it. You must provide the effort, but here are some ideas to help you with the strategy.

1. EXPAND BEYOND YOUR INNER CIRCLE

To get outside of your comfort zone, why not start with those in your comfort zone? Every friend you have has a friend you don't have. Begin with your inner-circle friends and expand the pool. What businesses are your closest friends in? Whom do they know who might benefit you? Think about the interesting people you've heard friends talk about. Also consider their interests. Who have they connected with through their hobbies and travels?

I bet for each of your friends, you could come up with a list of at least three or four—and in some cases as many as a dozen—people you would have interest in meeting through them. And chances are they would have just as much interest in meeting you! Why not start asking your friends to introduce you to some of them? Ask them to set up a lunch. Or ask if you can tag along as friends engage in their hobbies. Or simply ask for a phone number and make contact yourself. You'll be amazed by how quickly your circle expands in this first round. You can double, triple, or quadruple your circle

NOVELIST GWEN BRISTOW SAID, "WE CAN GET THE NEW WORLD WE WANT, IF WE WANT IT ENOUGH TO ABANDON OUR PREJUDICES, EVERY DAY, EVERYWHERE. WE CAN BUILD THIS WORLD IF WE PRACTICE NOW WHAT WE SAID WE WERE FIGHTING FOR."

of acquaintances almost overnight. And once you do expand the pool of people you know, be sure to touch base with your new friends periodically so that you remain connected.

2. EXPAND BEYOND YOUR EXPERTISE

I obviously value people who have experience in my field. In fact, I recommend that you "talk your craft" with others who share expertise in your area. But you should never limit yourself to connecting with people within your department or profession.

If you work in an organization of any size, one large enough to have multiple departments, then I recommend that you start by connecting with people in other departments. It doesn't matter what kind of an organization you're in, when there is connection and understanding between departments, everyone wins.

3. EXPAND BEYOND YOUR STRENGTHS

Even outside of work, I think we all tend to respect and gravitate to people whose strengths are like our own. Sports stars hang out together. Actors marry other actors. Entrepreneurs enjoy trading stories with other entrepreneurs. The problem is that if you spend time only with people like yourself, your world can become terribly small and your thinking limited.

If you are a creative type, go out of your way to meet people who are analytical. If you have a type-A personality, then learn to appreciate the strengths of people who are more laid back. If your thing is business, spend time with people who work

in non-profit environments. If you are white-collar, learn to connect with blue-collar people. Anytime you get a chance to meet people with strengths very different from your own, learn to celebrate their abilities and get to know them better. It will broaden your experiences and increase your appreciation for people.

4. EXPAND BEYOND YOUR PERSONAL PREJUDICES

French novelist André Gide said that "an unprejudiced mind is probably the rarest thing in the world." Unfortunately, that is probably true. I think all human beings have prejudices of some sort. We prejudge people we haven't met because of their race, ethnicity, gender, occupation, nationality, religion, or associations. And it really does limit us.

If we desire to grow beyond not only our circle of acquaintances but also some of the limitations created by our own thoughts, then we need to break down the walls of prejudice that exist in our mind and hearts. Novelist Gwen Bristow said, "We can get the new world we want, if we want it enough to abandon our prejudices, every day, everywhere. We can build this world if we practice now what we said we were fighting for."

What group of people do you find yourself disliking or mistrusting? Why do you hold such views? Has your vision been obscured by the actions of one or more individuals? The way to change your blanket likes and dislikes is to reach out to people of that group and try to find common ground with them. This may be the most

difficult of all circles to break out of, but it is well worth doing.

5. EXPAND BEYOND YOUR ROUTINE

One of the greatest impediments to meeting new people is routine. We often go to the same places all the time—the same gas stations, coffee shop, grocery store, and restaurants. We employ the same providers of services. We use the same companies for our business. It's just easy. But sometimes we need to shake things up and try something new. It's all about getting outside of your comfort zone.

I know that my ideas for expanding one's circle may not be revolutionary. They're really just practical thoughts. But the whole point is to remind you

that you can't wait for life to come to you. You need to initiate, invest, and do what's right when you don't feel like it—especially when it comes to cultivating relationships.

I can't remember a single time I've regretted getting outside of my comfort zone and trying to get acquainted with

someone I didn't know. Even if I failed to connect, or if there was no chemistry, or if the person turned out to be unpleasant, it always yielded some kind of benefit, either because I had a new experience, learned something new, or received an introduction to someone else I enjoyed meeting. It's an investment in time—and influence—that is always worth making. **C**

Dr. John C. Maxwell, known as America's authority on leadership, speaks in person to hundreds of thousands of people each year. He is the author of more than thirty books, including *The 360 Degree Leader*, and *The 21 Irrefutable Laws of Leadership*, which has sold more than a million copies. To learn more visit **www.injoy.com**.

Adapted from The 360 Degree Leader, *©2006 by John C. Maxwell. Used by permission of Nelson Books, a division Thomas Nelson Publishers, Nashville, TN. All rights reserved.*

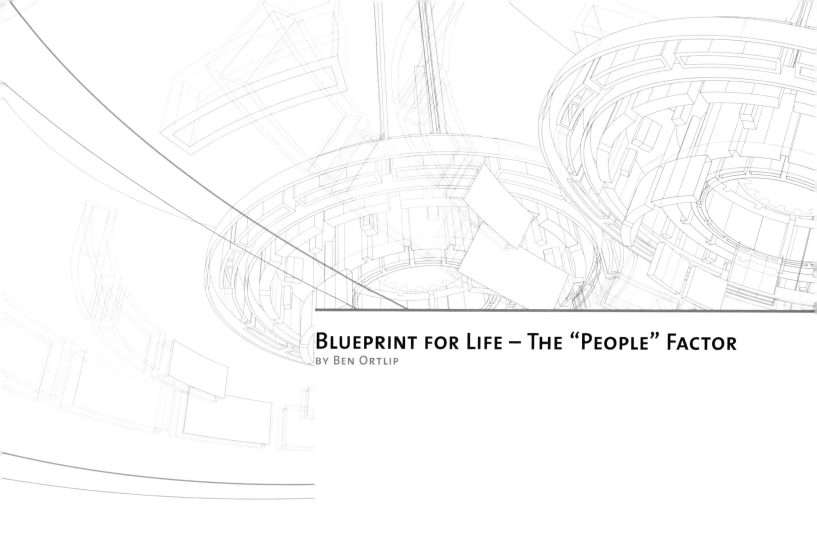

BLUEPRINT FOR LIFE – THE "PEOPLE" FACTOR
BY BEN ORTLIP

YOUR BLUEPRINT FOR LIFE BEGINS WITH A BLUEPRINT FOR PERSONAL NETWORKS.

Forget swimming against the current of culture. If you can just put a little space between you and certain other fish, you'll be well on your way. Of all the factors that influence your direction in life, none has more power than the people around you. Your goals, beliefs, values—even your faith—can be overwhelmed by a social tsunami. There's something about being in your inner circle that gives people the ability to shift your rudder.

In the early church, as today, life-on-life mentoring was the most effective method of discipleship. Paul wrote, "Let us not give up meeting together ... but let us encourage one another." (Hebrews 10:25 NIV) Your personal sub-culture (network of friends, associates) is one of the most important factors in your life. As my

pastor, Andy Stanley, tells young people, "Your friends can influence your decisions more than your parents ... or even God." The writer of Proverbs put it this way, "He who walks with the wise grows wise, but a companion of fools suffers harm." (Proverbs 13:20 NIV) That's true whether you're walking with a talented leader, an experienced parent, or someone who knows how to handle money. Whatever you hope to become, hang around those people long enough and good things will rub off on you. Hang around the alternative and you'll suffer for it.

Blueprint for Life divides life into five categories—Spiritual, Physical, Relational, Financial, and Professional. Most people assume that Spiritual is the most important category in a person's life. That may

be theologically true, but it's usually not the most influential category. When it comes right down to it, personal behavior is socially-dependent. We gravitate toward behavior that is like those around us. And despite all our goals and good intentions, eventually we end up doing what is reinforced by the people near us. That's why they call it a sphere of *influence*. Granted there are exceptions. But if you really want to change your life, try changing the people you hang around with. If you want to be a great tennis player, hang around great tennis players. If you want to be a great spiritual leader, find a way to sprinkle several into your monthly schedule. Whatever your aspirations, the best action step you can take is to become an engineer of your personal sub-culture. **C**

MY BLUEPRINT FOR PERSONAL NETWORKS

What people, if added to your personal network, would most enhance your ability to realize your Godly goals in each of the following categories? List their names in the space provided. Should any people be avoided?

BLUEPRINT FOR SPIRITUAL—TOP INFLUENCERS

BLUEPRINT FOR PHYSICAL—TOP INFLUENCERS

BLUEPRINT FOR RELATIONAL—TOP INFLUENCERS

BLUEPRINT FOR FINANCIAL—TOP INFLUENCERS

BLUEPRINT FOR PROFESSIONAL—TOP INFLUENCERS

Adapted by Ben Ortlip from Blueprint for Life, *used by permission. For more information, visit* **www.blueprintforlife.com.**

SEPARATED BY BIRTH, REJOINED IN MINISTRY

AN INTERVIEW WITH CHIP SWENEY AND BRYAN WHITE

CHIP SWENEY AND BRYAN WHITE JOKE THAT THEY ARE TWINS WHO WERE SEPARATED AT BIRTH. ON THE SURFACE, THE TWO ATLANTA-AREA PASTORS COULDN'T BE MORE DIFFERENT. CHIP, CAUCASIAN, IS AN ASSOCIATE PASTOR AT A LARGE, MOSTLY WHITE CHURCH CALLED PERIMETER. BRYAN, AFRICAN-AMERICAN, IS AN ASSOCIATE PASTOR AT A NEIGHBORING MEGACHURCH, HOPEWELL MISSIONARY BAPTIST CHURCH, WHICH HAS A MOSTLY AFRICAN-AMERICAN MEMBERSHIP. STILL, THE TWO MEN SHARE A COMMON PASSION FOR THEIR COMMUNITY THAT HAS CREATED A BROTHER-LIKE BOND BETWEEN THEM. AS THEIR FRIENDSHIP HAS DEVELOPED, SO HAS THE MINISTRY OF UNITE!, A COALITION OF ATLANTA-AREA CHURCHES. IN THIS INTERVIEW, THESE TWO PASTORS TALK ABOUT HOW THEY CROSS BOUNDARIES AND BUILD RELATIONSHIPS.

CVP: *A junior-high mission project is at the genesis of your story. Tell us about it.*

SWENEY: For a while we'd been looking for a way for students at Perimeter Church to build relationships with people in the community who had needs. This part of Atlanta includes "International Village," where a large number of immigrants live. As part of an annual mission project, we took hundreds of students to the apartment complexes in our area. I think that first year we were in about 12 to 15 different apartment complexes. And they went out for three straight days, three straight afternoons did block parties—provided food, hung out with kids, played games, did crafts, did dramas and did Bible lessons. Our church's involvement in community outreach (and specifically the apartment ministry) began with students catching the vision for it.

WHITE: There are about maybe forty to fifty different ethnic groups moving into this county. As a result we are finding that not only do we need to minister to them to get them into our churches or get them saved, but we need to serve them in a different kind of way to meet their needs. And that was one of the main focuses that we had in UNITE!

UNITE! was basically birthed out of that awareness—we can't do it alone. Right?

SWENEY: In Atlanta there are incredible challenges of disunity among churches, among denominations, among cultures, different ethnic groups. It's probably like any major big city, with groups that are not working together, doing their own thing.

WHITE: Every Tuesday a group of concerned clergy and community leaders would get together for lunch. We were there to discuss the problems and the concerns of the community and how we as a church could address those concerns. And during that meeting someone raised a question, "What would it look like if the churches would come together and see what we could do to help effect change?" It seems to me like if we were to come together as a group we can get more done.

SWENEY: At one of these pastors' luncheons, a few of us from Perimeter Church and a few from Hopewell were there, including Bryan and his pastor, Dr. William Sheals. We said, "You know, each of us are doing some great ministry in the community, what if we were to do it together? What if we were to join together, partner together and show the community that not only we love them, but we love them together as a united body of Christ?"

WHITE: It's one thing to say you love; it's another to show it.

SWENEY: This came about the same time as our church's 25th anniversary. Our church began to say, "What do we want the next 25 years to look like?" The junior-high mission project had planted some seeds, but as we launched the whole community outreach focus and emphasis, it was apparent that no one church was going to transform our community, our city. It was going to take the body of Christ working together. We intentionally said, "How can we begin to come alongside other churches such that we could have a much bigger impact than we ever could as one church?"

CVP: *The relationship between your two churches also produced a close friendship between you two as pastors.*

WHITE: It's really one of those things that I believe God orchestrated, because you need a vessel, you need a couple of vessels in order to show people what it is God's looking for in relationships when churches come together. Well, we are the church. And so if we demonstrate that kind of love and camaraderie and friendship, then we are an example to the whole church.

So as it turned out, Chip and I have become more than just Christian brothers; we became literally like brothers. I love this guy like I love my own self.

CVP: *Tell me about this phrase you use, "twins separated at birth." How has your friendship deepened through this experience?*

SWENEY: We couldn't be more different. Black, white; athletic, not-so-athletic. (We won't talk about hair.) But we've become best of friends.

WHITE: You know, we're not making a mockery of this whole relationship thing, but I believe that's how God sees us—as identical twins. He doesn't see us as any different from one another. He doesn't see a black Bryan; he doesn't see a white Chip. He sees children of God. And so because of this feeling that we have—we consider ourselves twins. I feel Chip. I feel what he feels. I've become very close to his family, his wife and his children. And I know for a fact that Chip feels the same way about me, so it's not a one-sided deal.

SWENEY: You know, we talk by phone if not every day—

WHITE: Every day! (laughter)

SWENEY: And so it's a deep friendship that goes way beyond talking about ministry things. We get into our own personal lives, our family. We're the best of buds. We enjoy hanging out with one another and hanging out with one another's families.

CVP: *How does your friendship serve as a model for the rest of UNITE!? How does it add to UNITE!'s ministry effectiveness and to the relationships of other churches and individuals?*

WHITE: The relationship that I have with Chip has filtered down into my congregation. They see how we interact. As a result of our relationship I've been able to do things at Perimeter; he's been able to do things in my church. We brought the two congregations together based on our relationship.

SWENEY: I think that's been one of the most powerful components of UNITE! is that of relationships, of friendships—that it's gotten deeper as it has gotten wider, particularly among those of us on the leadership team. There are about 10 churches on the leadership team, and about 90 churches involved overall. But it begins with Bryan and me, and expands from there among a number of us where relationships are deepening. And then out of relationships all kinds of different ministry and partnering takes place. **C**

For more from the Christian Vision Project and UNITE!, visit **www.christianvisionproject.com**.

© 2006 Christianity Today International. All rights reserved. Used by permission.

DAVID HODGES
GRAMMY AWARD WINNING MUSICIAN
Age 27, Los Angeles, California, www.myspace.com/tradingyesterday

DAVID JOINED A BAND CALLED EVANESCENCE IN 1999. THEY MADE A DEMO IN AN APARTMENT IN LITTLE ROCK, ARKANSAS THAT LANDED THEM A RECORD DEAL A YEAR LATER. THEY MOVED TO LA AND RECORDED THEIR DEBUT ALBUM RELEASED IN 2002. THE RECORD TOOK OFF BEYOND ALL THEIR EXPECTATIONS. SINCE LEAVING EVANESCENCE, DAVID HAS STARTED A BAND CALLED TRADING YESTERDAY WHICH IS ABOUT TO RELEASE THEIR DEBUT ALBUM "MORE THAN THIS." HE'S ALSO WRITTEN AND PRODUCED ON MANY PROJECTS FROM KELLY CLARKSON TO CHARLIE HALL.

CREATED TO CREATE
I feel very strongly that one of the main ways we are made in the image of God is through our creativity. Growing up, art was often taught to be a nice addition (at best) to the fundamentals of life, but never essential. It is my desire to dwell in and demonstrate the life-changing power of God using our eyes and ears and hands to create glimpses of Eden amidst our broken world.

PEOPLE ARE PEOPLE
I live in a city full of passionate people. Almost everyone I come across in L.A. is here to fulfill their destiny, to live out their dreams. I love that. It's not a very churchy crowd, so the vernacular is different than the "Christianese" I grew up with, but I am amazed at how we all talk about and care about the same things at the end of the day. People just want to be known and loved; they want to be part of something bigger than themselves.

THROUGH THE FLAWS
I try to be honest about my life—about how I am changed and how I am the same. I don't feel like God wants me to try to sell something that isn't real to me. When I pretend that my present brokenness doesn't exist, the rest of the world isn't fooled. My hypocrisy screams much louder than any pseudo-piety. But when the light of Christ genuinely and naturally shines through the flawed parts of my life, that is true evangelism.

LIVING LIFE WITH PEOPLE
Since my definition of evangelism has changed from trying to work Jesus into every conversation to simply living life with people around me, our natural community has become much more diverse. I'm used to most of my friends being like-minded Christians, but I am finding that the people we spend most of our life with now run the gamut from third generation Christians to agnostics to scientologists. What we do have in common is we all want to make art that changes people. And in giving relationships time to move to spiritual and even Christian questions, I have been amazed at how rewarding that process has been. Anything that is forced will seem forced. God's timing is much better than mine.

HUMILITY IN THEOLOGY
Being dogmatic about anything usually makes me look stupid down the road. It seems like every year I'm confident about something and the next God decides to broaden my perspective. God is big and I am very finite. For me to assume that I know everything about even one part of God's nature is foolish at best and often reckless. **C**

Bryan's Freedom Day

By Eric Haskins

I've been thinking about my community group lately. Marveling really. Because God has used this rag-tag bunch (myself included) to reveal to me how messy *and* exhilarating our spiritual journey can be.

Take Bryan. This past April we celebrated Bryan's Freedom Day. The day the Wisconsin Department of Corrections removed his not so stylish home monitoring ankle bracelet. That night, we counted down to 9:30 p.m. (Bryan's former DOC curfew) and cheered in celebration of his freedom. I'm struck by how this is a beautiful metaphor for our whole group.

In one way or another we are all journeying towards freedom. Freedom from what holds us captive from the life Jesus invites us into. Our journey is fueled by God's transforming grace; but God's transforming grace isn't solely an individual commodity. It's a commodity that God enables us as his body to be a catalyst for as well. Which is why I believe community is so important to our growth towards freedom in Christ.

I'm disappointed that it has taken this long in my journey with Jesus to embrace this as a way of life. This is what life in the church should be. Needs to be. Must be. When I say this, I hope you can sense I mean *really* embrace it. Not just give lip service to it. Not just to view this time of the week to be with friends, but to view this community as a transition point. A weekly check-point where I not only receive God's grace through others in the body, but a point in the week that God calls on me to dispense His grace to others as well.

Christ has called us to share his transforming life with any and all who come across our path. As we begin to accomplish this mission, church gets messy. We have people who come through our doors who are living messed up lives, have a messed up view of God, and are in desperate need of God's transforming grace.

This creates tension for many of us. Messy lives often show us that our well-rehearsed, Christian cliché answers and methods simply don't work anymore. It sends us scrambling.

This is good. It forces us to do what followers of Christ have always done: seek to make the changeless, grace-filled message of Jesus relevant in the midst of a changing culture. This is hard work, but it is some of the most rewarding work we can do. In the process God gives us the amazing pleasure of experiencing messed up lives put back together. Together, all of us messy but pieced together lives, turn right around to seek out more messy lives waiting for God's grace.

Several prominent authors have described community as a beautiful mess. Yep, that sums up my community, the people I do life with. But I wouldn't have it any other way. Paraphrasing Jesus, "I've come to seek those who are messed up." In my community, Jesus has hit the jackpot and so have I. My hope and prayer is that we will share the windfall. **C**

Eric Haskins lives with his wife Linda and daughter Mya in LaCrosse, Wisconsin. He serves as the Senior Pastor of Cornerstone Community Church (**www.cornerstonelacrosse.org**). Eric enjoys reading and drinking good coffee.

INTENTIONAL ABOUT COMMUNITY:

See your city from a new perspective. If you live in a metropolitan city, choose to take public transportation for one day. If you are in a small town, then ask a friend at work or school to car pool for one day. Is this normal for you, or counter cultural? Reflect on your experience and brainstorm other simple ways to be intentional about creating community.

Courageous in Calling

God has a unique purpose that He desires to carry out in me. To know this purpose I must first know Him. To fulfill this purpose, I must trust Him and have the courage to act on it, which may feel like a risk. My talents and heart converge to create my calling and purpose. I am competent in my calling because I am committed to further developing and honing my talents and skills. My foundational understanding of how God is working during my current season of life determines the specific way I apply this calling especially as it relates to the greater culture.

Do I have the courage to act on what God has called me to do? Do I understand and embrace my role in culture?

CONFESSIONS OF A RELUCTANT LEADER

FINDING THE COURAGE TO LEAD EVEN IF YOU'RE NOT WIRED THAT WAY

BY BILL MURRAY

TO BE HONEST, I'M NOT THE KIND OF GUY WHO REALLY FITS IN AT MOST LEADERSHIP CONFERENCES. YOU'D NEVER KNOW BY LOOKING AT ME. LIKE MOST PEOPLE, I CAN PUT ON MY GAME FACE, READ ALL THE RIGHT BOOKS FOR LEADERS, AND USE LEADERSHIP BUZZWORDS IN CONVERSATION. BUT IF I'M HONEST, THERE'S SOMETHING ABOUT THE WHOLE EXPERIENCE THAT LEAVES ME FEELING INADEQUATE. AT LEAST, IT USED TO. BEING SURROUNDED BY THOUSANDS OF TYPE-A PERSONALITIES AT A LEADERSHIP CONFERENCE ONLY CALLS ATTENTION TO THE FACT THAT I'M NOT REALLY WIRED LIKE THE NATURAL BORN LEADERS WHO FILL THE SEATS AT THOSE EVENTS. THEY'RE GREGARIOUS, CHARISMATIC, AND OFTEN A LITTLE PUSHY. IN CONTRAST, I'M INTROSPECTIVE, RESERVED, AND WOULD BE JUST AS HAPPY FOLLOWING IN SUPPORT OF GOOD IDEAS. SO DESPITE FINDING MYSELF IN CHARGE OF LARGE CHURCH GROUPS OVER THE YEARS, I'VE OFTEN WONDERED IF I WAS SWIMMING IN THE WRONG OCEAN. AM I REALLY CUT OUT TO BE A LEADER?

Through it all, I've come to realize that not all leaders are Natural Born Leaders. As I've observed, there's another kind of leader. And God wires these people to fill a very special role in His kingdom. I call them Reluctant Leaders.

When you think about it, some of the most important leaders in the Bible were Reluctant Leaders. Moses, Gideon, and Esther, to name a few. Ironically, their reluctance to lead was rooted in a deep sense of inadequacy that actually made them more godly leaders.

Shakespeare wrote, "Some are born great, some achieve greatness, and some have greatness thrust upon them." The same can be said of leadership. A Reluctant Leader is often the one who has leadership thrust upon him. That doesn't mean he isn't a great leader. Nor does it mean he doesn't want to lead. In fact, Reluctant Leaders bear the fingerprints of God's calling more visibly than any other type of leader; their success is less likely to be attributed to skill or determination and more likely to be credited to God.

At the same time, the Reluctant Leader faces unique obstacles. For starters, they often struggle to recognize and fully embrace their calling to be a leader. Even more confusing, their early attempts at leadership can be disastrous, because conventional leadership principles often presume you have the personality traits to back them up.

My suspicion is that a lot of next generation leaders out there are really Reluctant Leaders in disguise. They're passionate about engaging the culture with a revolutionary understanding of Christ. And it's clear that God has called them to a position of leadership. But when it comes to replicating the aura of their favorite young pastor, they aren't always gifted the same way. Everyone else seems to know instinctively how to get from point A to point B; but Reluctant Leaders simply don't have the same instincts. Nevertheless, God has called them to lead in such a time as this. And that will require learning a different approach to leadership.

NATURAL BORN DOUBTERS

My first official leadership role was as the Singles Minister at a large metro Atlanta church. I was optimistic and idealistic, but it didn't take long before a creeping self doubt set in. I was respected, so it was assumed I could lead. Whatever I was in charge of, everyone around me believed I could create momentum. But I never seemed able to make the critical leap into hyperspace. I felt like a back-up quarterback in a bowl game. The pressure was on and I wasn't sure how to be what I thought I was supposed to be.

My reluctance to lead comes naturally. My dad was a model servant. He was a gentrified blue collar man who owned a small hardware store in the upscale Atlanta suburb of Buckhead. His unhurried, gracious approach to business and customer service was a perfect fit for the mayors, senators, and local celebrities who patronized his store. His storefront remained basically the same for fifty years, while Buckhead grew to cosmopolitan proportions around him.

As a quintessential Southern gentleman, my dad's unspoken policy was: *Never, ever impose on others.* If you can't do it yourself, don't do it. Growing up with this philosophy definitely helped me learn how to be a nice guy. But too often this internal law has kept me from being an effective leader.

EMBRACING YOUR RELUCTANCE

My career in ministry leadership has been marked by three key stages on the way to embracing the calling of the Reluctant Leader. At first, I thought I was a natural born leader. Everyone else thought I could lead. I had an undeniable vision. So I must be a leader, right? Next, I suspected maybe I wasn't a natural born leader, but I was supposed to become one. You know, die to self, walk in the power of the Spirit, and go to lots of leadership conferences. I just needed to try harder. Finally, I learned to lead as what I really am: a Reluctant Leader.

Although we are wired differently, Reluctant Leaders have a lot in common with many of the natural born leaders I know. We see a culture that desperately needs to know the saving, grace-giving, liberating love of Jesus. And we see a church that hasn't engaged that culture very effectively. My personal burden to close that gap rivals my need for oxygen. I suppose I could just get a normal job and share the gospel with my co-workers and neighbors. But my calling and vision in this area are so strong that I won't be content until *the church* is doing its job. That's why I continue to be a leader even though I'm not wired that way. The watershed moment for a Reluctant Leader is the reality that we can't stand down from the calling God has placed on our lives—regardless of our personality, temperament, or giftedness.

"SOME ARE BORN GREAT, SOME ACHIEVE GREATNESS, AND SOME HAVE GREATNESS THRUST UPON THEM." THE SAME CAN BE SAID OF LEADERSHIP.

MY SUSPICION IS THAT A LOT OF NEXT GENERATION LEADERS OUT THERE ARE REALLY RELUCTANT LEADERS IN DISGUISE.

So here are a few principles I've learned along the way to help the Reluctant Leader lead courageously.

1. MAKE PEACE WITH WHO YOU ARE

Your calling in ministry is not a cannonball contest at the pool. It's a common mistake to judge success by the size of the splash. I'm like most guys. If I were pounding into the air as hard as I could from a diving board at the neighborhood pool, I'd go home in shame if my cannonball didn't make a big enough splash to reach the lifeguard stand. Especially if every other guy at the pool creates a tsunami. If others naturally draw the multitudes, it's easy to think that anything less is failure.

The truth is, I'm a small splash guy. That's because I'm a shepherding leader. I am irresistibly drawn into the hunt for and the nurture of the one errant sheep. When I look at the leaders of the burgeoning church in the book of Acts, I see myself in Barnabas. He championed the underdog. Interestingly, one of the biggest big splash leaders of all time, the Apostle Paul, initially needed the help of a Barnabas to get everyone else to give him the time of day. No one else was willing to trust him, but Barnabas was. In Acts 9, we're told: "When [Paul] came to Jerusalem, he tried to join the disciples, but they were all afraid of him, not believing that he really was a disciple. But Barnabas took him and brought him to the apostles." (Acts 9:26-27 NIV) Several years down the road, Barnabas championed John Mark in the same way. Paul—as is typical of most big splash leaders—didn't want anyone on his team who wasn't pushing ahead full tilt. Barnabas was willing to slow his pace a little for a young, possibly less-driven leader.

There was a time when the tension between shepherding and pastoring was so strong in me, I was ready to quit. My sweet spot is meeting with three or four guys for discipleship. When I see individuals flourishing spiritually, I feel like I'm doing my job. But I've always had this other job called pastoring. Pastoring has a way of keeping me from the job I really want to do. After all, pastoring means being a lot of things I am not; like a manager, a bureaucrat, and a CEO. When I'm plugging away at those roles it's like pushing water uphill. In the meantime, I have precious little time for the task I love most.

Finally, I confided in a friend of mine, Peter Lord, to unload my frustrations. Peter is a "big splash" pastor I've always admired. I'll never forget his advice. He affirmed my instincts— the strong inner stirrings that represent who I essentially am. And he told me to simply do what I love. Period. In other words, he gave me permission *not* to do all the things that make you look like a leader. Instead, just focus on my strengths.

The reality is that if we are to become catalysts for transformation in our culture, the church must operate with both kinds of leaders. So I began to recruit leaders and resources to fill in the gaps for our church. And I began to spend more and more time doing the things I know I'm called to do. That way, whenever I get diverted caring for the one sheep, I know there are leaders in place to look out for the 99. Bottom line: I found the freedom to pursue my calling when I made peace with who I am.

2. LEAD FROM YOUR CORE

I have discovered that reluctant leaders are not immune to criticism. No one in leadership is. When criticism and resistance come, you had better lead from something settled inside of you. Paul and Barnabas turned from the Jews to the Gentiles with this calling imbedded within them: "For this is what the Lord has commanded us: 'I have made you a light for the Gentiles, that you may bring salvation to the ends of the earth.'" (Acts 13:47 NIV) Yes, Barnabas was aptly named "Son of Encouragement," but he wasn't just a soft-hearted guy. He had been invested by God with a calling. He knew what that calling was and he was willing to incur the wrath of the Jews to follow it.

You cannot adequately defend something that isn't driven from your core. As a shepherding leader, one of the things I am adamant about is the basic survival needs of the sheep. That is part of who I am, and that is where I won't waver. That's why Barnabas was willing to go head to head with Paul to defend his decision to patiently bring along an inexperienced leader like John Mark.

I've watched my natural born leader friends with amazement at times. They are like the champions of the playground. Challenge them and they are ready to fight. And to them, most things look like a challenge. As a reluctant leader, I am not so quick to enter the fray. But when it comes to the calling that resides in my core – to protect my family, to shepherd the body of Christ, to engage the culture around me – I am just as ready to fight.

3. DEVELOP YOUR PLAN

To be successful, the natural born leader rarely needs more than a fuzzy plan and a cup of coffee. Reluctant leaders can't be so unscripted. We are more likely to be indecisive, so it's imperative that we have a clear plan in place. I have discovered that there are always people around who will lead if I don't. If I abdicate my responsibility as leader, someone else will step in to fill the gap. And that someone may lack the vision or even the integrity essential to leadership.

One day while playing basketball with some students from our church, I collapsed unexpectedly. The next thing you know, I was being airlifted to the intensive care unit of a major hospital. My first visitor in ICU was a retired pastor who had visited our church once or twice. He told my wife, "Tell Bill that I'll be glad to step in and take over. I'm experienced. I can take everything off of his shoulders for now."

My wife had a very strong sense that this man was up to no good, even though he seemed harmless. She asked one of our elders to do a little research, and we soon discovered this "harmless" pastor had embezzled money from his past church. And that was just the tip of the iceberg. A long list of evidence confirmed that he was a wolf in sheep's clothing. As a shepherd, I wasn't about to let him lead our church.

The problem was, I had not developed a clear plan. Our elders were left to lead during an extremely difficult time without a strategy. Most people in the church couldn't understand why this sweet older man with ministry experience wasn't allowed to lead. In the absence of a plan, his offer looked mighty good to many of our church members. By God's grace, and thanks to a group of elders with wisdom and integrity, the wolf didn't win. And I learned an important lesson the hard way: develop a plan.

4. IMPLEMENT YOUR PLAN WITH COURAGE

For a time, it was my habit to stand on our back porch every evening and gaze at the six o'clock train in the distance as it sped past our house. As my wife observed me, she wondered at the wistful expression she saw on my face every night as the rail cars rattled past and the engine blew its thin stream of smoke into the atmosphere. Thinking she would discover a boyhood love of trains or a latent wanderlust, she finally asked me about this nightly vigil.

I looked at her with a mix of frustration and longing on my face as I searched for a way to express my feelings. Finally I said, "I just love watching something move that I didn't have to push."

Natural born leaders don't get that story. Sure, they have frustrations. But most natural born leaders I know are freight trains. They need to work on harnessing the "go" that burns inside of them. Most of them were born to pull the train to the next destination.

As a leader whose task is to prod the church to engage an increasingly resistant culture with the radical message of the gospel, I must learn to motivate others with an agenda that often pushes them beyond their limits. That may be second nature for the freight trains out there, but it isn't for me. That's why it would be easy for me to back down when implementing a plan requiring that I impose on others. But, the truth is, a good plan always costs *something* to the people involved. There are two main areas where I have found it essential to lead courageously rather than let my overly merciful nature get the best of me: conflict and supervision.

Conflict is the bane of a Reluctant Leader's existence, so I have had to make a conscious decision not to avoid it. I had to learn how to have the tough conversations. I gave myself permission to be the bad guy when necessary. Or to defend the bad guy when one of my natural born leader colleagues drew fire for a gutsy leadership move. Again, I look at Barnabas and see someone who, although he wasn't necessarily a freight train, didn't back down from confrontation.

The second area of leadership that always involves imposition of some kind is supervision. As a leader, I am always supervising someone or something. I can't avoid it, but I've never enjoyed it. That is, until I realized that supervision is actually equivalent to discipleship. When I began to view my supervisory meetings with people as discipleship meetings, I began to actually enjoy holding people accountable to a task. What is discipleship if not helping people to bear up under the weight of responsibility? I call that growing in faithfulness. What is discipleship if not the supervision of a spiritual revolution in the life of a follower of Jesus?

ARE YOU A BARNABAS?

I like to think of Barnabas as a Reluctant Leader. He wasn't the prolific writer Paul was. He was never the main speaker. He was almost always mentioned in the context of a team, almost never as a one-man show. His very name implies he was more of a behind-the-scenes servant than a frontline leader. I could be wrong, but the few glimpses we get of him in Acts seem consistent with the Reluctant Leader profile. That doesn't mean Barnabas wasn't courageous. He risked the wrath of the very culture he sought to engage in order to be obedient to God's calling.

The first mention of Barnabas in Acts provides an example for leaders, whether you are the reluctant or the natural variety. As the church was just beginning to build momentum, we're told Barnabas "sold a field that belonged to him and brought the money and laid it at the apostles' feet." (Acts 4:37 ESV) The early church did the same thing. They "were of one heart and soul, and no one said that any of the things that belonged to him was his own." (Acts 4:32 ESV)

Barnabas began by divesting himself of what he owned. He laid it down. That is the first step of courage for any leader. Barnabas understood that anything he owned—including his gifts, his leadership style, his personality—would be made infinitely more valuable if offered as a sacrifice. That's because none of it was his in the first place. That means what really counts is not what style of leader I am, it's what I do with the leadership gifts I have.

If you want to be a part of the same movement of God's kingdom into our culture, your availability is more essential than your ability. What made the early church leaders usable were not their leadership personalities or styles, it was that God had access to everything they had and everything they were. They made their lives available, and the rest is history: "With great power the apostles were giving their testimony to the resurrection of the Lord Jesus, and great grace was upon them all." (Acts 4:33 ESV) **C**

Bill Murray is a Reluctant Leader at Midtown Community Church in Atlanta, Georgia where he serves as the Connections Pastor. (**www.midtowncommunitychurch.com**) He and his wife, Kitti, have four sons.

1. Are you a Reluctant Leader? Why would you describe yourself that way?

2. Do you compare yourself with Natural Born Leaders? How can you learn to make peace with the person God has created you to be?

3. What do you enjoy most about your job as a leader? In what ways does your leadership role require you to exhibit the traits of a Natural Born Leader?

4. How can your specific gifts be used in the mix to impact our culture with the gospel?

5. What steps should you take to develop a plan to lead from your strengths?

BILL HYBELS

E PLURIBUS UNUM

FLIPPING COINS

THE OPENING TOSS

I RECENTLY HAD THE CHANCE TO REVISIT THE CAMP WHERE I MET CHRIST IN MY LATE TEENAGE YEARS. I WASN'T SAVED AFTER A HIGH-PITCHED MEETING. NO ONE HAD JUST WITNESSED TO ME. I WAS WALKING FROM ONE SIDE OF THE CAMP TO THE OTHER LATE ONE EVENING, AND A VERSE CAME TO MY MIND. "NOT BY WORKS OF RIGHTEOUSNESS WHICH WE HAVE DONE, BUT ACCORDING TO HIS MERCY HE SAVED US." (TITUS 3:5 KJV) I REMEMBER STANDING ON THE SIDE OF A HILL GOING BACK AND FORTH IN MY MIND THINKING, "COULD THAT BE TRUE? MAYBE IT IS. MAYBE IT ISN'T." I COME FROM A FAMILY WITH A HUGE WORK ETHIC, AND I'D HAD TO WORK HARD FOR EVERYTHING UP TO THAT POINT IN MY LIFE. IT WAS DIFFICULT TO IMAGINE NOT NEEDING TO WORK HARD FOR THIS TOO.

I could have gone either way that night. It was almost like I was flipping coins, "Should I? Shouldn't I? Should I? Shouldn't I?" And then I thought to myself, "I'll just open up my heart and see what happens." And that's how I got saved. That's where it all began.

Thirty years later, I found myself in that exact same spot. Standing there it struck me that it could have gone either way. I remember flipping the coin. "Am I going to do this or aren't I? Should I or shouldn't I? Okay, yeah I will." That decision changed everything. I wound up leaving my father's business and starting a church. I wound up marrying a Christian woman, and raising a Godly family. As I looked back at the whole course of my life, I was overwhelmed by the significance of that moment.

A FIFTY/FIFTY CHANCE

Have you ever thought about what Ephesians 2 says? It starts ominously, "You were dead in your trespasses and sins." (Verse 1). And then it has this wonderful phrase, "But God who is rich in mercy." (Verse 4) *But God who is rich in mercy* raised us up, saved us, and adopted us.

I love that phrase, "But God who is rich in mercy." You see it in various places around the Scriptures where the story of someone's life is unfolding. They get to a certain point and their life could go this way or that way. The outcome could be good or bad; life giving or life ending. It's like they're flipping coins deciding which way to go, as I was on my salvation day. And then you read, "But God who is rich in mercy" and God steps into that situation and it all goes another way. And you think to yourself later about how life could have turned out so differently except for that *God who is rich in mercy.*

Some people want to look at my life and give me a nice award. They know about the success of Willow Creek, and they think it's all been based around some great organizational plan—as if it was just a matter of moving from one level to the next. But they have no idea how many times I've been in situations in the 30-some years of my Christian leadership where I was flipping coins. So many times, it could have gone this way or that way. *But God who is rich in mercy* intervened and had it go the Kingdom way, the right way, the life giving way.

HEADS OR TAILS?

Willow began like that. God had given me this incredible vision for starting an Acts 2 church, but I knew I needed lots of help. So I went to three guys I had served in youth ministry with.

I cast the vision, poured out my heart, asked for their help, the whole deal. Each one said no.

I kid you not, that night I'm in my bedroom flipping coins. "Maybe I shouldn't start this thing. Maybe I ought to play it safe, keep doing what I'm doing. Perhaps I should go back to the family business where I can make a lot of money." I'm just flipping coins. *But God who is rich in mercy* visited me that night and said, "I gave you this dream. Don't give up. Do it. Do it. Assemble a different team. Grab some different guys. These guys aren't going to make it or break it for you. You're the one with the dream. Get anyone who will come. But do it."

So the next day I go to three other guys. The first one has been my lifelong friend, Joel Jager. He's had polio since he was six weeks old, and has never walked a single step in his life without a horrendous limp. He was a C student in college. But we were lifelong friends and he followed me all over. So I said, "Joel would you help me with this?" And he said, "I'm in." Then I went to another high school buddy who was just getting over a bad marijuana habit that he had gotten into when he was in the military. He said, "Well you know I still have some stuff going on, but I'll do it." Then I went to a third buddy whose parents had dragged him off to the mis-

BUT THE RATE AT WHICH I WAS DOING THE WORK OF GOD WAS DESTROYING GOD'S WORK IN ME.

I'm telling you this because I'm past that era now and my inner world is working pretty well. Lynn and I have been married for over 30 years and we have two fantastic kids who love God and love the church. I have friends that matter to me. I go all the way back to that night right when the timid woman in my small group told me that I needed help. And I was flipping coins, I might get help, I might not. One of the real turning points of my life was the night *God who is rich in mercy* stepped in and guided me the right way.

TAILS.

Your life matters in the overall scheme of things so much more than you think it does. You probably don't know who you're going to become and the extent of the work that God wants to do through you. You may not know when you're flipping coins about if you'll launch that ministry or not, if you'll take that next step of faith or not, if you'll quit when it gets hard or not, if you'll face the demons of your inner world or not.

There have been so many times in my life where it all could have so easily gone the wrong way. Don't let yours be the life that so easily goes the wrong way. When you find yourself flipping coins—wondering if your decision is really that important—let the *God who is rich in mercy* come along side you. Let Him whisper and prompt and give you courage to pursue what He has called you to do—what will bring Him glory and advance his Kingdom. **C**

Bill Hybels is the founding pastor of Willow Creek Community Church (**www.willowcreek.org**) near Chicago. He also serves as chairman of the Willow Creek Association, a ministry that serves more than 10,000 churches worldwide. He is the bestselling author of numerous books including *Courageous Leadership* (Zondervan, 2002), *The Volunteer Revolution* (Zondervan, 2004) and *Just Walk Across the Room* (Zondervan, 2006).

Adapted from Bill Hybel's message at the 2005 Catalyst Conference, where he received the Catalyst Lifetime Achievement Award. www.catalystconference.com

sion fields in Paraguay. He didn't even like church. But he liked hanging out with us, and he said, "Well, I'll stay on the edges and help you lug stuff around." Thirty years later these guys are still with me. When I think back to that night when I was flipping coins, it could have gone this way or that way. Except for the God who is rich in mercy stepped in and helped me through that indecision.

CALL IT IN THE AIR

Willow began with a bang—we like to call them the wonder years. Every time we turned around there were a hundred more people at our services, people were getting baptized left and right, and we were growing like crazy. Things were going well to say the least.

And then I found out that one of our leaders was having an affair. The first thought that went through my head was this: "If I can keep this whole thing under wraps and not let it go public, then I can probably keep our church intact." I feared a scandal of that magnitude would wreck our church forever. At the same time, I knew that wasn't the right way to handle it. Sin is sin and it needs to be exposed. It needs to be confronted. The Bible is very clear on that.

I'm embarrassed to admit this, but I was flipping coins again. Back and forth, back and forth. Then the God who is rich in mercy came alongside and said, "Bill, if you'll handle this in the biblical way, I'll honor you for it."

Long story short, I got the elders together and exposed the problem. We dealt with it the best way we knew how at the time. It almost did blow up the church. It got messy and scandalous. The fallout was so ugly that one night I laid face down on the family room floor of our house—and for the very first time in the Willow ad-

venture—I thought I was going to quit. I was flipping coins again, thinking, "I can quit. I can go back to the family business." Or, "I can ride this out and keep preaching, keep leading, keep believing that some tomorrow is going to be better than today." And sometime before dawn, the *God who is rich in mercy* said, "If you will just trust me and get up in the morning and lead like I'm asking you to lead, I'll be in this with you. There will be a brighter day some day, there will be Bill."

I got up, and touched mystically by the power of the Holy Spirit, started leading. It took almost two years for us to get out of that phase—two really hard years. But we got through it and past it. Many times since then I've looked back and thought, "Wow, people don't know how close I came to quitting." I was flipping coins. Had it not been for the *God who is rich in mercy* it could have gone the other way.

DOUBLE SIDED COIN

Fast-forward about 15 years. Every single chart at Willow was going up and to the right. It almost seemed illegal—like the evil one just stayed away for a decade. But the pace of my life got out of control and I started skimming. Rather than communing with God, my prayer times were reduced to cries for help. I read the Bible because I needed a sermon. I reduced repentance to: "Whoops, we both know that was wrong" and then I'd move on.

I was skimming with my wife. I'd drive up into the driveway after work and say "Oh man, I hope she doesn't have a problem, because I've got no margin in my life." I was skimming with my kids. I'd hear that they were playing at a neighbor's house and breathe a sigh of relief because I simply didn't have the energy for them. Then I had staff members and good friends who were saying things to me like, "You know Bill, we used to hang out a little more.

We don't hang out much anymore." I was just skimming, and I really thought I could get away with it. But the rate at which I was doing the work of God was destroying God's work in me.

One night at my small group, I lost my patience with someone. Afterwards, a woman who was usually rather shy and soft-spoken, pulled me off to the side and said, "Bill you need *help*. I mean you need *help*. You don't see what's happening to you. But I think you need to go see a Christian counselor. I don't think you've ever looked deeply at your inner world." And then she said something I'll never forget. She said, "You're going to have to find out someday why you always commit to more than is healthy for you. Why do you always do that?"

I remember going to bed that night and I was flipping coins. I was like, "Yeah right, me go to a shrink and complain how my diapers were too right? Like that's going to work." I tried to convince myself that I could power up over it, get through it, fake it better. I'm going back and forth, back and forth, just flipping coins. But the *God who is rich in mercy* kept prompting me and saying, "You're only one-third of the way through your life, and you're already crumbling on the inside. You've got two-thirds of your life yet. What are you going to be like in another decade?"

So, I started going to a Christian counselor, and in the four years that followed I looked at stuff in my life I would never have looked at otherwise. I realized things about our family system that I had mythologized and talked myself into believing were lies. I had to answer the hardest questions and access stuff that I never thought I'd have to access.

No Gig is Too Small
By Margaret Feinberg

LAST YEAR I WAS ON A RATHER BUMPY FLIGHT BETWEEN SEATTLE AND DALLAS-FORT WORTH. AS WE APPROACHED THE AIRPORT, THE CAPTAIN ANNOUNCED THAT DUE TO STORMY WEATHER, THE PLANE WAS BEING REROUTED TO LAND AT A MILITARY BASE MORE THAN A HUNDRED MILES AWAY FROM DFW. ONCE WE TOUCHED DOWN, WE DISCOVERED THAT NONE OF THE PASSENGERS WOULD BE ALLOWED TO EXIT THE PLANE FOR SECURITY REASONS.

My husband and I sat on the plane—which was filled to capacity—for more than two hours waiting for the weather to clear in Dallas-Fort Worth. As the time passed, the passengers grew increasingly restless and hungry. After more than an hour the stewardess announced that food would be served. It turns out that the captain of the plane had gone to a nearby McDonalds and purchased enough cheeseburgers, fish and chicken sandwiches to feed everyone on our plane. He paid for the food out of his own pocket knowing that he wouldn't be reimbursed. But his simple act of kindness went one step further: He also purchased enough sandwiches for everyone on the airplane that was parked next to us!

This faceless American Airlines pilot committed an act of kindness that I will never forget. He went above and beyond the call of duty and helped make a difficult trip more comfortable through his generosity. Whether or not the pilot was a Christian, I do not know. But his act certainly demonstrated Christ-likeness. And it made an impact that lasted a lot longer than just the memories of a typical flight that weren't delayed—which I honestly don't remember much about.

The desire to make an impact is significant. While many people describe the desire increasing around the mid-point in their lives, many young adults desire to make an impact at an early age. "I don't want to get to 45 and wonder how to make the last half of my life significant," Brian Mosley says. "I want to live significantly now. How can I live a life that is valuable and not just self-serving?" Brian decided to do more than just talk about making an impact. During college, he joined his family on a trip to Africa that changed his life.

"Those four weeks (in Tanzania) were one of the most pivotal moments in my life," he says. "I never realized that missionaries weren't all pastors. In fact, there was a single girl teaching the missionary kids, a man who kept buildings and property in order, a Swiss-German family creating a written alphabet for the tribal language Sandawe, another single girl there as a nurse, and finally an associate pastor from Pennsylvania who moved his wife and three kids over to help start a church in the village. Talk about living out your faith."

The experience left Brian with one burning question: "God, what other opportunities are out there for me to use my video and communication skills to serve you?"

Brian realized that there were countless others who had a need for personal interaction to discover a good fit. He founded Rightnow (www.rightnow.org) in 2000 to serve as a connecting point between people looking for ways to serve overseas and the organizations that have the opportunities to do it.

As far as making an impact, Brian says there are a lot of people who think they have to be an expert, genius, Mother Teresa or Billy Graham to make an impact. "It is the group of people who think, I am worthless, how could I make an impact on anyone," Brian says. "It is fun to help people realize that their passion for motorcycles or design talent or sense of adventure or computer skills are God-given and can have an impact if you are willing to use what you've been given."

On the other side, there are some cases where it takes a very smart, experienced, strategic person to make the right kind of impact. "Not just any Joe Blow can go live in a tribal area creating the first written alphabet from a tribal language that has no written history," Brian says. "Sometimes people show up thinking that a willing heart is all they need to make an impact, but they really should be learning a trade or becoming knowledgeable in a certain field so they are more useful."

Another common misconception about making an impact is that you have to be involved in a full-time non-profit group or ministry in order to make a difference. You don't have to wear a cleric's collar or have a Masters of Divinity to reflect Christ. You can do it right where you are in your workplace. The Bible is filled with people who weren't in full time ministry but still used their professions and work to glorify God. Think of Esther, who became involved in politics, and was placed in leadership for what the Bible calls, "Such a time as this." Remember the innkeeper who provided a humble place for Jesus to be born. Consider Joseph of Arimethea who paid for the place where the Son of God was buried (granted, it was a short-term investment). The Bible tells of a man who provided the place and meal for the Last Supper. All these individuals were clearly used by God as they gave what they had to Him.

Reading the Gospels it becomes clear that Jesus wasn't concerned with what people did as much as how they did it. Zaccheus, a tax collector, was never told to change professions, but rather to stay in the same line of work and do it honestly. The Roman soldier, whose daughter was ill, was commended for his faith but Jesus never commented on his military occupation. The entire Sermon on the Mount is focused on how we treat others, not our

Every small initiative can make a tremendous difference

professions. Obviously, God is willing to use people in all different kinds of work to glorify Himself as long as we don't just automatically disqualify ourselves by saying we can't do it.

But this isn't just a New Testament phenomenon. When God wanted to build the Tabernacle, he used all kinds of individuals with different talents and gifts. God gave the workers the "skill, ability and knowledge" to create and design everything needed for the Tabernacle. They were blessed with talents for artistic design, and they could work with gold, silver, bronze, stone and wood. Every worker was able to use his talent and skill to build the Tabernacle, a place of worship to God and make an impact. (See Exodus 31:1-11)

As you seek to make an impact through your life, it is important to give others the time and space they need to make a difference, too. Give people room to be unique and different. 1 Corinthians 12:6 says, "There are different ways God works in our lives, but it is the same God who does the work through all of us." (NLT)

Another common misconception people have about making an impact is that you have to do something grandiose in order to make a difference. A mission or outreach doesn't have to involve travel or have a global impact in order to change people's lives. It is

great when one is large and successful, but change happens at multiple levels. We can make a difference on a personal, community, statewide and national level. Every small initiative can make a tremendous difference.

Michael, a 24-year-old, spent several years as a missionary before returning to the United States where he currently works as an assisted living worker with the mentally challenged. "I think about making an impact on the world probably about every day of my life," he says. "It affects everything I say and do. I try to make every opportunity count, and that's hard because in the place I work there is so much that I would like to say and do for the people but 99% of them couldn't understand me anyway. I sometimes feel that doing another job would be better because I would be able to speak the truth to people that could understand," he continues. "On the other hand I am able to take one of them to church and he blesses me every Sunday

while he has his hands raised worshiping and always making me point him to the right Scripture even though he can't read. I get to work with kids also who have problems, but I am able to see them change and become normal kids just through loving them. The reward might not be so visible but I know God is working through me and in every step I take and every word I speak to them. Sometimes we won't see the fruit of what we do, but that shouldn't discourage us from doing what is good. It should motivate us to (work) harder."

It simply comes down to being like Jesus to the people you work with and for. One of my close friends, Carol, is a full-time dental hygienist, but her gift is that she's used as a conduit of God's blessings. That may sound a little strange, but I have never met anyone so clearly used by God to provide for others on a regular basis. She'll have a single mom in her dental chair who says she's got a leaky roof she can't afford to fix, and two days later Carol will share the problem with a contractor who is in to have his teeth cleaned. Within a few weeks, the single mom's roof is fixed, the contractor has completed a kind and generous deed and Carol simply served as a vessel willing to be used to connect the two.

You can make an impact wherever you are. No matter how big or small the title or pay, you can use your job and your relationships to glorify God and serve as a representative of His kingdom here on earth. No gig is too small. **C**

Margaret Feinberg (**www.margaretfeinberg.com**) is an author and speaker who lives in Juneau, Alaska, with her husband Leif. She has written nearly 1,000 magazine articles and has contributed to written more than a dozen books including *Twentysomething: Surviving & Thriving in the Real World* released from W Publishing (W Publishing), *God Whispers: Learning to Hear His Voice* (Relevant Books) and *Just Married: What Just Might Surprise You About the First Few Years of Marriage* (Harvest House).

Adapted from What the Heck am I Going to Do With My Life, *©2006 by Margaret Feinberg, Tyndale House Publishers. Used by Permission.*

What's my motivation?

TO MAKE A LASTING IMPACT, YOU NEED TO KNOW WHAT MOTIVATES YOU. EVERYONE IS MOTIVATED DIFFERENTLY. WHAT MAKES YOU FLY INSIDE MIGHT MAKE SOMEONE ELSE CRASH. DO YOU PREFER TO BE MANAGED OR WORK ON YOUR OWN? WHAT MAKES YOU WANT TO WORK HARDER? IS IT MONEY? OR IMPACT? OR VERBAL AFFIRMATION? OR SOMETHING ELSE?

What motivates you is likely to change over time. You may be motivated by a few different factors at one age and another set of factors during a different age and stage in life. An interesting list of motivators was developed by H.A. Murray in the 1930's. Based on Murray's Manifest Needs, this list is designed to help you discover your motivational makeup.

Place checks by the categories that describe you best.

__ **Achievement.** You enjoy challenging tasks. You like setting goals and reaching them. You are willing to go the extra distance in your work. A little competition brings out the best in you.

__ **Affiliation.** You are a team player. You make friends with most people and enjoy healthy relationships at work. You enjoy being a member of a team and like working with others to accomplish a task.

__ **Aggression**. You can't help starting an argument just for the fun of it from time to time. You regularly become annoyed with your coworkers, even over the littlest things. You've been known to carry a grudge and get even with people who upset you.

__ **Autonomy**. You love your freedom. You find the less stress structure, the better. You can't do your best work when you're restrained or confined. If too many restrictions are placed on you, there's a temptation to rebel.

__ **Exhibition.** You love being the center of attention. You do things to win the attention of others and enjoy having an audience. Whether it's through your humor, drama or storytelling ability, you know how to capture the attention of others.

__ **Impulsivity.** You are spontaneous and often act on the spur of the moment. You openly speak your mind, but there are times you look back and wish you would have used discretion. You are ready to act on your immediate response to a situation.

__ **Nurturance.** You are always looking for ways to help and serve others. You provide sympathy and comfort to those in need. You are known as a "good friend" and you're willing to provide a listening ear to anyone who needs it.

__ **Order.** You work best when your work area is clean and tidy. You avoid clutter, confusion or lack of organization. You enjoy systems that keep information methodically organized.

__ **Power.** You aren't afraid to share your opinion. You enjoy the role of leader and assume that role in most of the situations you find yourself in. You often try to control the environment around you and have an influence on those people who are in direct contact with you.

__ **Understanding.** You enjoy learning and seek to understand. You value logical thought and ideas, especially when they satisfy an intellectual curiosity.

Each of these areas can serve as a motivational force in your workplace. Reflecting on the different areas, which best describe you? In which areas are you currently being motivated by what you do? Which areas are you using to motivate others?

CHAZOWN

By Craig Groeschel

I'M TRYING TO DECIDE HOW TO START THIS ARTICLE. SOME SAY THE FIRST SENTENCE IS THE MOST IMPORTANT. MY FIRST SENTENCE STINKS, BUT IT'S ALL I COULD COME UP WITH. LET'S SEE, WHERE DO I GO FROM HERE? HMMM. LET ME THINK. I GUESS I'LL JUST START TYPING AND MAKE IT UP AS I GO ...

I hope you're still reading, because I was just joking—to make a point.

If I continued rambling with no direction, you'd be wasting your time to read this. Truth is, I'd *never* write an article without any forethought or preparation, and neither would you. Yet most people are doing life that way—living day-to-day without vision.

That's why I wrote the book, *Chazown*. The title (which, granted, looks kind of odd) is a Hebrew word pronounced khaw-zone (not to be confused with calzone). It means *dream, revelation*, or *vision*. You can find this word in Proverbs 29:18: "Where there is no vision, the people perish." (KJV) Where there is no *Chazown*, most people stumble halfheartedly through life, hoping tomorrow will be better than today. Mostly just existing, hoping for a break. They keep turning the pages of their life's story, one after the other, until the final chapter.

It's not supposed to be that way.

Heartbreaking

I recently asked some of my church members, "Besides ministering to your family, what do you believe is the number-one, most important thing God wants to accomplish through you?" To their credit, the people were pretty honest. But I found their most common answer heartbreaking: It was "I don't know."

How disappointing!

Do we really think God sent His Son just so we would stumble around for years, ignorant of our reason for existence?

And we wonder why we're so unfulfilled.

What's Your Chazown?

The Bible makes it clear that we were designed from the beginning to live for a unique reason: for a dream, a big idea, a personal mission. That's why God calls us to live on purpose, keeping the end in view. As we seek Him, we can reach His and our greatest dreams. Anything less is a mistake, a lie, and a rip-off.

That raises the question, "How do I discover God's Chazown, His dream and vision for my life?" I recommend a simple approach that's proven helpful in thousands of lives, including my own. Begin your Chazown search by looking carefully at three areas, which we'll call the Three Circles. These are your **core values**, your **gifts**, and your **past experiences**. As we go, I'll demonstrate by showing you how my Three Circles point toward God's custom-designed *Chazown* for my life.

Let's start with **core values**. When God made you, He hardwired your heart with certain things you value deeply. These are the values that, if you were to follow the path God has for you, would become the driving forces of your life.

What are my core values? I deeply value integrity, evangelism, and stewardship. My heart beats to be the real deal, to reach people for Christ, and to be wise with God's resources. You, on the other hand, might value security, adventure, loyalty to home and family, justice and fair play, or caring for others.

What do you treasure? What do you stand for? What would you fight for? What do you *know* is so important that you'll let go of everything else to grasp it? God implanted your personal core values deep in your heart to help you aim for and hit the right target for your life.

Next, let's talk about your **gifts**. Just as your core values were placed in you by God, so were your special abilities. "We have different gifts, according to the grace given us." (Romans 12:6 NIV) These gifts are specially chosen to help you fulfill the Chazown He's calling you to.

When do people tell you, "You're so good at that it makes me sick—I wish I could do that"? Can you sing or dance? Are you good at gardening? How are you with numbers? Or leadership? Can you cook? Do others open up to you easily? Are you funny? Can you repair anything that breaks? (If you can, you make *me* sick.)

For as long as I can remember, God has given me the gift of leadership. Even in the second grade, I was a leader—a junior fire marshal. (If you're ever with me in a burning building, trust me—I'm your man.) God also gave me the gift of administration—and He finely tuned that gift through the years.

All the gifts and talents you possess came directly from God for a purpose. And He wants you to use them to benefit the body of Christ and be a blessing to the world.

Finally, let's examine your **past experiences**. These are events or seasons in your life that God has sent or allowed to prepare you to fulfill His future vision.

God tells us in Romans 8:28, "We know that in all things God works for the good of those who love him, who have been called according to his purpose." (NIV) The best part about "all things" is that it includes *all things*: the good things, the ordinary things, the not-so-good things, the truly (at the time) awful things. God has promised to use them *all* for good for those who love Him and have responded to His call to live out their Chazown for His purposes. This is important because your past often holds the key that unlocks your future.

In my life two shaping experiences stand out. First, after having a magician perform at my sixth birthday party, I started practicing magic (not the voodoo kind, but more of the rabbit-in-a-hat kind). By the time I was twelve, I was performing birthday shows for other kids, gaining confidence in front of audiences.

When I was young, I also found church to be the most boring, irrelevant place on earth. Those endless hours left a taste in my mouth that now motivates me to do church differently.

What do you think your past prepared you to do that you couldn't—or wouldn't—do otherwise? Think about the positive experiences that have been formative in your life. Maybe a business success has given you the confidence to lead a nonprofit organization toward greater impact. Maybe God healed you of cancer, and now you are able to offer that same hope to others.

Think also about the negative experiences that have shaped how you think, feel, and act. You lost a pregnancy and never thought you'd feel happy again. But because of God's emotional healing, now you can comfort other couples whose dreams have died. Maybe your marriage fell apart, but because of what God taught you through that experience, you now have wisdom that can reach through to people in relationship crisis.

Three Circles Converge
Bring your three Circles together, and find the place where they converge.

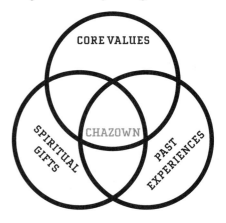

In almost every case, there's one identifiable "sweet spot" where these life-shap-

You've been created for something different, fulfilling, eternally important—and unique to you.

ing arenas come together—the one place where all dimensions are at full strength!

God has a divine destination for your life. At that place where your core values, your gifts, and your experiences meet, what destiny do you see? Look where your circles overlap. That's where you'll find your *Chazown*.

Finish this sentence: *"God has created me with a dream for my life, and I think it might be .."*.

The first time I overlaid my Three Circles, I was amazed at what I learned about my life's purpose. I realized that God had created me to make disciples. I'm on earth to lead people to become fully devoted followers of Christ. And I can do it best by serving as the pastor of a *different* kind of church.

God empowered and directed me to start a church that now meets in many locations. In a day when many nonbelievers are increasingly skeptical of Christ-followers, a commitment to the core value of integrity is a positive force to lead people to know Christ. By using technology and existing buildings, we can reach more people at a fraction of the cost of traditional church models—which happens to fulfill my core value of wise stewardship. After being in front of large audiences as a teenage magician, leading large groups is second nature to me. Using leadership and administration, I

can recruit, train, and release dozens of highly effective leaders and pastors. And because I was frustrated with the way church was for me, I started asking what church could become...

My dream might sound crazy to you. That's because it's not a vision that fits your passions and values and gifts and past experience. It wouldn't exactly get you out of bed every day with a jolt of enthusiasm.

And you're right. Because you're *you*. You've been created for something different, fulfilling, eternally important—and unique to you.

God's *Chazown* for Craig Groeschel fits me ... perfectly.

And yours will fit you. Perfectly!

Getting Started

You may be thinking, "Even if I figure out what my Chazown is, how do I start living it? Well, since a Chazown is a plan for a lifetime, it can seem pretty overwhelming. That's why you have to take it one small step at a time.

First, write a mission statement: a one-sentence description of where you're going and why. Once you get that nailed down, move on to some short-term goals. These are what you need to accomplish to make your Chazown a reality in the near future. As you write your goals, remember: to invite change, they must be specific and attainable—you have to actually be able to accomplish them. Move toward these goals one at a time. Having too many goals—or goals that are impossibly big—will only defeat you. Just take small steps.

If you have a goal to get more involved in church, your very next step might be to sign up for a membership class. Or call to volunteer as a greeter. Or set an appointment with a pastor. Or simply make a commitment to attend church this weekend. What's your next step?

Figure out what it is. Then take it.

You'll be on the path toward the dream of a lifetime. **C**

Craig Groeschel is senior pastor of LifeChurch.tv in Edmond, Oklahoma (**www.lifechurch.tv**). Since 1996, LifeChurch has grown from its beginnings in a rented dance studio to weekly attendance of more than 17,000; utilizing simulcast technologies to provide 30 worship experiences at seven locations in three different states. It is one of the top ten fastest-growing churches in America.

Adapted from Chazown: A Different Way to See Your Life *by Craig Groeschel, © 2006, Multnomah Publishers.*

GOD IS ALWAYS CALLING

**Because new aspects of our callings unfold with age,
we can always live expectantly**

By Andi Ashworth

LAST SUMMER I WROTE THE FOLLOWING E-MAIL TO A FRIEND, SUMMA-
RIZING THE PAST SEVEN DAYS OF MY LIFE. I WROTE IN ANSWER TO HER
QUESTIONS ABOUT WHAT I'D BEEN UP TO ...

*Yes, I've been writing, which also includes reading and studying, looking though journals
for material, and praying for direction. And yes, we've been receiving guests. It's the ongoing
thread of constancy in our lives. Steve Garber stayed with us on Thursday night. We had late
night quesadillas and conversation. He came to be part of the Blood:Water Mission board
meeting, which took place in our living room all day Friday. The organization, founded by
Jars of Clay, exists to promote clean blood and clean water supplies in Africa. Also on Friday
I cooked and delivered a meal to some of our extended family. They're just home from the
hospital with a new baby. Over the weekend we hosted an artist Chuck is working with.*

*Katy came last week for coffee and conversation. We talked of the vocations of hospitality,
marriage, and writing. Sandra came today and we met over cups of tea, our talk moving
through a range of subjects. And my small group from Gospel Transformation class is coming
tomorrow morning for brunch. Between preparing for guests, cooking, conversations, and
clean up—I have been immersed!*

*We're trying to pay closer attention to this particular work of receiving people in order to be
more aware of and more faithful to what God is doing in our midst. We're used to the work
of hospitality, caregiving, and mentoring, but I think I still miss really understanding our
vocation on some level, because it's so hard to name. Of course I'm referring to vocation in the
biblical/historical sense—meaning the whole of our life, not just one job or one task. Vocation is a subject that continually intrigues me and seems to hold deeper and broader meaning
as we age. It's also a topic that threads through many of our conversations with younger folks
as they yearn to understand the meaning of calling in their own lives.*

> Naming our calling helps us to be attentive to the particular life God is giving us.

FRAMING OUR CHOICES

One thing I know for sure as I approach my 50th year: Understanding one's calling is an ongoing process of discovery, and calling doesn't have to be limited to one area. I continue to find new aspects of calling announcing themselves in different chapters of our lives, and I don't suppose the revelation is over yet.

Young people of college age feel such pressure to decide what field of study to engage in, what kind of work to pursue. The age-old question, "what will you be when you grow up?" is haunting. I remember my daughter's anxiety as the need to declare a major loomed in her second year of college. Since my husband and I had grappled with the meaning of vocation for ourselves, we urged her to study what she loved, to move toward her true interests rather than worrying about the exact nature of her post-college life. We trusted that God would bring her to the work, people, and places that would fit the way He'd created her.

A WHOLE THAT'S A FIT FOR ME

As I survey my life from the perspective of middle age and vocation, this is what I see: I live in a small community west of Nashville. I'm continuing my seminary studies through Covenant's *Access* Distance Education Program. I am a wife, mother, mother-in-law, and grandmother. I'm part of an extended family in Nashville and California. I have a wide circle of friendships. I'm a member of Christ Community Church in Franklin, Tennessee, and the body of Christ universal. I have older woman/younger woman mentoring relationships. And I partner with my husband Chuck in the business of music—specifically artist development, recording, and music publishing, with my role primarily taking shape as "care and nurture through hospitality." All of these relationships have privileges, responsibilities, and time attached to them.

Because hospitality is so deeply woven into our calling, place is important. Our home, the Art House, a turn-of-the-century, remodeled country church, is central to who we are and what we do. It figures prominently in

our story and provides the setting for most of our work, especially that of receiving people. Though travel is a part of our life, our calling is rooted to a place, anchored to a spot on the map.

Our callings have developed over many years. There isn't one particular word or title that explains the work that Chuck and I do, though we've spent time trying to find precise definitions in order to get a better grasp on how to proceed. Chuck told *Christian Musician* magazine that for a decade he "wrestled with how to reconcile what seemed to be callings to several areas of word and work. I kept trying to narrow it down—you know, 'I'll just be a songwriter, no, I'll be a producer; no, I'll write books; yeah, and I'll go to seminary and be a pastor.' I don't wrestle with this anymore. Today all these different callings are neither seen or felt as separate, but instead make up a whole that's a fit for me. That said, I'll be busy writing books, speaking and teaching, developing artists, and helping them with their lives and work. I'll play a little jazz, co-run the Art House with Andi, write some songs, produce some music, and catch a few trout now and again. Stuff like that."

The Protestant doctrine of vocation, with its roots in the teachings of Martin Luther and John Calvin, helps us make sense of our life and attach importance to all its parts. From this perspective vocation consists of our stations in life and the avenues through which we relate to others: marriage, families, friendships, neighborhoods, citizenship in a city, state, and nation, and membership in the body of Christ—both locally and globally. In combination, our vocations come through the gifts and talents God has given us to be used for the sake of others. Through our roles, gifts, relationships, and the needs revealed in those relationships, the command to love God and neighbor becomes personal rather than abstract. In *Vocation: Discerning our Callings in Life,* Douglas Sherman points out that no one is called to be a Christian "in general." Rather, we all have concrete and specific geographic locations, relationships, and settings in which to use our gifts and serve God in our generation. Our calling to follow Jesus and be a certain kind of people is expressed through all of these. "Calling" is a comprehensive picture of the unique path laid out for each of us, consisting of the particular things God has asked us—and sometimes no one else—to do.

OUR UNIQUE PATH

When we look at our days through the lens of calling, life is infused with meaning, since there is no part that sits outside of life in Christ. And because new aspects of our callings continue to unfold with age, we can live expectantly. Callings are not always crystal clear. It takes reflection and assessment to figure them out. Since the path before us is uniquely ours, we must pay attention to what God is showing us through our relationships, inclinations, natural and spiritual gifts, and life circumstances. It's liberating to consider the things we love to do—and will always do in some capacity—because they are integral to the way God designed us.

Sometimes as a calling is forming in our lives, we're more filled with irritation and confusion than satisfaction and joy. It took years for me to adjust to the public nature of our home. Under God's tutelage and formation I've come to love this Art House life and can't imagine any other. But it's been a journey with many different seasons, some with overwhelming amounts of people and time demands, and each one contributing to an understanding of our limitations, our strengths, our weaknesses, and wisdom about how to continue.

As a further aid to understanding my callings, once or twice a week I write the content of recent days in my journal. This helps me recognize when something new is appearing and helps me see what is continual over time. As I look back through the pages I'm better able to discern what God is doing in our midst, how He's shaping my days and nights, the work of my hands and heart, and my prayers. I can then be more faithful in planning, preparing, responding, and making room for the life He's giving me individually and in partnership with my husband.

GIVING IT A NAME

Upon meeting new people we ask the question "What do you do?" When we reconnect with friends and family we inquire of each other "What have you been up to?" While filling out forms at the bank or the doctor's office there's one small space to answer the question "What is your occupation?" For any one of us, life and calling is so much more complex than a one-word answer or summary sentence. But still we must try to name things as best as we can, and for more important reasons than those medical forms. God is up to all kinds of things in His world and He gives His children the important work of participating. Modern life constantly confronts us with endless choices of how to give our time. Understanding and naming our callings helps us to be more inner-driven than outer-driven. It helps us in living faithfully through grace, with attentiveness to the particular life God is giving us.

From youth to old age we have a deep and human need for meaning and purpose, to know why we should get up in the morning. As I listen to my older friends and relatives I learn that age brings the possibility of loss: loss of spouse, friends, careers, health, and ways of life. Aging often brings new limitations, but it can bring just as many new opportunities. Young or old, those with eyes to see and ears to hear can recognize new callings. Eugene Peterson captures it beautifully in his paraphrase of Romans 8: "This resurrection life you received from God is not a timid, grave-tending life. It's adventurously expectant, greeting God with a childlike "What's next, Papa?" (The Message) **C**

Andi Ashworth is the author of "*Real Love for Real Life: The Art and Work of Caring.*" Andi partners with her husband Charlie Pecock-Ashworth in the work of the Art House.

This article first appeared in byFaith, *the bi-monthly magazine of the Presbyterian Church in America.* (**www.byfaithonline.com**)

FOR ALL HUMANITY

AN INTERVIEW WITH AMY LAURA HALL

THE ROLE OF TECHNOLOGY AT THE BEGINNING OF LIFE—WHETHER THE ISSUE IS STEM CELL RESEARCH, GENETIC ENGINEERING, OR ABORTION—IS ONE OF THE MOST PASSIONATELY CONTESTED AREAS OF OUR CULTURE. AS A PRO-LIFE CHRISTIAN ETHICIST, AMY LAURA HALL IS OFTEN FOUND AT THE CENTER OF THESE DEBATES IN THE NATIONAL MEDIA, AT SCIENTIFIC CONFERENCES, AND IN CHURCHES. A MOTHER OF TWO AND A PROFESSOR OF THEOLOGICAL ETHICS AT DUKE DIVINITY SCHOOL, AMY LAURA HAS HAD TO LEARN PERSISTENCE AND COURAGE IN ADVOCATING FOR THE WISDOM OF THE CHRISTIAN TRADITION'S REVERENCE FOR LIFE. SHE SPEAKS POWERFULLY ABOUT THE ABILITY TO FIND GRACE EVEN IN THE MIDST OF SUFFERING, RATHER THAN BY SEEKING AN ESCAPE FROM SUFFERING. AS SHE DESCRIBES IN THIS INTERVIEW WITH THE **CHRISTIAN VISION PROJECT**, SHE HAS BEEN ASKED TO BRING THAT MESSAGE TO SOME UNLIKELY PLACES.

CVP: *As a woman, a pro-life ethicist, and a Christian, there must be times when you feel out of place at a major research university.*

HALL: I've had quite a few moments when I felt like Jonah called into Nineveh!

In my first year at Duke, as a junior faculty member, I was asked to speak on a panel at an event celebrating Duke's Institute for Genome Sciences and Policy. I was the only woman on the panel, the only one under the age of 40, and the only non-scientist. And they wanted me to answer the question, "Does genomics pose new ethical problems?"

Duke is a very science-driven place, and I'm sure the organizers were expecting me to say that, sure, genomics poses interesting ethical problems, but nothing that would fundamentally challenge the whole project. At the time, seven years ago, the expectation among geneticists was that we would soon be able to identify all sorts of conditions in utero, and prevent disability through selective termination. Indeed, right now more than eight out of ten babies prenatally diagnosed with Down Syndrome are aborted. A presupposition of genomics is that if we can anticipate suffering, we can circumvent it through early detection and elimination.

It was very intimidating to try to bring a word of wisdom from God in this context: the Christian belief that God is present with us in the midst of suffering, and that God can work not even in spite of but through suffering. That God's will can work right in the midst of people's fragility and mortality.

So I went out and bought my first black suit—so I would look appropriately somber and more grown up than I was really feeling! But even with my black suit, I felt very out of place on that stage.

I talked about the complicated gift of being the caregiver for a child with a disability, and how people who care for children with disabilities, even very serious ones, speak of the gift that these children are to us. Even though they are not growing towards independence, and they're always going to be dependent, their lives are miraculous, gratuitous gifts as well.

CVP: *What was the reaction from the audience?*

HALL: You could see in people's faces how ridiculous, how absurd most of the people there thought this was. But afterwards two things happened that suggested God had used my words, foolish as these words sounded to most. A group of teenage girls from one of the local science-oriented high schools, not believers at all, came up to me and wanted to learn more about why I believed what I believe. "Being up there as a woman, being so courageous, must have been scary," they said. They had been drawn to me because I was a woman! What I had counted as a weakness, a handicap, was actually an entry point for them.

Then, as I was leaving, the guy running the sound board came up. "My son has autism," he said to me, "and I want to thank you for what you said. It's not as if it's easy, but he has been a gift to us. And I don't know if we would have had him if the technology had existed to predict that he would be autistic."

Those were amazing responses. But there were people on campus who quite literally wouldn't speak to me after that panel discussion, because I had been vocally pro-life in that context. On this campus, it's a given that it would be within a woman's rights to abort a child with a disability—but many would actually say it's a woman's responsibility to do so. To say otherwise, to say that a child with a disability is a gift from God, is deeply countercultural.

CVP: *Has your outspokenness hurt your professional prospects at Duke?*

HALL: Here's the amazing thing: not long ago Huntington Willard, director of the genomics institute, heard me give a talk on my research into the marketing of genomics and the language of hope in such marketing. And he asked me to teach a class this coming semester, and for the next three years, about how Protestant America has become aligned with the narrative of scientific progress. He has very graciously asked me to teach a class to these young, aspiring geneticists that will raise questions about the promotion of hope and progress through Western science.

And that may actually be trickier: I'm not going to be swooping in with my armor, dressed in my black suit, and then retreating. I'm going to be in long-term conversation with students who are aspiring to become geneticists, and trying to be a witness for wisdom.

CVP: *Where else does your calling require courage?*

HALL: I've learned courage from our neighbors. We live right next to a neighborhood of Durham, North Carolina, called Walltown. It traditionally has been a place where the cleaning and janitorial staff live—the people who actually do incarnate hospitality at Duke University. If I ask the woman who makes my bagel sandwich what she thinks of working at Duke, I'll get a different word from her on campus than I would on her front porch in Walltown.

A particular temptation, for those of us who have money, is to build a tree house—to pull our family up off the ground. But in doing so, we lose sight of how Christians live on the ground: how Christians live in public schools that are under-funded, how Christians are living in the midst of low-paying jobs, or how Christians live in the midst of persecution elsewhere. A family from Liberia, with seven children, has just moved in a block from our home. One of the blessings of friendship with their children is there is no yuppie-mom record-keeping of who owes whom a play date! They just show up, and we try to make time and room.

But before that story sounds too idyllic, I will say that they risk life and limb crossing the street to get to our house. There is no stop sign along the road that separates Walltown from Trinity Heights, the somewhat gentrified neighborhood where we live. There's no way for kids to cross over from Walltown into Trinity Heights safely.

I don't think that's an accident—it's symbolic. So we've decided not to give up until there's a stop sign. Which means doing the tedious, systematic work of getting the city council to approve a stop sign. It's a simple thing, but in some ways it turns out to be one of the hardest things to do in Durham, North Carolina.

CVP: *So just getting a stop sign put in requires effort and courage?*

HALL: More than I expected. The next step will be speed bumps! But first we're working on the stop sign. **C**

For more from the Christian Vision Project and Amy Laura Hall, visit **www.christianvisionproject.com**.

© 2006 Christianity Today International. All rights reserved. Used by permission

BRANDON MCCORMICK
FILMMAKER
Age 22, Atlanta, Georgia, www.whitestonemotionpictures.com

BRANDON CREATES SHORT FILMS WEEKLY FOR CROSSROADS COMMUNITY CHURCH (**WWW.CROSSROADSCONNECT.COM**). AS A TEENAGER, HE BEGAN PLAYING WITH A CAMERA FROM THE CHURCH. HE BEGAN TO IMAGINE GOD HAD GIVEN HIM TALENT AFTER WINNING MULTIPLE INTERNATIONAL FILM FESTIVALS. BRANDON HAS LAUNCHED A PRODUCTION COMPANY AND IS WORKING ON HIS FIRST FEATURE FILM.

HEART TO HEART
I believe God has called me to tell great stories. Not Christian stories or "Jesus" films, but real stories, honest stories, straight from the heart of the Father. Throughout human existence, God has chosen to teach through stories. It's a refined way of communication. Our hearts are knit for this kind of interaction. No matter the person, or what they believe or think, we are all wired to learn from a story. These stories come in different forms and genres, but in the end they pour from what God has placed in my heart. I'm not out to "make it" or become a big time Hollywood director. I'm hoping to tell, in whatever small part I can, this grand story that connects with everyone's heart.

BURIED ALIVE
I have noticed that when I tell people what I do, they don't quite understand what I'm talking about. When they visually experience the stories, something clicks. I often hear, "I never thought of it that way." My favorite conversations are when I create a short film on something that's really abstract or deep, like the concept of sin. In this case I made a short with a man who buries himself alive in the mud. It's a rather disturbing visual, but it did start conversations. People will say that until they watched something we created, they never really GOT it, deep down. But after the visual story, they grasped something on a profoundly spiritual level. This is an example of what I am called to bring to the culture at large.

BE IN IT
I think engaging culture means exactly what Christ meant when he spoke of being "in" yet not "of". I don't personally believe that we as Christians should be disconnected from culture, creating art or media for Christians by Christians. I think that we should be connected and inside culture, but choose to live our lives set apart, to a clearer and higher standard. At the core of it, we need to be in community with people who do not see things the way we do. We need to love and serve these people, and stay on target with what we are meant to do, unwavering and uncompromising.

WORD TO THE WISE
Listen. I cannot take one step without direction. When I hear, I move. To me it's as simple and as difficult as that, in everything I do. As a leader, it's scary. It takes courage. Sometimes it means telling people "I think God's saying this, so let's risk it." I try to encourage my team to listen and hear for themselves. When we share God's call, we work together for one purpose. When we can create with a unified passion, the end result will speak that same passion and the story will impact lives on many levels. **C**

THE END OF SUFFERING

By Tim Sanders

I believe that our mission in life is simple: Participate in the end of suffering. If we reduce suffering in the world, we enable the positive. We make a difference. You cannot make people happy and you cannot make them like you. You can, however, be a part of the solution instead of being part of the problem. Suffering is everywhere waiting to be addressed. It comes in many forms from physical needs like hunger to mental needs like uncertainty.

Happiness is like a ray of light that sits just beyond the dark clouds of suffering. When those clouds part, our joy shines through. We only get glimpses of this light because there is so much suffering in our lives.

Think about it, your greatest energy comes from your innate desire to end suffering. If you are bored, you find great energy to deal with that. If someone you care about needs something, you find it in yourself to give her your very best. This mission I suggest, the end of suffering, comes from your true nature as a compassionate being.

It is truly possible to unify our intentions and to align with others based on the mission we select in life. Currently, we have so many varied (and often selfish) missions that it is no wonder we think we are not like "them" and find ourselves largely divided.

When you choose the right mission, it gives you advice at every turn of your life. At work, your mission should tell you the difference between right and wrong and where to spend your time (and energy). Trying to achieve a vague professional mission is like trying to operate a business without a plan. It is difficult for you to separate your mission between personal and professional. How you are successful during the day is who you become in the evening. Conversely, your personal mission should guide your behavior towards your family, friends and acquaintances. If you find one mission that successfully guides you throughout your whole life, you have a blueprint for success. If your mission is aligned with others, you have a blueprint for community and cooperation.

It is my informed opinion that the most effective leaders in the world focus efforts towards the end of suffering. They are first and foremost happy and proactive in defending that happiness. They are sensitive to others' feelings and possess a connected form of emotional intelligence.

Think about this over the next few days. Ask yourself, "Do I have a unifying mission that guides me?" Then question, "Can I offer something towards the end of suffering or do I mostly create suffering?" You may decide to join me in my mission.

If you accept this mission, you must first address suffering in your own life. You need to make room for the needs of other people by dealing with your own. This is the road to self-reliance and peace. If you accept this mission, you will find yourself opting out of behaviors that could make others suffer, because you would "know better" as a result of your new focus on the end of suffering. If nothing else, just do an inventory in one week of how much suffering you created versus how much you addressed. The better you do, the more you are living on purpose. **C**

Tim Sanders is the one of the most sought-after speakers in America today. He is author of the *New York Times* and international bestseller, *Love is the Killer App: How to Win Business and Influence Friends* (Three Rivers Press, 2003), and most recently *The Likeability Factor* (2006). He is a frequent guest on radio and television programs around the country and is an irrepressible advocate for good values in the business world. He lives in northern California. Sign up for Tim's free newsletter at **www.timsanders.com**.

COURAGEOUS ABOUT CALLING:

Visit a library and research (or Google) "William Wilberforce". Take an hour and learn about his life. Consider how he discovered his calling, and the courage it took for him to pursue it. How does the example of William Wilberforce and his community influence your own calling?

Photo by Jeremy Cowart

WHAT WE ARE DOING ABOUT AFRICA ...

A SPECIAL REPORT ON THE CATALYST RWANDA WELLS PROJECT

"I THINK OUR AGE WILL BE REMEMBERED FOR THREE THINGS—THE DIGITAL REVOLUTION, THE WAR AGAINST TERROR, AND WHAT WE DID, OR DID NOT DO TO PUT OUT THE FIRES IN AFRICA. SOME SAY WE CAN'T AFFORD TO. I SAY WE CAN'T AFFORD NOT TO."

-BONO

THE CRISIS

Water is the basic foundation upon which every other thing in a community is built and sustained. Yet, in Africa, the water is often so filthy, you would hesitate to step in it, let alone drink it.

Most people in rural Rwanda do not have access to clean water. They fetch from swamps and rivers. Lack of clean water has led to poor hygienic conditions in schools, health units and among the communities.

In addition to this, most women and young boys and girls walk or ride bikes long distances to fetch water. This takes away time to complete home activities. School-goers score poorly because of the time wasted fetching water. Lack of clean water has led to the spreading of worms and other water-born diseases in those areas. Drinking contaminated water, cost families money for medicines, time away from schools, and even the lives of loved ones. Eighty percent of deaths in developing countries are caused by water-born illnesses.

The leadership of the Catalyst Conference, an annual event in October couldn't help but ask the question ... What would happen if 8,000 leaders and those they lead chose to act on this need?

We brought in a team from Rwanda to share the need in their country and see what might happen. It took just a few minutes to convey the stark reality to next generation church leaders.

A group of African orphans sang praise choruses in both their native tongue and English. Then, a young man from Rwanda named Pascel, who escaped the genocide, shared how he spent days as a child, fetching water from ditches in five gallon containers that he toted on his head for miles. The contaminated water killed his two siblings. More than a million lost their lives in the Rwanda genocide that turned their own people against one another in hand to hand battle during a 40 year war and 100-day massacre in 1994.

"It's hard to believe there's a Jesus when you see such dire conditions," he told us. But in the midst of death and despair on every front, he accepted Christ and shared how Christians in the United States are beginning to make a difference in his homeland not only spiritually, but by providing water.

His story was echoed by an African woman who told how the disease-laden water often spells the demise of thousands of children, but it is all a mother has to give. "The water here was given to you freely this morning. But to us, it's like gold," she said. "There are few wells with clean water."

A GENEROUS RESPONSE

On Friday, October 7, 2005 over 8,000 next generation leaders chose to act. In less than 10 minutes, an offering of $105,000 was generously donated by attendees. Through a partnership with Geneva Global[1], 100% of those funds are being used to provide approximately 35 wells to the people of Rwanda. (**www.genevaglobal.com**)

By identifying a specific need and doing something about it together, Catalyst demonstrated leadership in motion. The Rwanda Wells Project was the first time in the Catalyst Conference's six-year history that attendees were invited to participate as a community in a large-scale project.

While the outpouring of support was generous and more than imagined, the Catalyst team realizes it was just a small positive piece in a much bigger issue. However, the conference itself is designed to be just what it says ... a *catalyst* for influence. The hope was that as leaders went back home, they would determine how they can raise awareness in their own community and take positive action towards the needs in the nation of Africa.

TAKING IT HOME...

The Catalyst community has continued to respond. Many leaders returned home and shared the need with their own churches. To date, an additional $20,000 has been raised by individuals and congregations in support of the project!

We learned from our friends at Geneva Global that Colonial Hills Baptist church in Mount Morris, Michigan had contributed nearly $10,000 more dollars to the Rwanda Wells project—enough for three wells! Doug Klein has served as pastor of this congregation of 240 people for over 18 years. A five-year veteran of the Catalyst conference, he shares his first-hand account of Catalyst leadership in action:

Honestly, I was surprised. I had never really heard anything about the water problem in many parts of the world, specifically Rwanda. I was impacted by how great the need was, and impressed with the Catalyst community's response. They presented a compelling case for the church's role in helping people in need. What I liked most about the project was that all the money we gave would go directly to local churches in Rwanda, empowering and equipping them to build wells. I believed that having the churches build the wells would give them credibility and a platform for sharing the Gospel.

As they took up the offering that day at Catalyst, I began to think, "What if our church could help on a smaller scale?" When I got home, I began talking with our leadership team about raising $3,000 to build a well for a village in Africa. We presented it as

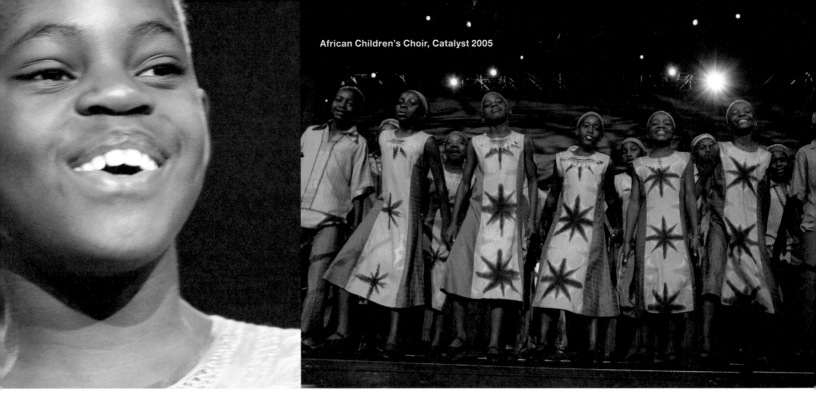

African Children's Choir, Catalyst 2005

our "Christmas present to a village in Rwanda". It would be a present that would keep on giving.

The Sunday after Thanksgiving, we handed out water bottles to every person in our congregation. We had printed up some statistics concerning the water problem around the world and taped them to the bottles. I asked our people to keep these water bottles visible as a reminder and to decide as a family what they could give to the project.

Our goal was to raise the $3,000 to build one well. "Oh me of little faith!" We had an overwhelming response. One person came forward at the end of the service and said that he wanted to contribute $3,000 himself! We increased our goal to build two or three wells. Our people generously responded and raised $9,832 for this project.

I hope that through projects such as these we are creating a culture of giving. Jesus said, "When we have done it unto the least of the brethren, we have done it unto Him." What if churches began asking themselves, "Who are the least of these in my community?" and then responded to meet their need? It will not only change your community, it will change you.

A DROP IN THE BUCKET

Since October 2005, the Wells Project has been impacting families and communities in Rwanda. So far, $115,367 has been invested impacting more than 20,000 lives.

The well projects are coming at the right time, as many people in Rwanda are ill or have died from contaminated drinking water. Here are three reports from field:

Project Goals: Water Collection and Training on Hygiene, Sanitation, and Maintenance of Water Sources

Local Grassroots Partner: Association des Eglises de Pentecote au Rwanda
As a result of this investment …

- Five collection areas and four wells will be built at six sites
- 180 trainers will gain skills in hygiene and sanitation
- At least 20,388 will improve their quality of life with reduction of water-borne ill nesses, including students, community members, and health clinic patients
- 1,080 will be discipled on the link between having a clean heart and a clean body

Local Grassroots Partner: Union des Eglises Baptistes au Rwanda
As a result of this investment …

- Water collection areas will be built on six sites in six provinces
- 3,000 people will improve hygiene and sanitation and pass that knowledge to their family members
- 7,580 people will access clean water and see water-born diseases reduced, school children will have higher scores
- 600 people will hear the Gospel, and an estimated
- 200 people will recommit or give their lives to Jesus

Local Grassroots Partners: Eglise Episcopal Rwanda Diocese of Kigali
As a result of this investment …

- 10 shallow wells will be built along with two rain catchments.
- Four natural springs will be protected
- Two units of six latrines each will be built at two schools
- 9,600 people will have access to clean water and 2,000 pupils will improve sanitation

JEFF SHINABARGER. ATLANTA, GA. CATALYST
REFLECTIONS FROM THE FIELD

The Rwanda Wells Project began as a humble moment with God. God woke me one morning at 3 a.m. with an idea that was bigger than me. It was bigger than the Catalyst Conference. It was the answer to the question, "What am I going to do about Africa?" I was overwhelmed by the Catalyst community's offering towards the Rwanda Wells Project in October. In April 2006 I had the opportunity to travel with a team to visit Rwanda and experience the progress on the projects happening there as a result of our offering. I visited two of the Catalyst wells—and even washed my face in the refreshing water. I was again humbled how God could use me and the Catalyst community to make such a difference for the people of Rwanda. The following are a few of my thoughts and reflections from the trip.

RWANDA
After traveling to the other side of the world and back with our team, I wanted to take a few moments to consider what we experienced together. Before we move too far back into our normal routine of life, I was hoping to stop for a moment and reflect on the opportunity that was given to us from so many different facets—society, humanity, influence, spirituality, justice, community, grace, history and opportunity.

GENOCIDE
Walking through one memorial, every single person broke down into tears. It was horrific, but it didn't seem real until we heard a personal story from a survivor. Then it moved from a museum or a movie to real life. My heart will forever be ashamed and hurt for what happened to some of the most beautiful people and children I have ever met. Yet at the same time, I have never seen or heard more powerful stories of restoration. We experienced an overwhelming environment of forgiveness that we may never see again in our lifetimes. The Rwandan people can forgive each other for the killings of friends and families, and we can't get over an argument in our marriages. How can we integrate that fragrance into the souls of our personal lives?

Grace and love ultimately will win.

WELLS
We saw a child that pumped the well, balanced the tin of water on his head, and then posed for us to take pictures. He is only one who gains. From that one well alone, we were told there are 2,999 others that smile just like him everyday. That was one of the proudest and most humbling moments of my life. We saw how the simplest modern convenience can change the health and hope of an entire village. This is so simple, yet could change humanity. What if today we worked to give everyone in the entire world an opportunity to have access to clean water? Can't you imagine the smile on that child's face multiplied by millions of different smiles from all over the world? Now that would be priceless.

A small offering has the ability to change a society.

MICRO-ENTERPRISE
We witnessed many successful micro-financing projects. From the environmentally conscious Sunflower Project to the generous women leading the Soap Project, there is no doubt that my mind was stimulated by the possibilities and importance of micro-enterprise in re-enabling and establishing the economy of third-world cultures.

Investing in Micro-Finance is a sustaining solution to the ending of poverty.

CHURCH
Taking a ride with Bishop Kolini, from the Anglican Church was a lesson in understanding the role of the Church in every culture. His self-defined personal role was to, "Reclaim the land as sacred and share the Gospel story of Grace with all." He does that in two very distinctive ways. First, he is loving and serving the people by addressing the social and physical needs of the community. Then, at the same time, he is preaching the need to understand justice and accept that grace is sufficient for all. There is no doubt the American Church can learn endless examples of how to live out the Gospel from his example.

There are living leaders globally in the Church to learn from today.

Catalyst Wells Project, Rwanda, April 2006

Photo by Jeremy Cowart

Photo by Jeremy Cowart

COMMUNITY

In Rwanda, people know how to live in Community. That is why they can forgive ... they must forgive because they are dependant on each other for ultimate survival. Everything is done in community and everyone has a role to play. Even 3-year olds, work and take part in the family. I have never been that dependant on others. For us to redeem the idea of community in our culture, we have much to learn from this pre-modern society.

Life is not meant to be lived alone.

PRESIDENT KAGAME

It occurred to me as we were in the room with President Kagame, the leader of the new Rwanda, that we could be standing with one of the most influen-tial leaders in the future history of the African continent. This man is taking steps in new territory comparable to what Nelson Mandela did for South Africa and Abraham Lincoln did for America. There is no doubt that God has placed the perfect leader for such serious times at the lead of the "heart" of all of Africa. He is restoring his country and setting a new standard for government leaders in the world. What an honor it was to admire the work he is doing for this beautiful nation and the influence he is gaining globally.

Great people of faith are rising in influence everywhere.

US

In closing, my final thought is the idea of possibility. We all personally saw a way we could get involved. I am en-couraged by the thousands who began this journey with us, and continue to contribute to it. You may have a riff to add to this list of thoughts from your own community, you may have a project to begin, or you may have an idea to wrestle with. There is never a better time to do something than now. This idea that woke me up in the middle of the night, is one of the greatest joys of my life. The Rwanda Wells Project is obviously an adventure that shouldn't just be a blip in your life, but rather a moment that will shape future thought and direction for years to come.

May we have compassion to care for the poor, widows, needy, hurting, and hungry. ⬛

WHAT OTHERS
ARE DOING ...

THE NEEDS IN AFRICA ARE GREAT, AND THE CATALYST COMMUNITY REALIZES THAT WE ARE ONLY PART OF THE BIGGER SOCIAL JUSTICE PUZZLE. THE FOLLOWING ARE A COLLECTION OF REFLECTIONS, BLOGS, AND STORIES FROM A FEW OF THE COUNTLESS OTHER INDIVIDUALS, GROUPS, CHURCHES, AND ORGANIZATIONS WHO ARE ANSWERING THE CALL TO ACTION. EACH TOLD FROM A DIFFERENT PERSPECTIVE, THESE WRITINGS REFLECT A COMMON PASSION TO CHANGE THE WORLD.

CORY LEBOVITZ. LAWRENCEVILLE, GA. CAUSE & AFFECT 3.31
A CONCERT WITH A CAUSE

It started as a thought ... "What could my friends and I do to help people who are in need?" Soon thoughts became ideas and ideas became plans. In conversation after conversation I cast vision for what it would look like for twenty-somethings to join together to raise awareness and money to help the devastation in Africa. I'm not Bono, but I knew the power of music to draw a crowd. So *Cause & Affect 3.31* was born.

It was more than just raising money for a specific project, it was also about inspiring people my age to get off the couch and do something. "I don't have a lot of money or power, but I want to affect the world." That phrase—affect the world—kept popping up all around me. God was convincing me that he had placed this desire in the hearts of my generation.

Partnering with our local church, Crossroads, we chose a special project through World Hope in Zambia, Africa. The money we raised would help give life back in a place where death reigned ... which is the very message of the Gospel. Gathering a team of like-minded individuals—who also happened to be my closest friends—we spent hours planning and praying together. I am so thankful for how God grew us together in community. Many times I felt like the task was too much, but God used these friends to keep me pushing towards the goal.

We did so many things to spread the word about the cause. We created a website and a MySpace page. We bought the biggest, ugliest van we could find, lined the inside with green shag carpet and painted a huge Africa logo on the outside. A street team was formed to go to local colleges to hang out with students and talk about the concert and Africa.

The night of the concert was amazing. Twenty-somethings used their gifts and creative abilities to pull off a multi-sensory experience of fun and compassion. Outside we had a fire-eater. Inside artists created auction-able paintings inspired by Africa. We started off the night with a drum circle by local musicians. We connected attendees to other local and international service opportunities.

The event was just a piece of the puzzle. As a result of the concert, a village in Zambia has renewed hope.

About a month after the concert I found a flyer on my car for a benefit concert some local bands were throwing to raise money for ... you guessed it ... Zambia, Africa. As I read the flyer, I realized the guys in those bands attended Cause & Affect. Digging a little more, I heard a statement that sums up the power of this revolution: "If they can do it, why can't we?" Each of us has something to give. Each of us has the power to affect the world.

RYAN BRICKER. DALLAS, TX. URBAN PLANNER
THE IRONY OF DEATH AND RESTORATION

Gulu, Uganda. It's on the map, it's in the news, but most undoubtedly it's "off the grid". The U.S. Embassy's standard quote hums drearily: *"We advise you not travel to the Gulu district. If you cross the Nile (northern Uganda) we cannot help you, and we will not be responsible for you. If you do go, write your last letter to your family."*

For twenty years in Northern Uganda there has been death, horror, rape, and mutilation on levels the human soul cannot comprehend. It encompasses not only governments and armies, but principalities and powers of the demonic world. And out of that desert of blood, grows the fertile fields of reconciliation unlike any place on earth. I've never known reconciliation to be anything we as humans and certainly not as cultures have ever truly practiced. Our world and our lives and our fundamental tenants of society stand on justice and vindication. and yet almost at a scale that only points to the disparity of the world that Jesus reconciled in his own sacrificial death, is the heart of a whole people group with hearts and arms huddled to receive the very ones who have raped and murdered their own.

Walking through the IDP (internally displaced peoples) camp where ten of thousands of people forced from their homes and villages and put into an African Mondrian masterpiece grid network of traditional African huts, is a wonderfully surreal scene. You'd expect the tight density of living to be equally a tight and potent sense of despair, and yet while they lived with almost nothing, I felt joy, contentment, hope and dignity.

In a scene that I shall never forget, a small sea of children rushed towards us with wide eyes and looks of amazement at the sight of someone so different. In their amazement and curiosity the children would all keep a safe distance just out of arms reach. It wasn't until I would reach out my own hand that they would stare, reach out to touch my hand, then look up slowly at me illuminated with joy. I couldn't help but to feel like Jesus himself as throngs of people were so enamored with my presence. But I wasn't a Messiah bringing healing and I wasn't bringing eternal truth with great sign and wonders, I was just there as a man, a friend.

You couldn't help but to feel if they had untied that colt and had palm fronds to spare they would create that triumphant entry for you. And yet all I could see was myself in their faces. Like them, I stand at a distance just being amazed, thinking I'm unworthy to touch and feel God and yet He extends not only his hand but his whole person. And while the throngs of people walk cautiously behind him in his wake, I long to be the one up on his shoulders. But I have to trust in the hand that is extended, the hand with nail scars. I have to get over the shame of my own filthy hands to touch a hand that's clean. .

Perhaps the greatest irony was that in a place so toxic—where diseases, viruses, parasites and bacteria abound—a person from a sanitized world could be so thoroughly cleansed. I will forever be in awe that the ones the whole world rushes in to help are themselves the ones who provide, restore and teach.

GARY HAUGEN. WASHINGTON, DC. INTERNATIONAL JUSTICE MISSION
7.13.2006—FROM RWANDA

The agenda for the day was to take my friends on a 1-2 hour drive outside Kigali to a genocide site: a typical small, rural church that became a bloody, mangled massacre site for thousands of innocent people. The site has now been transformed into a genocide memorial. When I first arrived at this small church in 1994 with a team of six other U.N. investigators, it was simply a busted-up brick church sitting on a grassy slope surrounded by maize and banana fields. Rotting bodies were strewn in the dirt and grass around the church, and a massive pile of corpses had decomposed into bones and trash in the sanctuary.

Our task was to conduct a preliminary investigation that would assess the existing physical and testimonial evidence of the massacre. All murder investigations begin with the bodies, and so we began with pulling the skulls out from the putrid pile of corpses, blood-saturated clothing, shoes, government identity cards, jerry cans, machetes, and clubs. We were there to do a very basic accounting of how many victims (male, female, child) and cause of death; and the skulls would get us that far. We began building grotesque columns of skulls in the church yard:

woman-machete/child-machete/woman-blunt instrument/man-machete/child-machete, etc., etc., etc.

Now I was back with friends 12 years later. The yard was all cleaned up and given a fenced perimeter and protective roofing. Some of the columns of skulls had been placed on shelves, and other piles of skeletal remains and personal effects were collected for display. Such physical sites are extremely important for historical memory and stand as an indispensable and relentless record of the ordinary man's capacity for evil. And I do think you have to see the artifacts to actually hold in your mind the reality of what human beings are capable of; the aggressive, intentional, malicious torture and butchery of completely innocent and defenseless human beings by otherwise normal, common neighbors down the street.

Two basic truths are simply inescapable from the story in hindsight: Ordinary human beings are perfectly capable of committing such atrocities and human beings can fail to stop such atrocities even when they are perfectly capable of doing so. I took the opportunity to share with my friends the Psalm that came to speak to me so powerfully when I was there in 1994—Pslam10, an aching passage that begins by asking where God is in the midst of such brutality. For me, the answer from Scripture drew me to the conclusion that we know where God is. The more interesting question to ask: Where are God's people?

My dream after leaving Rwanda was to hope that the next time a disaster like Rwanda should raise its ugly head in our world that the Body of Christ would be better prepared to respond because 1) we would have a heart for what was happening in the larger world; and because 2) we would know the sin of injustice when we saw it and know what to do. And now through IJM, I can see indisputable evidence that such a movement of change is taking place among God's people—and that His people are actually moving beyond fear and triviality and into contention with the very real forces of evil, violence, sexual exploitation, slavery and oppression. And even on this trip one can see how the movement calls everyone to a role; the lawyers and cops, yes, but also the social workers, the pastors, the business people, the teachers, the moms, the photo journalists, and even the rock stars.

JEREMY COWART. NASHVILLE, TN. PHOTOJOURNALIST
JENNA LEE. NASHVILLE, TN. BLOOD:WATER MISSION
HOPE IN THE DARK

Twenty-five years ago, AIDS was unknown in sub-Saharan Africa. Today it's overwhelmingly the continent's biggest killer. In *Hope in the Dark*, photojournalist Jeremy Cowart documents the hope and pain of Africa's AIDS generation—a generation beset by poverty and fear, a generation in which children in some countries are more likely to die of AIDS than not. But despite the sickening odds, Cowart captures brief glimpses of beauty, optimism and joy as he makes his way across the continent.

Also on the documenting trip, where more than 5,000 images were taken, was Jena Lee, the executive director of Blood: Water Mission, a nonprofit organization dedicated to reducing the impact of the HIV/AIDS pandemic and promoting clean blood and clean water in Africa.

"Jeremy Cowart and I went to Africa with a desire to learn and a willingness to have our worldviews shattered," Lee says. "It's easy to romanticize our perceptions of Africa; it's much harder to come, on a human level, to realize that we're not all that different from one another."

Lee pens the thoughts, captions and stories behind the photos throughout the book. Together, through this collection of startling, remarkable images, the lens uncovers not just the magnitude of the problem, but also the places where God is undeniably present in the midst of it. "I hope [the photos] allow you to connect with the people; to understand their stories, struggles and hope; and to join with them to do something," Cowart says. "You don't have to move to Africa ... But I do hope that you will allow these images of people who changed me to change you, too."

JASON RUSSELL. LAREN POOLE. BOBBY BAILEY.
SAN DIEGO, CA. INVISIBLE CHILDREN
CAN A STORY CHANGE THE WORLD?

In the spring of 2003, these three young Americans traveled to Africa in search of such a story. What started out as a filmmaking adventure in Africa transformed into much more, when these three boys from Southern California found themselves stranded in Northern Uganda. What they found was a tragedy that disgusted and inspired them—a story where children are the weapons and the victims. They discovered children being abducted from their homes and forced to fight as child soldiers. The footage they captured revealed, for the first time, the tragic (and untold) story.

The *Invisible Children: Rough Cut* film exposes the effects of a 20-year-long war on the children of Northern Uganda. They originally screened the film in June 2004 for friends and family and soon expanded to high schools, colleges and religious institutions. From suburban living rooms to Capitol Hill, with coverage on Oprah, CNN, the National Geographic Channel, and more, this film has taken on a life of its own. Today, an estimated 1.5 mil-

lion people have viewed and been impacted by the film, all due to the efforts of those on the grassroots level who have spread it by word of mouth. This wonderfully reckless documentary is fast-paced and truly unique. To see Africa through young eyes is humorous and heartbreaking, quick and informative—all in the same breath.

After people viewed the movie, the one question repeatedly asked was, "What can I do?" As a result, in September 2004, the non-profit, Invisible Children, Inc. was born from a film. It has grown to become the awareness, mobilization, and fundraising effort taking place throughout America and other countries around the world by people who are inspired to act. The goal is to empower the individual viewer to become a part of the story and "be the change they wish to see in the world" through action.

And that's just what people are doing: nine-year-olds are individually collecting money at their churches, while fourteen-year-olds are

coordinating garage sales that both screen the film and send all proceeds to Invisible Children. Youth pastors are leading their students in fundraising for the cause. This past April, more than 80,000 people, inspired by the film, walked from their homes to spend the night outside in their cities to raise awareness for the Ugandan children at an event called the Global Night Commute.

Invisible Children is committed to helping the people of Northern Uganda with resources that provide hope through the Education Program and Bracelet Campaign, bringing health care, safety, education and employment to an area ravaged by war. It is their belief that we need to live for more, because the invisible children need more to live.

Three adventurous guys took up the challenge from one Ugandan child, "Please don't forget me," and have inspired the world. Become a part of the story and check out **www.invisiblechildren.com**. ◪

WHAT ARE YOU DOING ABOUT AFRICA?

Find out more and get involved by checking out the websites below.
Visit **www.fermiproject.com** to learn how you or your church can stay involved in the
Rwanda Wells project.

Geneva Global	www.genevaglobal.com
P.E.A.C.E	www.purposedriven.com/peace
Hope Rwanda	www.hoperwanda.org
Compassion International	www.compassion.com
Lifewater International	www.lifewater.org
World Vision	www.wvi.org
World Hope	www.worldhope.org
The ONE Campaign	www.one.org
Invisible Children	www.invisiblechildren.com
Blood:Water Mission	www.bloodwatermission.com

FOOTNOTES

SESSION 01:
ENGAGED IN CULTURE

Catalyst Study: The 7 Languages of Culture

1. In *The Five Love Languages* (Moody Publishers, 1996), seasoned marriage counselor Gary Chapman says people feel most loved in a marriage in one of five ways: quality time, words of affirmation, gifts, acts of service, and physical touch. Though we have a primary love language, we can learn a second language so that our spouse's needs are met.

William Wilberforce:
A Name You Need to Know

1. Lester J. Cappon, ed., *The Adams-Jefferson Letters* (Chapel Hill: University of North Carolina Press, 1959), p. 349, cited by David Mc Cullough, *John Adams* (New York: Simon & Schuster, 2001), p. 285.

2. Paul Helm, The Callings (Carlisle, Penn.: Banner of Truth, 1987), pp. 54-55.

3. William Wilberforce, *The Speech of William Wilberforce, Esq., Representative for the Country of York, on the Question of the Abolotion of the Slave Trade* (London: Logographic Press, 1789), p. 18.

4. The two-dimensional work of art depicted in this image is in the public domain worldwide due to the date of death of its author, or due to its date of publication. Thus, this reproduction of the work is also in the public domain. (**www.wikipedia.com**)

SESSION 02:
AUTHENTIC IN INFLUENCE

Catalyst Study: I Smell Dead Fish

1. Patton Dodd, *"Whose Passion,"* The New Pantagruel, ©*2003*.

The Calcutta Paradox

1. Renzo Allegri, Mother Theresa: The Early Years, August 1996, <http://www.ewtn.com/library/ISSUES/EARLYYR.HTM>.

2. Jim Collins, *Good to Great* (New York, NY: Harper Collins, 2001), 27-30, 33-35.

SESSION 03:
UNCOMPROMISING IN INTEGRITY

Love: The New Integrity

1. Gregory McNamee, *Gila: The Life and Death of an American River* (New York: Orion, 1994), 147-48.

2. James H. Olthuis, *The Beautiful Risk* (Grand Rapids, MI: Zondervan, 2001), 71.

3. James H. Olthuis, "Cross the Threshold," *Hermeneutics of Charity*, ed. James K.A. Smith and Henry Isaac Venema (Grand Rapids, MI: Brazos, 2004), 38.

4. "Do you expect a pat on the back?" Luke 6:32, MSG.

5. J. Davis, "Literature Cultures, Oral Asides," *TLS: Times Literary Supplement*, 30 July 1999, 6.

SESSION 04:
PASSIONATE ABOUT GOD

Sabbath/Shabbat

1. Nan Fink, *Stranger in the Midst: A Memoir of Spiritual Discovery* (New York: Basic Books, 1997), 95-96.

SESSION 05:
INTENTIONAL ABOUT COMMUNITY

Catalyst Study:
The Coming Loneliness Epidemic

1. Social Isolation in America: Changes in Core Discussion Networks over Two Decades; McPherson, Smith-Lovin, Brashears

2. ibid

3. Psychological Sense of Community, Springer Jennifer L Hillman Jan 1, 2002

4. RUBIN, ALAN M., PERSE, ELIZABETH M. & POWELL, ROBERT A. (1985) LONELINESS, PARASOCIAL INTERACTION, AND LOCAL TELEVISION NEWS VIEWING. *Human Communication Research* **12** (2), 155-180. doi: 10.1111/j.1468-2958.1985.tb00071.x

5.http://www.gravity7.com/articles_investigations.html

BONUS SESSION

What We are doing about Africa?
A Special Report from the Catalyst
Rwanda Wells Project

1. **Geneva Global** is a private philanthropy that holds the promise of solving problems, building communities and changing lives. Geneva Global offers philanthropic opportunities that are purposeful investments in lasting change in places where change is needed the most by supporting effective charitable programs, not ineffective charitable work. (**www.genevaglobal.com**)

2. *Article author/contributor information:*

Doug Klein is pastor of Colonial Hills Baptist church in Mount Morris, Michigan. Contact the church at **chbc@prodigy.net.**

Terry Wilhite is a communications and multimedia specialist who regularly contributes to Pastors.com and other internationally-recognized ministry leadership web sites and publications. He's a regular attendee of the Catalyst Conference. Find more about his work at **www.terrywilhite.com**.

Shannon Sedgwick is the Vice-President of Geneva Global, Inc. For more information on Geneva Global or the Rwanda Wells Project, contact her at **shannon@genevaglobal.com**.

Jeff Shinabarger is the lead experience designer for the Catalyst conference and Executive Editor of the *Catalyst Groupzine*. He is a founder of the *FERMI Project* and *Q*, an exclusive boutique event designed to inform and expose church leaders to future culture. Jeff lives in Atlanta with his wife Andre and dog Max. Email him at **jeff@fermiproject.com.**

Kerry Priest is managing editor of the *Catalyst Group-Zine* and the *Catalyst Monthly* online magazine. She is also a full-time graduate student at the University of Georgia, studying leadership education. Email her at **kerry.priest@injoy.com.**

3. Photos from *Hope in the Dark* (2006, Relevant Books). Copyright © by Jeremy Cowart Photograpy, **www.jeremycowart.com**.

TAKE YOUR GROUP TO A PLACE...

...WHERE THEY CAN SEE PEOPLE'S NEED IN A NEW WAY

...WHERE THEY CAN UNDERSTAND THEIR CALLING

...WHERE THEY WILL LEARN HOW THEIR FAITH CAN SHAPE CULTURE

INTERSECT|culture

This compelling 6-session DVD and corresponding curriculum helps your group experience and envision how followers of Christ can be a counterculture for the common good. Together you'll experience stories of other believers who changed the culture around them. You'll watch how their journeys unfolded, their challenges, and their breakthroughs. Also included on the DVD are insights from trusted pastors and Christian leaders such as Tim Keller, Lauren Winner, James Meeks, Brenda Salter McNeil, and Ken Fong.

To purchase, or for more information about the Christian Vision Project, visit **www.catalystspace.com.**

NELSON IMPACT
A Division of Thomas Nelson Publishers
Since 1798

The Nelson Impact Team is here to answer your questions
and suggestions as to how we can create more resources
that benefit you, your family, and your community.

Contact us at Impact@thomasnelson.com

We spend the best hours of our days at work so make them count.

In this **Life@Work GroupZine**, gifted teachers and practitioners tackle the integration of faith and work by revealing **The Essential Qualities of a Life@Work Leader: Skill, Calling, Serving, & Character.**

With relevant articles, book excerpts, curriculum, study questions, hands-on planning exercises, and much more, this practical resource is ideal for individuals, small groups, and mentoring relationships. If you are committed to **growing in your faith** and **making the most of your career**, the **Life@Work GroupZine** series is for you!

Visit us online at www.lifeatworkgroupzine.com.

NELSON IMPACT
A Division of Thomas Nelson Publishers
Since 1798

**SHARE THIS UNIQUE RESOURCE
WITH YOUR SMALL GROUP**

**Call 800.333.6506 today
for Special Group Pricing!**